Karen Brown's

Italy

Charming Bed & Breakfasts

Written by
NICOLE FRANCHINI

Illustrations by Elisabetta Franchini
Cover Painting by Jann Pollard

Karen Brown's Guides, San Mateo, California

Karen Brown Titles

Austria: Charming Inns & Itineraries

California: Charming Inns & Itineraries

England: Charming Bed & Breakfasts

England, Wales & Scotland: Charming Hotels & Itineraries

France: Charming Bed & Breakfasts

France: Charming Inns & Itineraries

Germany: Charming Inns & Itineraries

Ireland: Charming Inns & Itineraries

Italy: Charming Bed & Breakfasts

Italy: Charming Inns & Itineraries

New England: Charming Inns & Itineraries

Portugal: Charming Inns & Itineraries

Spain: Charming Inns & Itineraries

Switzerland: Charming Inns & Itineraries

Alla
Piccola Sofia,
Benvenuta al Mondo!

Editors: Karen Brown, June Brown, Clare Brown, Nicole Franchini, Iris Sandilands, Lorena Aburto, Cathy Knight.

Illustrations: Elisabetta Franchini; Cover painting: Jann Pollard; Web designer: Lynn Upthagrove.

Maps: Susanne Lau Alloway—Greenleaf Design & Graphics.

Copyright © 1992, 1994, 1996, 1997, 1998, 1999, 2000, 2001 by Karen Brown's Guides.

This book or parts thereof may not be reproduced in any form without obtaining written permission from the publisher: Karen Brown's Guides, P.O. Box 70, San Mateo, CA 94401, USA, e-mail: karen@karenbrown.com.

Distributed by Fodor's Travel Publications, Inc., 280 Park Avenue, New York, NY 10017, USA.

Distributed in Canada by Random House Canada, 2775 Matheson Boulevard. East, Mississanga, Ontario L4W 4P7, Canada, phone: (905) 624 0672, fax: (905) 624 6217

Distributed in the United Kingdom, Ireland, and Europe by Random House UK, 20 Vauxhall Bridge Road, London, SW1V 2SA, England, phone: 44 20 7840 4000, fax: 44 20 7840 8406.

Distributed in Australia by Random House Australia, 20 Alfred Street, Milsons Point, Sydney NSW 2061, Australia, phone: 61 2 9954 9966, fax: 61 2 9954 4562.

Distributed in New Zealand by Random House New Zealand, 18 Poland Road, Glenfield, Auckland, New Zealand, phone: 64 9 444 7197, fax: 64 9 444 7524.

Distributed in South Africa by Random House South Africa, Endulani, East Wing, 5A Jubilee Road, Parktown 2193, South Africa, phone: 27 11 484 3538, fax: 27 11 484 6180.

A catalog record for this book is available from the British Library.

Library of Congress Cataloging-in-Publication Data

Franchini, Nicole, 1959–
   Karen Brown's Italy : charming bed & breakfasts / written by Nicole Franchini ; illustrations by Elisabetta Franchini ; cover painting by Jann Pollard.
      p. cm. -- (Karen Brown's country inn series)
    ISBN 1-928901-08-5
    1. Hotels--Italy--Guidebooks. 2. Italy--Guidebooks. I. Title: Italy. II. Brown, Karen, 1956- III. Title. IV. Series.

TX907.5.I8 F73 2001
647.9445'03--dc21
                                     00-039729

Contents

ITALIAN FARMER'S POEM

Our memories are crouched
in silence within the belly of the earth.
Yet it takes only a day of sunshine,
an impromptu storm in the sky,
the perfume of freshly cut hay,
and immense fields dotted with golden haystacks,
to ignite in us the memories
of certain evenings spent full of gaiety.

It was at sunset when we used to join together
in the barn filled with grain
to celebrate the end of the harvest.
The "gioanassa" musician friend,
pressing the keys of his worn-out accordion,
succeeding in emitting the notes
to a waltz or mazurka, leaving us
drunk with happiness.

One more glass of wine before the night
fades into day.
One more toast to bid farewell
to another summer
that crossed the path of our youth.

Anonymous

Introduction

BED AND BREAKFAST ITALIAN-STYLE—*agriturismo,* as the bed and breakfast activity is called in Italy, has made great strides over the past decade or so. The bed and breakfast concept is relatively new to Italy, which followed suit after France and England originated the trend. Accommodations vary from simple farmhouses to noble country villas, all promising unique and memorable stays. "*Agritourism*" travel offers visitors to Italy the unique opportunity to observe daily life "up close" as a guest in someone's home. It is a superb way to interact directly with Italians, experiencing their way of life as a participant rather than just an observer. It offers a more intimate contact with the country's traditional ways of life than can ever be experienced during hotel stays. It is the alternative vacation for curious visitors who wish to explore the back roads of this fascinating country and depart with a more in-depth understanding of Italians and their lifestyles than they could possibly get from city stays and sightseeing alone. The individual who will benefit most from agritourism will have an open, inquiring mind and a certain amount of flexibility. In return, agritourism rewards the traveler with a feeling of being "at home" while abroad. The warm welcome and the value you'll receive will tempt you back to the agritourism track year after year.

HISTORY: *Agriturismo*, defined as agricultural tourism, was launched in 1965 as part of the Italian government's national agricultural department's plan to make it possible for farmers to supplement their declining income in two ways: through offering accommodation to tourists and through direct sales of their produce.

After World War II, during reconstruction and the subsequent industrial boom, Italians abandoned the countryside in droves in search of employment in urban centers, reducing the rural population from eight to three million people. Consequently, farmhouses, villas, and castles all across the country were neglected and went to ruin. This phenomenon also disrupted the centuries-old tradition of passing customs and property from one generation to the next.

The agritourism concept, with its government funding, proclaimed tax breaks, and an increasing need to escape congested cities, has lured proprietors back to their land and ancestral homes, providing them with the incentive to restore and preserve these historical buildings (with many treasures among them), without spoiling the natural landscape. An additional consequence is an improved distribution of tourism between Italy's overcrowded cities and the countryside, which serves to raise awareness of the many marvelous historical and cultural attractions, from art and architecture to scenery and cuisine, that await tourists off the beaten track.

Each of Italy's 20 regions participates in agritourism, with a full 60% of participants concentrated in Tuscany and Trentino-Alto Adige. This edition of *Italy: Charming Bed & Breakfasts* includes selections from 14 of Italy's regions. Unfortunately, this type of accommodation is still very scarce in Italy's southernmost regions such as Calabria,

Basilicata, and Campania. We are happy to offer a selection of bed and breakfasts in Sicily, where a law permitting agritourism activity was passed just a few years ago.

In practical terms, agritourism was developed to stimulate the local economy in rural areas by encouraging the creation of accommodations (rooms, apartments, and campgrounds) in places where they had never before been available. In a more long-term and idealistic sense, it was hoped that the promotion and development of tourism in rural Italy would also bring about greater environmental awareness and rescue traditional folklore and customs, such as regional cuisine and handicrafts, from oblivion.

For Italians, agritourism facilitates an exchange of views between farmers and urbanites who come in search of a peaceful vacation surrounded by natural beauty. In fact, agritourism and the rich culture of the farmer represent for many an affirmation and validation of their heritage. Lamentably, some Italians still have a misconception of agritourism because it was originally organized as an exchange of very basic room and board for work in the fields. A wave of positive press in recent years and higher quality standards have helped enormously to change this outdated image.

Controversy also surrounds the fact that there are few established regulations governing this type of activity, and they differ greatly from one region to another. Consequently, few clearly defined quality standards exist and those participants with limited economic resources resent wealthier proprietors, whom they accuse of running accommodations resembling hotels more than farm stays. Moreover, it does not simplify matters that agritourism is organized in typical Italian fashion, with responsibility divided among three associations, each with its own regulations, politics, and guidelines. Each association produces a directory (in Italian) and may be contacted by writing to:

AGRITURIST, Corso Vittorio Emanuele 101, Rome 00168, Italy
Email: agritur@confagricoltura.it
TERRANOSTRA, Via 14 Maggio 43, Rome 00187, Italy
Email: terranostra@coldiretti.it
TURISMO VERDE, Via E. Franceschini 89, Rome 00155, Italy, Email: info@turismoverde.it

About Bed & Breakfasts

Our goal in this guide is to recommend outstanding places to stay. All of the bed and breakfasts featured have been visited and selected solely on their merits. Our judgments are made on charm, setting, cleanliness, and, above all, warmth of welcome. However (no matter how careful we are), sometimes we misjudge an establishment's merits, or the ownership changes, or unfortunately sometimes standards are not maintained. If you find a recommended place is not as we have indicated, please let us know, and accept our sincere apologies. The rates given are those quoted to us by the bed and breakfast: please use these figures as a guideline only and be certain to ask at the time of booking what the rates are and what they include.

Please supplement this book with the Karen Brown website (*www.karenbrown.com*). Our site contains not only a wealth of information for planning your vacation but also post-press updates on our guides, and is a handy source for Michelin maps. Several of the properties in this guide are featured there (their web addresses are on their description pages) with photos and direct links to their email and personal websites.

ACCOMMODATION

The most important thing to remember as you consider an agritourism vacation is that you will be staying in the private homes of families that are obligated to run their bed and breakfasts without hiring additional personnel aside from family and farmhands. Do not forget that, in most cases, the primary responsibility of your hosts is the running of their farm, so, with a few exceptions, do not expect the service of a hotel. **Rooms may not necessarily always be cleaned daily** (sometimes linens are changed every three to seven days). Nevertheless, do anticipate a comfortable and enjoyable stay, because the proprietors will do everything possible to assure it. Cost will vary according to the level of service offered. (For the traveler's convenience, some city hotels have been included that are similar to a bed and breakfast in style, but go by the name *Albergo*, *Pensione*, or Hotel.)

ROOMS: Agritourism accommodation should not be thought of strictly in terms of the British definition of bed and breakfasts, as in Italy they vary greatly according to each proprietor's interpretation of the concept. The bed and breakfasts in this guide have been described in terms of the criteria used in their selection—warmth of hospitality, historic character, charm of the home, scenery, proximity to sites of touristic interest, and quality of cuisine. Obviously, all of these attributes are not always found in each one. Most of them have an average of six rooms situated either within the family's home or in a separate guesthouse. We have tried to include only those with en-suite bathrooms, as our readers have requested (although for the budget traveler this may not be a priority). Having another bed or two added to a room at an extra charge for families with small children is usually not a problem. According to laws of the European Community, all new or renovated establishments must now offer facilities for the handicapped. It is best to enquire about the individual bed and breakfast's facilities when making reservations to see if they have accommodation that is suitable for you.

APARTMENTS: Since more and more travelers are learning that it is much more advantageous to stay for longer periods in one place (distances are so short between towns within a specific region), apartment-type accommodations with fully equipped kitchenettes are flourishing. And, in fact, jumping around from one place to another for one or two nights defeats the purpose of a more intimate contact with host families. Apartment accommodation is offered either within the farmhouse along with other units for two to six persons, or as a full house rental for six to ten persons. They are rented by the week from Saturday to Saturday throughout the country, the exception being during the low season. No meals are included unless the bed and breakfast also has a restaurant or makes special arrangements for breakfast. Rates include use of all facilities, unless otherwise indicated, linens, and utilities. There is usually an extra charge for heating and once-a-week cleaning. Average apartments for four persons run $700 weekly, a rate hotels cannot beat.

FOOD

A highlight of the agritourism experience is without a doubt the food. Most travelers would agree that a bad meal is hard to find in Italy, a country world-famous for its culinary skills. In the countryside you'll be sampling the traditional recipes from which Italian cuisine originates. Since, whenever possible, all of the ingredients come directly from the farms where you'll be staying, you'll discover the flavorful difference freshness can make. A peek into the farm kitchen is likely to reveal pasta being rolled and cut the old-fashioned way—by hand. Many country cooks prefer to prepare food using traditional methods, and not rely on machines to speed up the process. Guests are usually welcomed into the kitchen for a look around and actual cooking lessons are becoming very popular.

MEALS OFFERED: Bed and breakfasts often serve only a Continental breakfast of coffee, tea, fresh breads, and jams. However, many prepare other meals and offer (sometimes require) half- or full-board plans. Half board means that breakfast and dinner are both included in the daily per-person room rate. Full board includes the room and all three meals and is less common, since most guests are out and about during the day, or prefer one lighter meal. Dinner is a hearty three-course meal, often shared at a common table with the host family, and normally does not include wine and other beverages. Menus might be set daily, according to the availability of fresh produce, or a limited choice may be given. Some farms have a fully fledged restaurant serving non-guests as well. Travelers who are not guests at a particular bed and breakfast may take advantage of this opportunity to sample other fare. It is advisable to reserve in advance.

ENGLISH

English spoken at each bed and breakfast has been indicated as follows: fluent, very well, well, some, little, or none. We would like to note, however, that this is just an indication, as the person who speaks English may or may not be there during your stay. In any case, it is helpful (not to mention rewarding) to have a few basic Italian phrases on hand. A phrase book or dictionary is indispensable. And when all else fails, the art of communicating with gestures is still very much alive in Italy!

LENGTH OF STAY

Agritourism is most advantageous for those who have more than the standard one week to travel. Bed-and-breakfast accommodations take longer to reach, for one thing, and **often they are neither set up nor staffed for one-night stays**, which increase costs and defeat the purpose. There are numerous exceptions, however, especially in bed and breakfasts near cities, where overnight guests are accepted. It is noted in the description where a minimum stay is required.

WHEN TO VISIT

Since agritourism accommodation is usually in permanent residences, many remain open all year, but most are open only from Easter through November. If you are traveling outside this time, however, it is worth a phone call to find out if the bed and breakfast will accommodate you anyway (at very affordable rates). The best time for agritourism is without a doubt during the spring and fall months, when nature is in its glory. You can enjoy the flowers blossoming in May, the *vendemia*, or grape harvest, at the end of September, the fall foliage in late October, or olive-oil production and truffle hunts in November and December. Southern Italy can be mild and pleasant in the winter, which might be perfect for travelers who like to feel they are the only tourists around. The vast majority of Italians vacation at the same time, during the month of August, Easter weekend, and Christmas, so these time periods are best avoided, if possible.

WHAT TO SEE AND DO

Bed and breakfast proprietors take pride in their farms and great pleasure in answering questions about their agricultural activity. They will often take time to explain and demonstrate procedures such as wine making, olive pressing, or cheese production. They are the best source for, and are happy to suggest, restaurants and local itineraries including historic sites, picturesque villages, and cultural activities. Your hosts feel responsible for entertaining their guests and many have added swimming pools or tennis courts if they are not already available in the vicinity. Other activities such as archery, fishing, hiking, and biking are sometimes offered. Horseback riding has made an enormous comeback and farms frequently have their own stables and organize lessons and/or excursions into the countryside. In most circumstances, a charge is made for these extra activities.

PLANNING YOUR TRIP

Italian Government Travel Offices (ENIT) can offer general information on various regions and their cultural attractions. They cannot offer specific information on restaurants and accommodations. If you have access to the Internet, visit the Italian Tourist Board's websites: *www.italiantourism.com* or *www.enit.it*. Offices are located in:

Chicago: Italian Government Travel Office, 500 N. Michigan Ave., Suite 2240, Chicago, IL 60611 USA; tel: (312) 644-0996, fax: (312) 644-3019. (Mail, fax, or phone only.)

Los Angeles: Italian Government Travel Office, 12400 Wilshire Blvd., Suite 550, Los Angeles, CA 90025, USA; tel: (310) 820-1898, fax: (310) 820-6357.

New York: Italian Government Travel Office, 630 5th Ave., Suite 1565, New York, NY 10111, USA; tel: (212) 245-4822, fax: (212) 586-9249.

Montreal: Italian Government Travel Office, 1 Place Ville Marie, Suite 1914, Montreal, Quebec H3B 2C3, Canada; tel: (514) 866-7667, fax: (514) 392-1429.

London: Italian State Tourist Office, 1 Princes Street, London WIR 8AY, England; tel: (020) 7355-1557, fax: (020) 7493-6695.

Sydney: Italian Government Travel Office, Level 26, 44 Market Street, Sydney NSW 2000, Australia; tel: (61292) 621.666, fax: (61292) 625.677.

Rome: ENTE Nazionale Italiano per il Turismo (Italian Government Travel Office), Via Marghera, 2, Rome 00185, Italy, tel: (06) 49711, fax: (06) 4463379.

RATES

Room rates vary according to size, location, season, and level of service. Rates range from $65 to $200 for a double room with breakfast (indicated as B&B in the following descriptions) and from $75 to $150 per person for room with half board (dinner also included). The majority of the bed and breakfasts selected for this guide have private bathrooms. **Approximate prices for 2001 are indicated in lire and are by no means fixed**. Rates include tax and breakfast unless otherwise indicated, and are **confirmed at the time of reservation**. Many hotels now give rates in both lire and Euro currency as preparation for the changeover programmed for 2002. Because of its cost advantages, agritourism is an ideal choice for a family vacation. Children under eight are offered a discount and hosts will almost always add an extra bed for a small charge. There are some wonderful benefits to traveling in the low season (November to March with the exception of holidays) in Italy. The considerable reduction in bed-and-breakfast rates combined with irresistibly low air fares makes for a super-economical vacation. And then, there's the ultimate advantage of not having to fight for space with crowds of other tourists. Italy is all yours!

CREDIT CARDS

Credit cards are rarely accepted, cash being the preferred method of payment. When "plastic payment" is taken, the type of card accepted will be indicated as follows: AX: American Express; MC: MasterCard; VS: Visa; or all major.

Introduction–About Bed & Breakfasts

RESERVATIONS

Whether you plan to stay in several bed and breakfasts or decide to remain for an extended period in just one, **advance reservations are preferred**. Not only do many of the bed and breakfasts have only a few bedrooms available, but also they are usually in private homes that are not prepared to take walk-in traffic. There are several ways to make a reservation:

Email: This is our preferred way of making a reservation. If the bed and breakfast is on our website, we have included their email address in the listing details and added a direct link on their Karen Brown web page. (Always spell out the month as the Italians reverse the American month/day numbering system.)

Fax: If you have access to a fax machine, this is a very quick way to reach a bed and breakfast. If the place to stay has a fax, we have included the number in the description. At the end of this section we provide you with a reservation request letter in Italian with an English translation. (See comment above about spelling out the month.)

Letter: You can write to the bed and breakfast (allow up to six weeks for an answer because mail to and from Italy is very slow). Make photocopies of the sample reservation-request letter. (Again, be sure to spell out the month.) Frequently a deposit is requested in order to confirm the reservation.

Reservation Service: If you want to pay for the convenience of having the reservations made for you, pre-payments made, vouchers issued, and cars rented, any of the bed and breakfasts in this guide can be booked through **Hidden Treasures of Italy**, a booking service run by the author of this guide, Nicole Franchini. Further information can be found at the back of this book.

Telephone: You can call the bed and breakfast directly. This is very efficient since you will get an immediate response. (The level of English spoken is given in each bed and breakfast description.) To telephone Italy from the United States, dial 011 (the international code), then 39 (Italy's code), then the city area code (with the "0" since the new system was established in October 1998), and then the telephone number. Italy is six hours ahead of New York.

BED & BEAKFAST or HOTEL NAME & ADDRESS—clearly printed or typed

Vi richiediamo la seguente prenotazione:
We would like to request the following reservation:

Numero delle camere o appartamenti _____ con bagno o doccia privata a _____ posti letti
Number of rooms or apartments with private bath or shower for how many persons

Numero di adulti _____   Numero di bambini _____ Età _____
Number of adults   *Number of children and ages*

Numero delle camere o appartamenti _____ senza bagno o doccia privata _____ posti letti
Number of rooms or apartments without private bath or shower for how many persons

Numero di adulti _____   Numero di bambini _____ Età _____
Number of adults   *Number of children and ages*

Data di arrivo _____   Data di partenza _____
Date of arrival   *Date of departure*

Tipo di servizio richesto:
Type of meal plan requested:

____ Pernottamento con prima colazione (*B&B*)

____ Mezza Pensione (*Half Board—breakfast and dinner included*)

____ Pensione Completa (*Full Board—all three meals included*)

Costo giornaliero: B&B (two persons) _____

Daily rate   MP (Half Board—per person) _____

PC (Full Board—per person) _____

Ci sono ulteriori sconti per bambini e quanto? _____
Is there a discount for children and what is it?

E necessario una caparra e quanto? _____
Is a deposit necessary and for how much?

Ringraziando anticipatamente per la gentile conferma, porgo cordiali saluti,
Thanking you in advance for your confirmation,

YOUR NAME, ADDRESS, TELEPHONE & FAX NUMBER—clearly printed or typed

Reservation Request Letter in Italian

FINDING YOUR BED AND BREAKFAST

At the back of the book is a key map of the whole of Italy plus 13 regional maps showing each recommended bed and breakfast's location. The pertinent regional map number is given at the right on the *top line* of each bed and breakfast's description. To make it easier for you, we have divided the location maps with grids of four parts—a, b, c, and d—as indicated on each map's key. Directions to help you find your destination are given after each bed and breakfast description. However, they are only a small clue, as it would be impossible to find the space to give more details, and to know from which direction the traveler is arriving. The beauty of many of these lodgings is that they are off the beaten track, but that characteristic may also make them very tricky to find. If you get lost, a common occurrence, first keep your sense of humor, then call the proprietors and/or ask locals at bars or gas stations for directions. As previously mentioned, detailed maps for the area in which you will be traveling are essential. It is important to know that addresses in the countryside often have no specific street name. A common address consists of the farm name, sometimes a *localita* (an unincorporated area, or vicinity, frequently not found on a map) and the town name followed by the province abbreviated in parentheses. (The bed and breakfast is not necessarily in that town, but it serves as a post office reference.) The *localita* can also be the name of the road where the bed and breakfast is located, to make things more confusing. We state the *localita* as the third line of the bed and breakfast information.

TRANSFERS INTO CITIES: Travelers from abroad normally arrive by plane in Milan, Rome, or Venice (sometimes Florence) and pick up their rental car at the airport. However, if your first destination is the city and you plan on picking up your car after your stay, approximate transfer rates are as follows:

MILAN

From Malpensa to city by taxi (70 min)	Lire 145,000
From Malpensa to Cadorna station by train (every 30 min)	Lire 15,000
From Malpensa to central station by bus (every 20 min)	Lire 13,000–22,000
From Linate to city by taxi (20 min)	Lire 50,000
From Linate to city by bus (every 20 min)	Lire 4,000

ROME

From Da Vinci to city by train (every 30 min)	Lire 16,000
From Da Vinci to city by taxi (45 min)	Lire 90,000–120,000

VENICE

From airport to city by waterbus (1 hour)	Lire 17,000
From airport to city by private waterbus	Lire 140,000
From station to city by waterbus (15 min)	Lire 8,000
From station to city by private waterbus	Lire 140,000

FLORENCE

From airport to city by taxi (30 min)	Lire 40,000

REGIONAL FARM NAMES

The following names for farms, seen throughout this guide, vary from area to area.

azienda agricola—a general term meaning farm, not necessarily offering hospitality

borgo—a small stone-walled village, usually of medieval origins

casale, casolare—variations of farmhouse, deriving from "casa"

cascina and ca'—farmhouse in Piedmont, Lombardy, and Veneto

fattoria—typically a farm in Tuscany or Umbria

hof and maso—terms meaning house and farm in the northern mountain areas

locanda—historically a restaurant with rooms for travelers passing through on horseback

masseria—fortified farms in Apulia, Sicily

podere—land surrounding a farmhouse

poggio—literally describes the farm's position on a flat hilltop

tenuta—estate

torre—tower

trattoria—a simple, family-run restaurant in cities and the countryside

villa and castello—usually former home of nobility and more elaborate in services

Introduction–About Bed & Breakfasts

About Italy

The following pointers are given in alphabetical order, not in order of importance.

BANKS

Banking hours are Monday through Friday from 8:30 am to 1:30 pm and 3 to 4 pm, with some city banks now opening on Saturday mornings. Cash machines accepting U.S. bank cash cards and credit cards are widely distributed throughout Italy. *Cambio* signs outside and inside a bank indicate that it will exchange traveler's checks or give you cash from certain credit cards. Also privately run exchange offices are available in cities with more convenient hours and comparable rates.

CAR RENTAL

An International Driver's Permit is not necessary for renting a car as a tourist: a foreign driver's license is valid for driving throughout Italy. Readers frequently ask our advice on car rental companies. In the U.S.A. we always use Auto Europe, a car rental broker that works with the major car rental companies to find the lowest possible price. They also offer motor homes and chauffeur services. Auto Europe's toll-free phone service from every European country connects you to their US-based, 24-hour reservation center (ask for the card with European phone numbers to be sent to you). Auto Europe offers our readers a 5% discount, and occasionally free upgrades. Be sure to use the Karen Brown ID number 99006187 to receive your discount and any special offers. You can make your own reservations via our website, *www.karenbrown.com* (select Auto Europe from the home page), or by phone (800-223-5555).

DRIVING

A car is a must for this type of travel—most bed and breakfasts are inaccessible by any other means of transportation. A car gives the traveler a great deal of independence (public transportation is frequently on strike in Italy), while providing the ideal means to explore the countryside thoroughly. It is best to reserve a vehicle and pre-pay by credit card before your departure to ensure the best rates possible.

Italy is not quite the "vehicular-free-for-all" you may have heard about, at least not outside big cities (particularly Rome, Florence, and Milan). When visiting Rome, it's advisable to do so at the beginning or end of your trip, before you pick up or after you drop off your car, and, by all means, avoid driving within the city. Italians have a different relationship with the basic rules of the road: common maneuvers include running stop lights and stop signs, triple-parking, driving at 100 mph on the highways, passing on the right, and backing up at missed highway exits. But once out of the city, you will find it relatively easy to reach your destination. Road directions are quite good in Italy and people are very willing to help.

DISTANCES: Distances are indicated in kilometers (one kilometer equals 0.621 mile), calculated roughly into miles by cutting the kilometer distance in half. Distances between towns are also indicated in orange alongside the roads on the Touring Club Italiano maps. Italy is a compact country and distances are relatively short, yet you will be amazed at how dramatically the scenery can change in an hour's drive.

GASOLINE: Gas prices in Italy are the highest in Europe, and Americans often suspect a mistake when their first fill-up comes to between $45 and $80 (most of it in taxes). Most stations now accept Visa credit cards, and the ERG stations accept American Express. Besides the AGIP stations on the autostrade, which are almost always open, gas stations observe the same hours as merchants, closing in the afternoon from 12:30 to 4 and in the evening at 7:30. Be careful not to get caught running on empty in the afternoon! Many stations have a self-service pump that operates on off-hours and accepts only 10,000- or 50,000-lire bills.

MAPS: An above-average map of Italy is absolutely essential for this type of travel. The Touring Club Italiano maps, in an easy-to-read three-volume format divided into North, Central, and South, are a superior selection. Even the smallest town or, better, *localita* is indicated in the extensive index. Another fine choice is the Michelin series of maps. We use the Michelin 400 series maps (six regional maps) and the *Michelin Tourist and Motoring Atlas of Italy* (a book of maps). To outline your visit to Italy you might want to consider the one-page map of Italy, Michelin map 988. We sell these and regional Michelin green guides (sightseeing guides) in our website store at *www.karenbrown.com*.

ROADS: Names of roads in Italy are as follows:

Autostrada: a large, fast (and most direct) two- or three-lane tollway, marked by green signs bearing an "A" followed by the autostrada number. As you enter you receive a ticket from an automatic machine by pushing a red button. Payment is made at your exit point. If you lose your card, you will have to pay the equivalent amount of the distance from the beginning of the autostrada to your exit.

Superstrada: a one- or two-lane freeway between secondary cities marked by blue signs and given a number. Speed limit: 110 kph.

Strada Statale: a small one-lane road marked with S.S. followed by the road number. Speed limit: 90 kph.

Raccordo or *Tangenziale*: a ring road around main cities, connecting to an autostrada and city centers.

ROAD SIGNS: Yellow signs are for tourists and indicate sites of interest, hotels, and restaurants. Black-and-yellow signs indicate private companies and industries.

TOLLS: Tolls on Italian autostrade are quite steep, ranging from $15 to $28 for a three-hour stretch, but offering the fastest and most direct way to travel between cities. Fortunately for the agritourist, tollways are rarely necessary. However, if it suits your needs, a *Viacard*, or magnetic reusable card for tolls, is available in all tollway gas stations for 50,000 or 100,000 lire, or a MasterCard or Visa card can now be used in specified lanes (the lines for these automatic machines are always the shortest).

HOLIDAYS

It is very important to know Italian holidays because most museums, shops, and offices are closed. National holidays are listed below:

New Year's Day (January 1)   Assumption Day (August 15)
Epiphany (January 6)   All Saints' Day (November 1)
Easter (and the following Monday)   Christmas (December 25)
Liberation Day (April 25)   Santo Stefano (December 26)
Labor Day (May 1)

In addition to the national holidays, each town also has its own special holiday to honor its patron saint. Some of the major ones are listed below:

Bologna—St. Petronio (October 4)   Palermo—Santa Rosalia (July 15)
Florence—St. John the Baptist (June 24)   Rome—St. Peter (June 29)
Milan—St. Ambrose (December 7)   Venice—St. Mark (April 25)

The Vatican in Rome has its own schedule. The museums are closed every Sunday, except the last Sunday of each month when admission is free.

REGIONS

For reference, the 20 regions of Italy from north to south, with their capital cities in parentheses, are as follows:

NORTH—Valle d'Aosta (Aosta), Liguria (Genova), Piedmont (Torino), Friuli Venezia Giulia (Trieste), Trentino-Alto Adige (Trento & Bolzano), Lombardy (Milan), Veneto (Venice), and Emilia-Romagna (Bologna).

CENTRAL—Tuscany (Florence), Umbria (Perugia), Marches (Ancona), Lazio (Rome), Abruzzo (L'Aquila), and Molise (Campobasso).

SOUTH—Campania (Naples), Apulia (Bari), Calabria (Cantazaro), Basilicata (Potenza), Sicily (Palermo), and Sardinia (Caliari).

SAFETY

If certain precautions are taken, most unfortunate incidents can be avoided. It is extremely helpful to keep copies of passports, tickets, and contents of your wallet in your room in case you need them. Pickpocketing most commonly occurs in cities on buses, train stations, crowded streets, or from passing motorbikes. WARNING: At tollway gas stations and snack bars, **always** lock your car and beware of gypsies and vendors who try to sell you stolen merchandise. This practice is most prevalent south of Rome. In general, **never** leave valuables or even luggage in the car. Also, **never** set down luggage even for a minute in train stations.

Introduction—About Italy

SHOPPING

Italy is a shopper's paradise. Not only are the stores brimming with tempting merchandise, but the displays are works of art, from the tiniest fruit market to the most chic boutique. Each region seems to specialize in something: in Venice hand-blown glass and handmade lace are popular; Milan is famous for its clothing and silk; Florence is a center for leather goods and gold jewelry; Rome is a fashion hub, where you can stroll the pedestrian shopping streets and browse in some of the world's most elegant shops boasting the latest designer creations. Religious items are also plentiful in Rome, particularly near St. Peter's Cathedral. Naples and the surrounding area (Capri, Ravello, and Positano) offer delightful coral jewelry and also a wonderful selection of ceramics. You will be enticed by the variety of products sold at the farms such as wines, virgin olive oil, jams and honeys, cheese, and salami, along with local artisans' handicrafts. NOTE: For reasons of financial control and the tax evasion problems in Italy, the law states that clients **must** leave commercial establishments with an official receipt in hand, in order to avoid fines.

For purchases over 300,000 lire an immediate cash refund of the tax amount is offered by the Italian government to non-residents of the EU. Goods must be purchased at an affiliated retail outlet with the "tax-free for tourists" sign. Ask for the store receipt **plus** the tax-free shopping receipt. At the airport go first to the customs office where they will examine the items purchased and stamp both receipts, and then to the "tax-free cash refund" point after passport control.

US customs allows US residents to bring in $400-worth of foreign goods duty-free, after which a straight 10% of the amount above $400 is levied. Two bottles of liquor are allowed. The import of fresh cheese or meat is strictly restricted unless it is vacuum-packed.

TELEPHONES

The Italian phone company (TELECOM) has been an object of ridicule, a source of frustration, and a subject of heated conversation since its inception. Although more modern systems are being installed, it remains one of the most archaic and costly communication systems in the developed world, though touch-tone phones are now found in parts of the major cities. Telephone numbers can have from four to eight digits, so don't be afraid of missing numbers. Cellular phones have saved the day (Italians wouldn't be caught dead without one) and are recognized by four-digit area codes beginning with 03.

IMPORTANT NOTE: Since October 1998, all calls to Italy need to include the "0" (previously dropped) in the area code, whether calling from abroad, within Italy, or even within the same city.

Dial 113 for emergencies of all kinds—24-hour service nationwide.

Dial 116 for Automobile Club for urgent breakdown assistance on the road.

Remember that no warning is given when the time you've paid for in a public phone is about to expire (the line just goes dead), so put in plenty of change. Unused coins will be refunded. There are several types of phones (in various stages of modernization) in Italy:

Regular rotary phones in bars, restaurants, and many bed and breakfasts, which you can use *a scatti*, meaning you can pay the proprietor after the call is completed.

Bright-orange pay phones, which accept 500-, 200-, and 100-lire coins as well as *gettoni*. Bright-orange pay phones as above with attached apparatus permitting insertion of a *scheda telefonica,* or reusable magnetic card worth 5,000 or 10,000 lire.

NOTE: Due to the ongoing modernization process of telephone lines, phone numbers are constantly being changed, making it sometimes very difficult to contact lodgings (many times they are not listed under the lodging's name). A recording (in Italian) plays for only two months indicating the new number. If you are calling from the United States and your Italian is not up to par, we suggest you ask the overseas operator to contact the Italian operator for translation and assistance.

To call the United States from Italy, matters have been eased by the ongoing installation of the Country Direct System, whereby with one 200-lire coin you can reach an American operator by dialing either 172-1011 for AT&T or 172-1022 for MCI. Be patient and wait the one to two minutes before a recording or US operator comes through. Either a collect call or a credit-card call can then be placed. If you discover this system doesn't work from some smaller towns, dial 170 to place a collect call, or, in some cities, try dialing direct (from a *scatti* phone), using the international code 001 + area code + number.

TIPPING

Hotels: Service charges are normally included in four- and five-star hotels only. It is customary to leave a token tip for staff.

Restaurants: If a service charge is included, it will be indicated on the bill, otherwise 10–15% is standard tipping procedure.

Taxis: 10%.

TRAIN TRAVEL

Although a car is an absolute necessity to reach most bed and breakfasts, it is often convenient and time-saving to leave the car and take a train for day trips into the city. NOTE: Your ticket must be stamped with the time and date **before** you board the train; otherwise, you will be issued a 40,000-lire fine. Tickets are stamped at small and not very obvious yellow machines near the exits to the tracks. Unstamped tickets may be reimbursed with a 30% penalty. In order to avoid long lines at the station it is strongly advised that you purchase your ticket (including seat reservation) in advance through a local travel agency when you arrive in Italy or contact CIT train reservation service to book tickets from the States (tel: 800-248-8687). The IC and EC trains to major cities are the most efficient.

We wish you the best in your travels to Italy and always welcome your comments and suggestions. *Buon Viaggio!*

Bed & Breakfast Descriptions

Ostellato, Belfiore

In the heart of the wine valley of Piedmont, just above the town of Alba, lies the stately, cream-colored villa belonging to Giuliana Pionzo, her doctor husband Giuseppe, and sons Andrea and Fabrizio—Cascina Reine's gracious hosts. The guest book overflows with compliments and praise for their incredibly warm hospitality. Accommodation is offered within the ivy-covered main house, each room finely decorated with antiques, paintings, and the family's personal objects. A suite consisting of a bedroom, sitting room with two extra beds, bath, kitchenette, and large terrace is ideal for a family of four. Other equally charming rooms and apartments (one with facilities for the handicapped) are on the ground and first floors of the adjoining wing, one with its own private terrace. A full breakfast is served either outside under big umbrellas overlooking the vineyards and woods or inside in the pristine dining room with vaulted ceilings. There is a small above-ground pool to the side of the house. Alba boasts some of the finest restaurants in Italy and is also famous for its regional wines and prized truffle festival. The Giacosas have a piece of land dedicated to experimentation (with Torino University) of the cultivation of truffles, which are hunted by moonlight with trained dogs. *Directions*: From Alba follow signs for Barbaresco and Mango. Halfway up the hill on a large curve, watch for a small yellow sign indicating a gravel road on the left and then the wrought-iron gates of the property at the end of the road.

CASCINA REINE
(Villa La Meridiana)
Hosts: Giacosa family
Localita: Altavilla 9
Alba (CN) 12051, Italy
Tel & fax: (0173) 440112
5 rooms, 4 apartments
Lire 110,000–150,000 double B&B
Breakfast served, dinner upon request
Open all year, Handicap facilities
English spoken well, Region: Piedmont

Seven kilometers from historic Bergamo and within easy reach of beautiful Lakes Como, Iseo, and Garda is the home of the region's agritourist president, Gianantonio Ardizzone. On the property, next to the recently constructed residence where he and his family live, is a sprawling 15th-century farmhouse and barn quad complex of the type known in Lombardy as a *cascina.* Installed within the cascina are five guest apartments, each including one or two bedrooms, bathroom, and kitchen. The apartments are furnished modestly but comfortably, with a decidedly rustic ambiance within and without. Breakfast is served. The cascina is nestled in pretty surroundings, looking onto the small town of Nese and backing onto the green hills where well-tended riding horses are kept. Gianantonio delights in showing guests his hobbies—a collection of antique farm tools, fruit orchard, and ostrich breeding—and wife Lalla takes care of guests' daily requests. A nearby trattoria adequately appeases the appetite, or you may want to do some shopping before you arrive and come ready to prepare your own meals. The Grumello offers self-catering, conveniently located accommodation and outstanding value. Your hosts are exceptionally helpful and sincerely warm. *Directions:* Exit from the A4 autostrada at Bergamo and follow signs for Alzano Lombardo, Valle Seriana. Exit at Alzano after 6 km and follow hospital signs; go straight on for Nese and turn left on Via Grumello after 300 meters.

CASCINA GRUMELLO
Hosts: Gianantonio Ardizzone family
Localita: Fraz. Nese
Alzano Lombardo (BG) 24022, Italy
Tel: (035) 510060, Fax: (035) 738703
5 apartments
Lire 50,000 per person B&B
Breakfast only
Open all year, Credit cards: VS
Handicap facilities
Some English spoken, Region: Lombardy
www.karenbrown.com/italy/cascinagrumello.html

The southernmost tip of Umbria bordering Lazio offers a myriad of interesting sights and villages up for discovery and La Palombara is a splendid base from which to explore them. Signor Baldoni, a yacht broker from Rome, bought the 400-year-old country home made of stone with its six bedrooms mainly for entertaining. He enjoys the place so much that he had the one-story barn converted into a guesthouse with two apartments each containing three bedrooms, three bathrooms, and living room with kitchenette. They can be rented out either as separate rooms or as an entire apartment. The decor, as in his own home, is one of refined elegance, full of precious antiques and leather sofas. Coordinated color schemes in rooms follow through in English wallpaper, fabrics, and bathroom tiles. The large windows look out to the surrounding garden lined with hydrangeas, which includes a rose garden with many rare species. Guests relax poolside in the summer and are treated to a very special candlelit dinner prepared by the Count himself in the enormous veranda overlooking the pool. Gourmet cooking lessons mingled with the Count's advice on proper service and etiquette (*bon ton*) are an exceptional experience. In the colder months, afternoon tea is served before the fire in the Count's lovely home. A romantic retreat. *Directions*: Before entering Amelia, take a right for Acquasparta and follow the road for 4.5 km, staying left for Castel dell'Aquila. 2.5 km after Sambucetole turn left for Collicello. La Palombara is the first house on the left.

LA PALOMBARA
Host: Count Giancarlo Baldoni
Strada di Collicello 34
Amelia (TR) 05022, Italy
Tel: (0744) 988373, Fax: (0744) 988414
6 rooms with private bathrooms (or 2 apartments)
Lire 200,000 double B&B
3-night minimum stay
Breakfast served, dinner upon request
Open all year
English spoken well, Region: Umbria
www.karenbrown.com/italy/palombara.html

Borgo Argenina has all the elements of a "bestseller" bed and breakfast: the perfect location in the heart of Chianti, very comfortable accommodation within an ancient stone farmhouse, glorious countryside views, and, above all, Elena, the Borgo Argenina's doting and gregarious hostess. She left behind a life and successful fashion business in Milan and bought an entire abandoned village, restoring two of the stone houses for herself and the bed and breakfast. She chose the best artisans in the area and literally worked with them to create the house of her dreams. Everything from painting stenciled borders in rooms through restoring furniture to sewing quilted bedspreads is executed exclusively by Elena herself. Her enviable energy level and fierce determination has allowed her to overcome the many obstacles involved in the restoration work. The downstairs living rooms and breakfast room are beautifully done in rich cream and soft yellows that complement perfectly the brick-vaulted ceilings and terra-cotta floors. Elena is up at dawn baking cakes for breakfast accompanied by classical music. Every little detail has been attended to in the pink-and-blue bedrooms adorned with white eyelet curtains, patchwork quilts, and dried flower arrangements. The adorable independent house for three persons with terrace and views and two of the bedrooms have kitchen facilities. *Directions*: Follow route 408 from Siena for Gaiole and turn off to the right at Monti. Just before Monti and S. Marcellina there is a sign on the right for Argenina.

BORGO ARGENINA
Hostess: Elena Nappa
Localita: Argenina-Monti
Gaiole in Chianti (SI) 53013, Italy
Tel & fax: (0577) 747117
6 rooms with private bathrooms, 1 house
Lire 220,000 double B&B
* 280,000 house daily*
Breakfast only, Open all year
English spoken well
Region: Tuscany
www.karenbrown.com/italy/argenina.html

Nestled in the breathtaking scenery of the Subasio Mountains flanking Assisi is a cluster of stone houses known as Le Silve, once a village that served as a haven for 10th-century pilgrims traveling from the Adriatic coast to Rome. Carrying on that tradition of excellent meals and gracious hospitality, Daniela has added her own touch of elegance to the rustic setting. The guestrooms are tastefully appointed with pressed wildflowers framed over beds and antiques, which meld harmoniously with the preserved medieval architecture. The main house holds bedrooms on different levels divided by an occasional sitting area, reception area, living room with fireplace, and superb views onto the surrounding mountains. The adjacent house has a charming, beamed, stone-walled dining room with spacious bedrooms in the adjoining, single-level wing, each with its own front terrace. Daniela's twin sons are the dynamic young chefs while her husband runs the vast 600-plus-acre farm made up of woods, groves, and a deer reserve. Scattered about the property are various farmhouses that have been converted into apartments for weekly stays. This combination inn/agritourist facility has many amenities plus two swimming pools and tennis courts. *Directions:* From Assisi go in the direction of Gualdo Tadino and take the winding uphill road right at the sign for Armenzano, following it for 10 km. The hotel is just after Armenzano village and is well marked.

LE SILVE DI ARMENZANO
Hosts: Daniela Taddia family
Localita: Armenzano
Assisi (PG) 06081, Italy
Tel: (075) 8019000, Fax: (075) 8019005
20 rooms with private bathrooms
* 7 apartments*
Lire 280,000–300,000 double B&B
All meals served
Open March to November, Credit cards: all major
Fluent English spoken
Region: Umbria

The delightful Malvarina farm with its charming, country-style accommodations, excellent local cuisine, warm and congenial host family, and ideal location has been a long-time favorite of our readers. Just outside town, yet immersed in lush green vegetation at the foot of the Subasio Mountains, the property is comprised of the 15th-century stone farmhouse where the family lives and four independent cottages (converted barn and stalls) divided into bedrooms and suites with en-suite bathrooms, plus three apartments with kitchenettes for two to four persons. *Casa Angelo* holds several bedrooms plus a sweet breakfast room with a corner fireplace and cupboards filled with colorful Deruta ceramics. Great care has obviously been taken in the decor of rooms, using Mamma's family's heirloom furniture. The old wine cellar has been cleverly converted into a cool and spacious taverna dining room with long wooden tables for dining *en famille* if not out on the veranda terrace. Cooking classes are very popular here. A collection of antique farm tools and brass pots cover walls near the enormous fireplace. Horses are available for three- to seven-day trekking trips into the scenic national park just beyond the house, led by gregarious host, Claudio. A welcome addition is the new swimming pool for guests. *Directions*: Exit at Capodacqua from the Perugia-Spello route 75. Turn right then left on Via Massera (Radio Subasio sign) and follow the road up to Malvarina.

MALVARINA
Hosts: Claudio Fabrizi family
Localita: Malvarina 32
Assisi (PG) 06080, Italy
Tel & fax: (075) 8064280
Email: malvarina@umbria.net
10 rooms with private bathrooms, 3 apartments
Lire 160,000 double B&B (3-night minimum stay)
* 130,000 per person half board*
Breakfast & dinner served
Open all year, Credit cards: all major
Some English spoken, Region: Umbria
www.karenbrown.com/italy/malvarina.html

Fabrizio and Bianca, the Milanese hosts originally from this part of Umbria, restored their inherited La Fornace farmhouse, situated in the very desirable touring location of Assisi, with their guests' comfort foremost in mind. With careful attention to detail, four comfortable apartments were fashioned within the three stone houses, each with one or two bedrooms, bathroom, fully equipped kitchenette, and eating area. Interesting decorating touches such as parts of antique iron gates hung over beds, terra-cotta and white ceramic tiles in the immaculate bathrooms, and antique armoires give the accommodations a polished country flavor. *Le Pannocchie*, the largest of the four, includes a corner fireplace, while *Papaveri* looks out over the flat cornfields up to magnificent Assisi and the Subasio Mountains beyond. The Cascioli family looks after guests when the owners are away and stocks each apartment with breakfast fixings. At guests' request guided tours are arranged to Umbria's top sights. Besides a lovely swimming pool for guests, bikes, ping-pong, and games for children are on hand. *Directions*: From Perugia-Spoleto highway 75, exit at Ospedalicchio on route 147, turn left for Tordibetto after the bridge, then right for Assisi and follow signs for La Fornace.

PODERE LA FORNACE
Hosts: Bianca & Fabrizio Feliciani
Via Ombrosa 3
Tordibetto di Assisi (PG) 06081, Italy
Tel: (075) 8019537 or (0330) 282154
Fax: (075) 8019630
4 apartments
Lire 145,000–315,000 per apartment daily
3-night minimum stay
Breakfast included with weekly stays
Closed February, Credit cards: all major
English spoken well (hosts)
Region: Umbria

After many years of traveling to Italy at any free opportunity, Jennie and Alan left England to move to Tuscany and fell in love immediately with Villa Mimosa, a rustic, 18th-century home with a shady front courtyard facing the street in town. Alan got to work right away with restoring and transforming the upstairs into guest quarters, creating three sweet bedrooms, each with a different theme. He added small, but very practical bathrooms in each room. A cozy sitting room and library with grand piano are reserved upstairs for guests and decorated with their own antiques shipped over from England. Jennie and Alan's idea with offering a few rooms was to share their passion for this part of the country known as Lunigiana (very near the Cinque Terre coastal area and one hour from both Parma and Lucca) and give their guests lots of personal attention, while making them feel right at home. Guests are treated to breakfast on the terrace overlooking the vegetable garden and Apennine Mountains and delight in Jennie's creative cuisine based on fresh garden vegetables and local recipes. *Directions*: Exit from the A15 autostrada (Parma-La Spezia) at Pontremoli from the north or Aulla from the south and head north alongside the autostrada to Villafranca, then Bagnone. Enter town through the gateway and turn left at Via N. Quartieri. Go uphill to Corlaga for 3 km and Villa Mimosa is on the right-hand side before the church.

VILLA MIMOSA
Hosts: Jennie & Alan Pratt
Localita: Corlaga
Bagnone (MS) 54021, Italy
Tel & fax: (0187) 427022
3 rooms with private bathrooms
From lire 160,000 double B&B
Breakfast served, dinner upon request
Open all year
Fluent English spoken
Region: Tuscany

In the heart of the Veneto region, south of Vicenza, lies the Castello winery and estate, a handsome 15th-century villa watching proudly over the sweet town of Barbarano Vicentino and the home of the Marinoni family for the past century. Signora Elda, along with her two young children, Lorenzo and Maddalena, carries on the tradition. The large walled courtyard with manicured Renaissance garden is bordered by the family's home, the guesthouse (originally farmer's quarters), and converted barn, where concerts and banquets are organized. A lovely courtyard overlooks the family's expansive vineyards from which top-quality (D.O.C.G.) red wines are produced. The independent two-story guesthouse overlooking the garden can be rented out as one house or divided into three apartments. It has recently been renovated, with each apartment having one or two bedrooms, bathroom, and kitchenette with sitting area, and decorated simply but pleasantly with the family's furnishings. This is an excellent, economical base from which to visit the Veneto region. It's an easy drive to Padua and Venice where you may opt to leave your car and take the train. *Directions*: Exit from the A4 at Vicenza Est towards Noventa Vicentino, then Barbarano Vicentino. Follow signs to Castello (20 km).

IL CASTELLO
Hosts: Elda Marinoni family
Via Castello 6
Barbarano Vicentino (VI) 36021, Italy
Tel & fax: (0444) 886055
Email: castellomarinoni@tin.it
3 apartments
Lire 40,00-45,000 per person daily
3-night minimum stay
No meals served
Open all year
English spoken well
Region: Veneto
www.karenbrown.com/italy/ilcastello.html

The area around the city of Alba is true wine country, where vineyards cover every possible inch of land, making Chianti look almost barren! Of course, where there is good wine, there is good food and the region abounds in famous restaurants. Giovanna, an independent producer of wine, admirably manages her grandparents' farm and bed and breakfast single-handedly—a childhood dream of hers. She abandoned the business world for a more tranquil pace and loves welcoming travelers who are looking for a home away from home, wholesome foods, and the simple pleasures of country life. The mustard-colored house backed by striped hillsides has a separate guest entrance. A large informal living room filled with books and local wine itineraries includes a corner kitchen where guests sit at a table for a self-service breakfast. Upstairs are the three country-style bedrooms, each with a different color scheme. The pink room has twin beds and a vineyard view while the green and blue rooms have queen beds. They each have new, immaculate bathrooms, and are decorated with grandmother's lace curtains, old photographs, brass beds, and patchwork quilts. Three apartments for longer stays accommodating two to four persons have just been completed. *Directions*: From Alba (6 km) follow signs for Barbaresco. Before town at the sign for Tre Stelle, look for Cascina delle Rose on the left. From Asti follow signs for Alba-Barbaresco-Treiso. After Barbaresco, on the road towards Alba, watch for Tre Stelle and the bed and breakfast on the right.

CASCINA DELLE ROSE
Hostess: Giovanna Rizzolio
Localita: Tre Stelle
Barbaresco (CN) 12050, Italy
Tel: (0173) 638292, Fax: (0173) 638322
3 rooms with private bathrooms, 3 apartments
Lire 160,000 double B&B
2-night minimum stay (rooms)
4-night minimum stay (apartments)
Breakfast only, Open all year
English spoken well, Region: Piedmont

La Casa Sola is just that—an ancient villa standing alone on a hilltop surrounded by bucolic countryside. The gracious proprietors and hosts, a noble Genovese family, are assisted by the local Regoli family who tend to this gorgeous 400-acre vineyard estate in the heart of Chianti. Their prestigious production of Chianti Classico, Cabernet, Merlot, and olive oil is of the highest quality. There are six large guest apartments on two floors of a rose-covered stone farmhouse down the road from the main villa. All the apartments are comprised of a living room, kitchen, bedrooms, and baths, with private entrances and garden. Each apartment is furnished in style with selected country antiques, numbers 3 and 5 being the loveliest. Details such as botanical prints hung with bows, eyelet curtains, fresh flowers, and a bottle of wine are welcome touches. Number 5, for up to eight people, is the most spacious, with three bedrooms, fireplace, and magnificent views over the Barberino Valley and cypress woods. *Il Capanno* in the converted barn is a delightful "nest" for honeymooners. An inviting swimming pool overlooks the valley surrounding the main villa. An ideal touring base in a tranquil, romantic setting. *Directions*: Leave the Firenze-Siena superstrada at San Donato in Poggio. 1.5 km after San Donato at the church, turn right for Cortine/Casa Sola, and follow it for 2.5 km.

FATTORIA CASA SOLA
Hosts: Count Gambaro family
Localita: Cortine
Barberino Val d'Elsa (FI) 50021, Italy
Tel: (055) 8075028, Fax: (055) 8059194
6 apartments
Lire 750,000–3,500,000 weekly (July & August)
  (heating/cleaning extra)
Breakfast & dinner served upon request
Open all year
English & French spoken well
Region: Tuscany

Strategically positioned midway between Siena and Florence sits the square stone farmhouse with cupola (actually one of the bedrooms!) dating to 1700 owned by Gianni and Cristina, a couple from Milan who have dedicated their lives to the equestrian arts. The Paretaio appeals particularly to visitors with a passion for horseback riding, for the de Marchis offer everything from basic riding lessons to dressage training, and day outings through the gorgeous surrounding countryside. In fact, the Paretaio is recognized as one of the top riding "ranches" in Tuscany. On the ground floor is a rustic living room with country antiques, comfy sofas, and piano enhanced by a vaulted brick ceiling and worn terra-cotta floors. Upstairs, the main gathering area is the dining room, which features a massive fireplace and a seemingly endless wooden table. Acccss to most bedrooms is from this room, and each is decorated with touches such as dried flowers, white lace curtains, and, of course, equestrian prints. A vast collection of over 300 pieces with an equestrian theme is displayed about the home. Il Paretaio also organizes courses in Italian and is an excellent base for touring the heart of Tuscany. The swimming pool gives splendid views over olive groves and vineyards. *Directions*: Head south from Barberino on route 2 and after 2 km take the second right-hand turnoff for San Filippo and continue on 1.5 km of dirt road to the house.

IL PARETAIO
Hosts: Cristina & Giovanni de Marchi
Localita: San Filippo
Barberino Val d'Elsa (FI) 50021, Italy
Tel: (055) 8059218, Cellphone: (0338) 7379626
Fax: (055) 8059231, Email: ilparetaio@tin.it
6 rooms with private bathrooms, 2 apartments
Lire 80,000–170,000 double B&B
  110,000–130,000 per person half board
  800,000–1,000,000 weekly per apartment
Breakfast & dinner served, Open all year
English & French spoken very well, Region: Tuscany
www.karenbrown.com/italy/ilparetaio.html

Sitting among woods along a small river is the Molino dell'Argenna, a 16th-century grain mill miraculously transformed into an elegant bed and breakfast. Liliana and Pierpaolo, the cordial hosts, took on the challenging project of restoring the stone mill. Pierpaolo provided the know-how, having worked on the restoration of homes for many years, while Liliana added style in her careful selection of antiques, rich fabrics, and soft colour schemes in rooms. Five romantic bedrooms accessed from the exterior of the mill have smart travertine bathrooms and many hotel amenities, with special touches such as embroidered linen sheets. The charm of the home comes not only from its decor, but also from its being built on different levels with terraces, balconies, and archways leading to private corners. Guests have breakfast served either in bedrooms or out on private patios, as well as in the intimate dining room where Pierpaolo fulfills his passion for creative cooking. Divine gourmet dinners are accompanied by a very selective list of wines. Close to the house is a large swimming pool with Jacuzzi. Behind the home is the *Molinetto*, a miniature version of the mill where a delightfully private one-bedroom loft with living room and terrace is offered. *Directions*: Conveniently located near the main road. Exit at S. Donato from the Florence-Siena highway and after S. Donato town follow signs for Castellina. Turn left on a dirt road after the La Ripa sign at km 9.5.

RELAIS MOLINO DELL'ARGENNA   **New**
Hosts: Liliana Cajelli & Pierpaolo Porcù
Localita: S. Silvestro 17
Barberino Val d'Elsa (FI) 50021, Italy
Tel: (055) 8072354, Fax: (055) 8072310
Cellphone: (0368) 7563003
5 rooms with private bathrooms
Lire 220,000 double B&B
  Lire 1,500,000–2,000,000 weekly per loft
2-night minimum stay
All meals served, Open all year
Very little English spoken
Region: Tuscany

When the Caccetta family and three other families purchased the 250-acre property just over 20 years ago, they were true pioneers in agritourism. After many years of restoring both the land and historic 16th-century hunting lodge, today they have a self-sufficient organic farm producing top-quality Chianti, white and rosé wines, grappa, and olive oil. Spacious guestrooms are divided between the main house, with two suites and three bedrooms, and an adjacent house. All are decorated with care and attention to detail using lovely family antiques, which blend in perfectly with the overall refined ambiance. The very cozy common rooms include a living room with fireplace and stone walls, card room, small bar area, and dining rooms where breakfast and dinner are served. Amiable hosts Gianfranco and Damiano take care of guests. During the warmer months, a buffet breakfast and dinner are served outside under the pergola overlooking deep woods. A set four-course dinner consists of traditional Tuscan recipes using primarily fresh vegetables and aromatic herbs. A swimming pool, grass tennis courts, many hiking trails into the surrounding woods, and horseback riding at a nearby stables are all available. *Directions*: From the Siena-Florence highway, exit at San Donato, drive to Tavarnelle then Barberino, and turn right at the La Spinosa sign. Take the dirt road to the very end.

LA SPINOSA
Hosts: Caccetta, Presezzi, Ossola & Videsott families
Via Le Masse 8
Barberino Val d'Elsa (FI) 50021, Italy
Tel: (055) 8075413, Fax: (055) 8066214
Email: info@ laspinosa.it
5 rooms, 4 suites with private bathrooms
Lire 240,000–280,000 double B&B
  170,000–190,000 per person half board
3-night minimum stay
Breakfast, light lunch & dinner served
Open March to November, Credit cards: MC, VS
English spoken very well, Region: Tuscany
www.karenbrown.com/italy/laspinosa.html

The Bad Dreikirchen is situated up in the Dolomite foothills with an enchanting view over a lush green valley and distant snowcapped mountain peaks. The young and energetic Wodenegg family works diligently at making guests feel at home in their lovely residence and at running the busy restaurant, which serves typical local meals to non-guest patrons as well as guests since it shares the site of a unique historical monument— *Le Tre Chiese*, three curious, attached, miniature medieval churches. This unique inn is accessible only by taxi or Jeep, or on foot. An exhilarating half-hour hike takes you up to the typical mountain-style chalet with long wood balconies in front. The most charming rooms are those in the older section, entirely wood-paneled, with fluffy comforters and old-fashioned washbasins. The rambling house has several common areas for guests as well as a swimming pool. This is truly an incredible spot, near the Siusi Alps and Val Gardena where some of the best climbing in Europe can be found. *Directions*: Exit from the Bolzano-Brennero autostrada A22 at Chiusa, cross the river, and take S.S.12 south to Ponte Gardena. Take the road on the right up to Barbian and call the hotel from the village for a pickup by Jeep (22,000 lire).

BAD DREIKIRCHEN
Hosts: Annette & Matthias Wodenegg family
San Giacomo 6
Barbian, (BZ) 39040, Italy
Tel: (0471) 650055, Fax: (0471) 650044
Email: wodenegg.matthias@rolmail.net
30 rooms, 20 with private bathrooms
Lire 60,000–111,000 per person half board
Breakfast & dinner served
Open May 11 to November 4
English spoken well
Region: Trentino-Alto Adige
www.karenbrown.com/italy/baddreikirchen.html

Just 2 kilometers outside Barolo in the area where the famous wine is produced sits the long rectangular farmhouse of Raffaella Pittatore, passed down to her from her grandparents. After years of working for a major tour-operator company, and living in many parts of the world, she has come back home with her young son, ready to impart her hospitality experience to her own guests. She is a natural hostess, friendly and accommodating, with a *joie de vivre* that is truly refreshing. One year after opening, four bedrooms in the attached former barn were added to the four already existing on the first floor. These are simply furnished with the family's country furniture and each has its own bathroom, with one having a kitchenette. Downstairs you find an informal living room and breakfast room with original brick ceilings and floors. Guests can use the kitchen or barbecue, if desired, and breakfast is served out on the front patio in fine weather. Although there are no particular views, the crossroads location is convenient for touring this beautiful Piedmont wine country, the price economical, and the hospitality exceptional. Raffaella has put together many interesting local itineraries including quaint villages, castles, wine museums, and vineyards. *Directions*: From Alba (10 km) follow signs for Barolo and at the turnoff stay to the left. The entrance to the bed and breakfast is on the right-hand side of the road just at this fork.

IL GIOCO DELL'OCA
Hostess: Raffaella Pittatore
Via Crosia 46
Barolo (CN) 12060, Italy
Tel & fax: (0173) 56206, Cellphone: (0338) 5999426
8 rooms with private bathrooms
Lire 110,000–130,000 double B&B
Breakfast only
Open all year
Credit cards: MC, VS
English spoken very well
Region: Piedmont

The expansive Pomurlo farm, home to the congenial Minghelli family, covers 370 acres of hills, woods, and open fields and is an excellent base for touring Umbria. A winding dirt road leads to the typical stone house, which contains a restaurant featuring organically grown, farm-fresh specialties. An antique cupboard and old farm implements on the walls enhance the rustic setting. A nearby converted stall houses two adorable independent rooms looking out over the lake. Other guestrooms and apartments are found in two large hilltop homes commanding a breathtaking view of the entire valley with its grazing herds of longhorn cattle. The main house, a 12th-century tower fortress where the inn's personable hostess Daniela resides, accommodates guests in three additional suites of rooms. Breakfast fixings are provided in rooms. The acquisition of the neighboring property has resulted in a center (*Le Casette*) offering more service—three stone farmhouses containing several other rooms and a restaurant around a large swimming pool. Comfortable and cheerful, all rooms are decorated with wrought-iron beds, colorful bedspreads, and typical regional country antiques. Activities such as tennis, soccer, and mountain biking are available. *Directions*: The farm is conveniently located near the Rome-Florence autostrada. Take the Orvieto exit from the A1 and follow signs for Todi, **not** for Baschi. On route N448 turn right at the sign for Pomurlo.

POMURLO VECCHIO
Hosts: Lazzaro Minghelli & family
Localita: Lago di Corbara
Baschi (TR) 05023, Italy
Tel: (0744) 950190 or 957645, Fax: (0744) 950500
25 rooms & apartments
Lire 85,000–105,000 per person half board
Trattoria on premises
Open all year, Handicap facilities
Some English & French spoken
Region: Umbria

Only 30 kilometers from Milan, the Cascina Maremma is the pure definition of agritourism: a 100-acre working farm using strictly organic methods; offering accommodation and meals using more than 80% of the farm's own produce; and organizing lessons in organic production and the agri-ecosystem. It is also part of the Ticino River Park reserve, which can be explored by bike, horse, or foot only. The typical *cascina* in northern Italy is a quad formation with large inner courtyard lined with houses, stalls and barns. Over the years the very involved hosts, Alberto and family, have vastly improved the comfort level and charming decor of the accommodations, which are situated in two side-by-side colorful ex-farmers' houses. Cheerful rooms (with air conditioning), two with external private bathrooms, have country furnishings and beamed ceilings and are accented with matching floral curtains and bedspreads. The delightful downstairs dining rooms maintain their true country flavor with antiques, fireplace, and wood-burning oven dating to the 1600s. On weekends people from the city come to enjoy the excellent, wholesome meals. Within reach are Malpensa airport, the lake region, Vigevano, and Morimondo. *Directions*: Exit Autostrada A7 (Genova-Milano) at Rinasco and head towards Castrate Primo, Besate. In the small town of Besate look for a sign for the cascina and follow this country road for 2 km to the farm.

CASCINA MAREMMA   *New*
Hosts: Alberto Romani family
Strada per il Ticino
Besate (MI) 20080, Italy
Tel & fax: (02) 9050020
10 rooms with private bathrooms
Lire 100,000–120,000 double B&B
* 75,000–90,000 per person half board*
Breakfast & dinner served
Open all year, Credit cards: MC, VS
English spoken well
Region: Lombardy

The Locanda, a pale-yellow-and-brick house dating from 1830, sits on the border between Tuscany and Umbria and is an excellent base from which to explore this rich countryside. The villa's dining room features a vaulted ceiling in toast-colored brick, an enormous fireplace, French windows opening out to the flower garden, and antiques including a cupboard adorned with the family's blue-and-white china. The upstairs quarters are reserved primarily for guests, and contain five comfortable rooms all off one hallway and an inviting sitting room and library. The cozy bedrooms have mansard ceilings, armoires, lovely linens, and washbasins. Additional guestrooms are located on the ground floor of the converted barn between the house and a small garden. These are more spacious, private, and modern in decor. Cordial hostess Palmira assists with local itineraries. Excellent regional fare including divine vegetarian dishes with local produce is prepared by local cooks. Siena is only 45 kilometers away, and the quaint medieval and Renaissance villages of Pienza, Montepulciano, and Montalcino are close by. *Directions*: Exit from the Rome-Florence autostrada at Val di Chiana. Head toward Bettolle, then bear right toward Siena. Follow signs for La Bandita.

LOCANDA LA BANDITA
Hostess: Palmira Fiorini
Via Bandita 72
Bettolle-Sinalunga (SI) 53040, Italy
Tel & fax: (0577) 624649
Email: info@locandalabandita.it
9 rooms with private bathrooms
Lire 160,000 double B&B
Breakfast served, dinner with reservation
Open all year
Credit cards: all major
English spoken well
Region: Tuscany
www.karenbrown.com/italy/locandalabandita.html

The vast Torre Burchio property is immersed in 1,500 acres of wooded wildlife preserve where wild boar, deer, hare, and pheasant abound. Seemingly far away from "civilization," this Italian version of a ranch offers a relaxing holiday in close touch with nature, while still being in reach of Umbria's top sights. The reception, restaurant, and six guest bedrooms are within the main 18th-century farmhouse, which maintains the ambiance of the original hunting lodge with hunting trophies on the walls, large open fireplace, cozy living room, and library. The upstairs breakfast room, from which the bedrooms lead, is lined with colourful Deruta ceramics. An additional eight bedrooms are found in a single-story house just across from the lodge, while the eight very comfortable apartments with kitchenettes are in a beautifully restored 230-year-old stone house with inner courtyard 4 kilometers down the road. The rooms and apartments are very nicely appointed with antiques, pretty fabrics, paintings, and large bathrooms, and have telephones and televisions. Guests gather in the busy restaurant in the evening for a hearty meal based on organic products from the farm. Many activities such as cooking classes, horseback-riding weeks, and sports are available. *Directions*: 20 km from either Perugia or Assisi. From the center of Bettona, follow signs for 5 Cerri-Torre Burchio and follow the dirt road through the woods for 5 km to the main house/reception.

TORRE BURCHIO   New
Hosts: Maria Casavecchia & Alvaro Sfascia
Localita: Bettona
Bettona (PG) 06084, Italy
Tel: (075) 9885017, Fax: (075) 987150
14 rooms, 8 apartments
Lire 130,000–170,000 double B&B
  95,000–115,000 per person half board
  600,000–1,400,000 weekly per apartment
3-night minimum stay, All meals served
Closed January
English spoken well
Region: Umbria

Luisa and Sergio left their fashion business in Parma and settled in this peaceful and varied landscape 3 kilometers from the coast after the stone farmhouse was extensively restored. The stylish, impeccable home clearly reflects the personalities of the warm and reserved hosts who themselves tastefully designed both the exterior and interiors. The idea of offering hospitality was a natural one since the four corner bedrooms upstairs each has its own large private terrace and beautiful floral-tiled bathroom. All offer beds made with linen sheets and splendid views over fruit orchards and olive groves to the sea. While the hosts occupy the cupola, guests have a separate entrance to the upstairs rooms, giving utmost privacy to all. Common areas include the living room and open kitchen with large arched window and doors looking out to the surrounding garden. An ample fresh country breakfast with cakes all prepared by Luisa is served here. A separate cottage next to the main house offers a double room and beamed living room with stone fireplace and kitchen. Day trips include Elba Island, Volterra and San Gimignano, Lucca, Siena, private beaches, Etruscan itineraries, visits to the wine estates of Bolgheri, and biking in the nearby nature park. *Directions*: Exit from Aurelia on route 1 at Bibbona and turn left. Pass through the town of La California and turn left for Bibbona. Podere Le Mezzelune is before town, well marked to the left. Pisa airport is 40 km away.

PODERE LE MEZZELUNE
Hosts: Luisa & Sergio Chiesa
Via Mezzelune 126
Bibbona (LI) 57020, Italy
Tel: (0586) 670266, Fax: (0586) 671814
Email: mezzelune@pop.multinet.it
4 rooms with private bathrooms, 1 cottage
Lire 235,000–265,000 double B&B
  1,350,000–1,650,000 cottage weekly
Breakfast only
Open all year, Credit cards: MC, VS
No English spoken, Region: Tuscany
www.karenbrown.com/italy/mezzelune.html

This guide includes some small urban hotels for the convenience of travelers who would like to do some metropolitan sightseeing. For some reason, the city of Bologna is often bypassed by visitors, despite its rich past, beautiful historic center, arcaded streets, and elegant shops. Cristina, Serena, and Mauro Orsi, the owners of the splendid, four-star Hotel Corona d'Oro, mentioned in another of our guides, *Italy: Charming Inns & Itineraries,* own two other centrally located, smaller hotels: the Orologio and the Commercianti. Just steps away from Bologna's main piazza and Basilica you find the recently renovated Orologio, so-called because it looks onto city hall with its clock tower. The reception desk on the ground floor leads upstairs to a large sitting and dining room where a buffet breakfast is served. From this level there is an elevator up to the newly remodeled rooms with lovely antiques, fabric walls, and white and gray marble bathrooms. The elegantly decorated rooms have all amenities and most have views of the square. Bicycles are available free of charge to our readers to visit the city's historical center and main monuments. The owners also organize personalized cooking classes, tickets for special events, and private tours of Bologna and surrounding cities. *Directions*: Located in the heart of the old city. Private garage facilities are available upon reservation (restricted traffic in historical center).

HOTEL OROLOGIO
Hosts: Cristina Orsi family
Via IV Novembre 10
Bologna 40123, Italy
Tel: (051) 231253, Fax: (051) 260552
Email: hotoro@tin.it
31 rooms with private bathrooms
Lire 305,000–525,000 double B&B
  Lire 395,000–770,000 daily per suite
Breakfast only
Open all year, Credit cards: all major
English spoken well, Region: Emilia-Romagna
www.karenbrown.com/italy/hotelorologio.html

Bed & Breakfast Descriptions   47

Bolsena is a quaint, ancient village 18 kilometers from Orvieto right on picturesque Lake Bolsena with its small ports and two islands. Marco Zammarano, with his long hotelier experience in Rome, took over the family's 60-acre hillside farm property just above town and opened lovely bed and breakfast accommodation within two stone farmhouses. The main house holds eleven beamed bedrooms each with en-suite bathroom, satellite TV, and fridge, simply but comfortably appointed with a mix of wicker furniture and country antiques. All but two have gorgeous views over the manicured garden and swimming pool out to the lake. The remaining four bedrooms are farther up the wooded road in another house with its own swimming pool. A third residence with an additional ten rooms was being completed when we visited. A restaurant for guests only has an ample outside terrace enjoying sunsets over the lake and takes advantage of ingredients fresh from the farm. Here you have the convenience of being near town and many interesting Etruscan sights while being immersed in utter tranquillity. The lake itself offers many activities including a fascinating boat ride to the small, historic island of Bisentina. *Directions*: Exit the A1 autostrada at Orvieto and follow signs for Bolsena. Just before town at the Trattoria Castagneta, turn right up to La Riserva. Shuttle service is available from the Rome airport or Orvieto train station.

LA RISERVA MONTEBELLO   *New*
Host: Marco Zammarano
Strada Orvietana Km 3
Bolsena (VT) 01023, Italy
Tel: (0761) 799492, Fax: (0761) 798965
Cellphone: (0335) 5310801
15 rooms with private bathrooms
Lire 140,000–180,000 double B&B
* 110,000–140,000 per person half board*
All meals served
Closed January, Credit cards: all major
English spoken well
Region: Lazio

A pocket of absolutely stunning yet unexplored countryside is the Oltrepo Pavese hills, 60 kilometers south of Milan. It is predominantly wine country producing top-quality Cortese, Pinot, Barbera, and Riesling. Less than an hour's drive away is the Alba/Asti wine region of Piedmont and the Italian Riviera. Also not to be missed are historic Pavia and its celebrated Certosa monastery. What better place to set up a home base than the Castello di Stefanago where a variety of accommodation is available. The two Baruffaldi brothers work diligently at producing wines and maintaining their 600-acre property. The 12th-century castle perched atop a hill and taking in spectacular views houses the host families and five lovely suites for two to five persons. Each has a bathroom, living area, and kitchenette and has been decorated appropriately with the family's period furniture. Below the castle on the road is a restored farmhouse, *La Boatta*, where a restaurant and six sweet double bedrooms are available. Each room has coordinated Provençal-patterned spreads and curtains with spotless bathrooms. Typical meals are served using fresh produce directly from the farm. (Fixed menu 45,000 lire.) *Directions*: Exit at Bereguardo/Pavia on the A7 autostrada from Milan. Follow it to Pavia (skirting the city) and then Casteggio. Drive on to Montebello-Borgo Priolo-Fortunago-Stefanago and up the long drive to the castle.

CASTELLO DI STEFANAGO
Hosts: Patrizia & Giacomo Baruffaldi
Borgo Priolo (PV) 27040, Italy
Tel: (0383) 875227 or 875413, Fax: (0383) 875644
6 rooms with private bathrooms, 5 suites
Lire 100,000–260,000 double B&B
All meals served
Open February to November
Credit cards: all major
Some English spoken
Region: Lombardy
www.karenbrown.com/italy/stefanago.html

Just off the busy road that connects the major towns of Umbria—Perugia, Assisi, Spoleto, and Todi—is the elegant country house Giulia, which has been in the Petrucci family since its 14th-century origins. Later additions were built on to the main stone villa, one of which Signora Caterina has opened up to guests. Time seems to have stood still in the six bedrooms, all but one with en-suite bathroom, and filled with grandmother Giulia's lovely antique wrought-iron beds, armoires, and period paintings. They are divided among three floors, accessed by a steep stone staircase, the largest having a ceiling fresco depicting the local landscape. Another room with handicapped facilities has been added on the ground floor. Breakfast is served either in the chandeliered dining room upstairs, with Oriental carpets, lace curtains, and a large fireplace, or under the oak trees in the front garden during the warmer months. The family's frescoed quarters can be rented out for weddings. Part of the barn has been converted into two independent units, which include a fully equipped kitchenette for up to four persons. Although the large swimming pool overlooks a rather barren field and the distant main road, it is a welcome respite after a full day of touring, which guests do a lot of from this strategically convenient location. *Directions*: Just off the Perugia-Spoleto route 75 between Trevi and Campello.

CASA GIULIA
Hostess: Caterina Alessandrini Petrucci
Via S.S. Flaminia km.140.1
Bovara di Trevi (PG) 06039, Italy
Tel: (0742) 78257, Fax: (0742) 381632
7 rooms, 6 with private bathrooms
 2 apartments
Lire 170,000–190,000 double B&B
 120,000–200,000 daily per apartment
Breakfast only, Open all year
Some English spoken
Region: Umbria

The town of Brisighella is a gem and comes to life during the first half of July with its annual Medieval Festival when games of the period are re-enacted, and medieval music, literature, and dance are produced. Locals attire themselves in appropriate costume and torches illuminate the village's narrow streets nightly for the occasion. Just out of town sits the sweet farmhouse of Ettore (a former architect) and Adriana, with its 10 hectares of organically cultivated vineyards and orchards. Guests can learn about the production of the hosts' excellent Sangiovese and Chardonnay wines. The renovated barn next to their small brick house holds two guestrooms and a rustic dining area with exposed beams and a large fireplace where guests gather for typical Romagna-style meals. A third bedroom is within their own home and the ex-barn provides a cozy apartment for two to five. Breakfast is served out on the covered terrace overlooking a quiet valley lined with vineyards. Rooms are decorated with simple country furnishings. The atmosphere is casual and the value excellent. "Must sees" are the mosaics in Ravenna, Bologna's historical center, and the international ceramic museum in Faenza. *La Torre* golf club is 8 kilometers away. *Directions*: Take the Faenza exit from the A14 between Bologna and Rimini. Follow signs for Brisighella or Firenze. At town turn left for Terme/Modigliana. Il Palazzo is the third identical house on the left after the Hotel Terme.

IL PALAZZO
Hosts: Ettore Matarese family
Via Baccagnano 11
Brisighella (RA) 48013, Italy
Tel & fax: (0546) 80338
Email: ematarese@racine.ra.it
3 rooms with private bathrooms, 1 apartment
Lire 120,000 double B&B
  700,000–900,000 weekly per apartment
3-night minimum stay
All meals served, Open March to October
English spoken well, Region: Emilia-Romagna
www.karenbrown.com/italy/ilpalazzo.html

Yet another addition to the fast-growing agritourism sector is the lovely 300-acre countryside property of the Toscano brothers. Giovanni transferred from Florence to be a permanent resident at his grandfather's vineyards. After years of meticulous restoration work on the group of three stone houses, they opened doors to guests, offering very comfortable accommodation within eight apartments of varying size (one to four bedrooms). One pale-yellow building holds two large apartments while the third stone structure holds the remaining apartments and has an arched loggia on the second floor. Rooms are tastefully decorated with antiques and country fabrics, enhancing the original beams and brick floors. Among the many services offered are individual telephones, satellite television, barbecue facilities, and bike rentals. The landscaping with its many cypress trees is as impeccable as the general ambiance. Attention to detail is evident also in the organization of activities such as wine-tastings, cooking lessons, and guided itineraries to Florence, Siena, and Arezzo. Beautiful scenery surrounds you, especially by the pool, seemingly part of the natural setting. Breakfast and other meals can be taken in the dining room overlooking the pool. *Directions*: From the A1 autostrada exit at Valdarno for Montevarchi, Bucine (8 km). From town follow signs up to Iesolana, passing over a stone bridge (2 km) to the end of the road.

IESOLANA
Hosts: Giovanni & Isabelle Toscano
Localita: Iesolana
Bucine (AR) 52021, Italy
Tel: (055) 992988, Fax: (055) 992879
Email: iesolana@val.it
8 apartments
US $120–$180 double B&B
  US $930–$2,600 weekly per apartment
3-night minimum stay
Breakfast served, lunch & dinner upon request
Open Easter to October, Credit cards: MC, VS
English spoken well, Region: Tuscany
www.karenbrown.com/italy/iesolana.html

After living in South Africa for 20 years, the Tosi family returned to their homeland in search of a piece of land that in some way resembled their beloved Africa. The gorgeous Montebelli property, situated in Maremma, the wild west of Italy, fit the bill with its 300-plus acres of mountain, hills, and plain, all close to the sea—the one essential element, according to Lorenzo, which brings people *allegria*. Lorenzo, his *simpatica* wife, Carla, and son, Alessandro, now divide their time and energy between their guests and production of wines and olive oil. At the foot of the hills is the main guesthouse where most of the rooms are situated. Others, each with separate entrance, are in two one-story wings connecting to an outdoor dining area. The best rooms are in the main house, decorated tastefully with antiques and including all the amenities of a regular hotel. The half-board requirement allows guests to sample the marvelous cuisine of the area within the characteristic dining room featuring the stone wheel from the original press. This is unexplored territory, full of historical treasures and Etruscan remains. And if that's not enough, scenic walks on marked trails (a must for the views!), a swimming pool, tennis courts, horse riding, and summer concerts are available right on the property. *Directions*: From the north, exit at Gavorrano Scalo from Aurelia route 1 for Ravi then Caldana. Two km past Caldana, turn at the Montebelli sign and follow the dirt road to the end.

MONTEBELLI
Hosts: Carla & Lorenzo Tosi
Localita: Molinetto, Caldana (GR) 58020, Italy
Tel: (0566) 887100, Fax: (0566) 81439
Email: aziendamontebelli@libero.it
21 rooms with private bathrooms
Lire 130,000–180,000 per person half board
2-night minimum stay, 1 week high season
All meals served, Open March to November
Credit cards: all major, Handicap facilities
English spoken well, Region: Tuscany
www.karenbrown.com/italy/montebelli.html

The quaint medieval village of Calvi is just on the border between the regions of Lazio and Umbria and conveniently located at 15 kilometers from the autostrada and 70 kilometers from Rome. Sandro and his charming wife, Louise from Sweden, divide their time between Rome and the countryside where their farm's activities include production of wine and olive oil, and horse breeding. The fascinating family residence in town is a historic palazzo dating back to the 15th century filled with period furniture, paintings, and frescoed ceilings. From their windows they look onto the bright-yellow farmhouse where hospitality is offered within four comfortable apartments, each with private garden area. Accommodations on the first and second floors are a combination of one or two bedrooms, living room with fireplace, fully equipped kitchen, bathroom, and outdoor barbecue. The house has been restored with new bathrooms and tiled floors while maintaining original beamed ceilings and a country flavor in antique furnishings. Fresh fixings for breakfast are left in the apartments and special arrangements have been made with local restaurants for guests. Besides wandering around the many villages of the Sabina area, you can conveniently visit Orvieto, Todi, and Spoleto, under an hour away, take hikes to the lake, or relax by the swimming pool overlooking the beautiful hillside. *Directions*: Leave the Rome-Firenze autostrada A1 at Magliano Sabina. After Magliano, follow signs for Calvi. Just before Calvi are signs for San Martino on the right.

CASALE SAN MARTINO
Hosts: Louise & Sandro Calza Bini
Colle San Martino
Calvi (TR) 05032, Italy
Tel: (0368) 435100, Fax: (0744) 710644
4 apartments
Lire 110,000–250,000 daily per apartment
2-night minimum stay, 1 week July & August
No meals served, Open all year
English spoken well, Region: Umbria
www.karenbrown.com/italy/casalesanmartino.html

The Villa Bellaria, situated right in the picturesque village of Campagnatico with its stone streets and houses and magnificent views over the Ombrone Valley and up to Mount Amiata, retains the authentic flavor of a noble country home from centuries past. Credit goes to gracious hostess Luisa who oversees the 900-plus-acre property, once belonging to such powerful families as the Aldobrandeschi and Medici. It was partially destroyed during World War II, and completely restored by the Querci della Rovere family. Talented Luisa runs not only the hospitality activity but the entire farm as well, while her husband produces Morellino wine from another property. With its large surrounding balustraded park with cypress-lined trails and swimming pool, one forgets that it is all part of the actual town (with its many conveniences). Two apartments are situated in a wing off the main villa and the other newer but characteristic ones are spread out on three floors in the transformed olive press building. They have either one or two bedrooms, bathroom, and sitting room with kitchenette and are appointed with the family's country furniture. This is a lovely base from which to explore a vast number of prepared and varied itineraries. *Directions*: From Siena (55 km) or Grosseto (20 km) exit from highway 223 at Campagnatico and continue for 4 km to the town. The villa is the second right in town—drive up to a green gate.

VILLA BELLARIA
Hostess: Luisa Querci della Rovere
Campagnatico (GR) 58042, Italy
Tel & fax: (0564) 996626 or (0577) 281716
Cellphone: (0335) 6097438
Email: villabellaria@libero.it
10 apartments
Lire 150,000 daily per apartment
2-night minimum stay
No meals served
Open all year
English spoken well, Region: Tuscany
www.karenbrown.com/italy/bellaria.html

For those who have a passion for horseback riding, or with an urge to learn, La Mandria provides the opportunity to do either while on holiday. Host and horseman Davide Felice Aondio's horse farm has been in existence for over 35 years and has been a model for riding resorts. Situated near the foothills of the Alps and between the cities of Turin and Milan, the vast, flat property borders a 5,000-hectare national park, offering spectacular scenery and endless possibilities for horseback excursions. The complex is made up of horse stables, indoor/outdoor ring, haylofts, guestrooms, dining room, and the private homes of the proprietor and his son Marco's family. The whole forms a square with riding rings in the center. As a national equestrian training center, lessons of every kind are offered for all ages. Six very basic bedrooms with bath are reserved for guests, and good local fare is served in the rustic dining room. Golf, swimming, and tennis facilities are available nearby. Two side trips that must not be missed are first, to lovely Lake Maggiore, and then to the intriguing medieval town of Ricetto where the houses and streets are made of smooth stones. *Directions*: Take the Carisio exit from the Milan-Turin autostrada. Head toward Biella, but at the town of Candelo turn right for Mottalciata. La Mandria is on the right.

LA MANDRIA
Hosts: Marco Aondio family
Candelo (VC) 13062, Italy
Tel: (015) 2536078, Fax: (015) 2530743
6 rooms with private bathrooms
Lire 120,000 double B&B
  100,000 per person half board
All meals served
Open all year
English spoken well
Region: Piedmont

Poetically named after a classic Italian tale by Cesare Pavese, a native of this area, the Luna e i Falo (meaning the moon and the fire) farmhouse was lovingly restored by congenial hosts Ester and Franco Carnero. The ritual described in the story is still performed in August every year when local farmers burn old grapevines under the full moon in hopes of a good crop. On that night, the bonfires dotting hills surrounding the farm create quite a spectacle. The Carnero's brick home has arched windows and arcaded front and side terraces, with three double or triple rooms and one apartment for four persons within the villa which they have made available to visitors. For a country home, the spacious living/dining area is elaborately furnished with Renaissance period pieces. The bedrooms reveal a combination of old and new decor and sweeping views of the countryside, known for its wineries. The emphasis at the Luna e i Falo is on the cuisine: the proprietors previously owned a top-rated restaurant in Turin, and continue to practice their culinary skills, producing delicacies from ancient recipes to guests' delight. Regardless of the language barrier, they have a way of making guests feel right at home. *Directions*: From Asti follow the signs for Canelli and, before town, take a right up the hill to Castello Gancia. The farmhouse is on the right after Aie.

LA LUNA E I FALO
Hosts: Ester & Franco Carnero
Localita Aie 37, Canelli (AT) 14053, Italy
Tel & fax: (0141) 831643
3 rooms with private bathrooms, 1 apartment
Lire 180,000 double B&B
 140,000 per person half board
2-night minimum stay
Breakfast & dinner served
Open March to November
No English spoken (French)
Region: Piedmont

North of Florence between Prato and Pistoia is a pocket of little-known, yet entrancing countryside encompassing the Calvana Mountains and Bisenzio Valley. Grazia, Mario, and their three children have lived there all their lives and love sharing their enthusiasm for the area by offering accommodation to visitors. Although access to the rather plain-looking house is by a congested side entrance, the property is beautifully situated overlooking a wooded valley and private lake at the back. What really counts here is the hosts' warmth and their sincere effort to make their guests feel at home. The bedrooms for two to three persons with accompanying immaculate baths are sweet and simple, decorated with comfortable, old-fashioned furniture. Guests convene downstairs for breakfast and dinner in the rustic dining room with exposed beams and fireplace. Off the dining room is the kitchen, where you can watch fresh pasta being rolled out for meals that reflect the influence of the bordering regions of Tuscany and Emilia. A visit to the welcoming Ponte alla Villa offers an opportunity to familiarize yourself with the customs of an area off the beaten track. *Directions*: From Prato, take route 325 north for 25 km to Vernio, then bear left toward Cantagallo. Watch for signs for the bed and breakfast at Luicciana.

PONTE ALLA VILLA
Hosts: Grazia Gori & Mario Michelagnoli
Localita: Luicciana 273-La Villa
Cantagallo (PO) 59025, Italy
Tel: (0574) 956244, Fax: (0574) 956094
8 rooms with private bathrooms
Lire 90,000 double B&B
* 70,000 per person half board*
2-night minimum stay
All meals served
Open all year—weekends only during winter
Very little English spoken
Region: Tuscany

The turreted medieval village of Capalbio, perched on a hilltop, has the double advantage of being close to one of the prettiest seaside spots—Argentario—plus having the beautiful countryside and villages of Maremma to explore. Corinna and her daughter Monica, a local family, run an efficient little bed and breakfast operation, having left a long career in the restaurant business. Breakfast, composed of fresh homemade cakes, breads, and jams is served in the stone-walled dining room or out on the patio. Ten rooms in a row, each with independent entrance from the garden, are situated next door to the main house. They are nicely decorated in a uniform blue or pink color scheme, and have such amenities as television, telephone, hairdryer, and air conditioning. This comes in handy on hot summer evenings, although there is always a cool breeze passing through (hence the Etruscan name "Iced Woods"). The farm property extends over 30 acres of olive groves, and fields of grain and oats. Not to be missed is an unforgettable meal at Tullio's famed restaurant in town, run by relatives of the Olivi family. *Directions*: From Rome on the coastal highway 1, exit before Capalbio at Pescia Fiorentina. At Pescia stay left for 3 km. Ghiaccio is just 1 km after the fork for Manciano.

GHIACCIO BOSCO
Hostesses: Monica Olivi & Corinna Bonucci
Strada della Sgrilla 4
Capalbio (GR) 58011, Italy
Tel & fax: (0564) 896539
10 rooms with private bathrooms
Lire 120,000–180,000 double B&B
Breakfast only
Open all year
Some English spoken
Region: Tuscany

Up in the northeastern reaches of Tuscany bordering Umbria and near several nature reserves in mountains reaching heights of 1500 meters is the newly opened agritourism bed and breakfast, Borgo Tozzetto. Owning a bed and breakfast is nothing new to Luciano Fabrizi, whose family owns the very popular La Malvarina in Assisi. Luciano fell in love with this lesser-known, virgin countryside and has put the business in the capable hands of a young local couple, Daniela and Marco. Tozzetto is located in a group of private homes, encompassing two restored stone houses plus a mini apartment in the transformed stalls (*Gnacco*). The *Contadina* is a large apartment on two floors with three bedrooms and kitchen/living room in the same building as the stone-walled taverna dining room where Daniela serves local specialties. Just across from this is a small house with two identical one-bedroom apartments on each floor, enjoying sweeping views over the bucolic hillsides. All rooms are immaculate and neat, with simple reproduction country furniture and fresh paint in soft hues set off by stencil motifs. There is a park in front with an above-ground pool (this should become a permanent one this year) and playground for children. The impressive city of Arezzo with its beautiful historical center and antique market is 45 kilometers away. *Directions*: Exit at Arezzo from the A1 autostrada and drive towards Sansepolcro, Anghiari, and Caprese Michelangelo (Michelangelo's birthplace and museum). In town there are signs for Tozzetto—2 km.

BORGO TOZZETTO   New
Hosts: Daniela & Marco Fontana
Localita: Tozzetto
Caprese Michelangelo (AR) 52033, Italy
Tel: (0575) 793853 or 799811, Fax: (0575) 793545
4 apartments
Lire 110,000–250,000 daily per apartment
2-night minimum stay, Breakfast & dinner served
Open all year
Very little English spoken
Region: Tuscany

La Minerva is located in a quiet section of Capri, slightly off the beaten track, yet still quite central, permitting easy access to the more bustling areas of town—a walker's paradise with no motorized transportation allowed. The hotel has evolved over the years from a bed and breakfast with the Esposito family in residence to a full-fledged hotel with many amenities, now run by son Luigi (third generation). Glass entrance doors look straight through the capacious reception/sitting area across glossy blue-and-white tiled floors out to a view of the sea through another set of glass doors at the opposite end of the room. The captivating sea views through umbrella pine trees will strike you every time you come and go, as well as from most bedrooms. Rooms, all below this level, are reached by elevator, as is a small breakfast area, although most guests prefer breakfast served in rooms on their private balconies. The entire hotel has been recently renovated and the royal-blue-and-white tile theme follows through in the luminous guestrooms (standard or larger superior doubles), which are accented by an occasional antique piece. A rooftop solarium is an unusual bonus. *Directions*: Stop at the tourist office as you get off the hydrofoil in the port for a detailed map indicating Via Occhio Marino. The *funicolare* cable car or a taxi takes you from the port to the piazza at the center of town. From there it's a ten-minute walk to the hotel. Prearrange to have your luggage picked up at the port, otherwise, pack lightly!

LA MINERVA
Host: Luigi Esposito
Via Occhio Marino 8
Capri (NA) 80073, Italy
Tel: (081) 8377067, Fax: (081) 8375221
18 rooms with private bathrooms
Lire 210,000–350,000 double B&B
Breakfast only
Closed February, Credit cards: all major
English spoken well
Region: Campania

The Villa Krupp is a delightful, small, family-run hotel, whose claim to local fame can be found in its guest book, boasting such illustrious names as Lenin and Gorky. The warm Coppola family has owned the property since the turn of the century and in the '60s turned it into a hotel. The charming accommodation contains 12 bedrooms in a somewhat modern and boxy white building alongside the host's own residence. The Krupp is dramatically situated in one of the most beautiful corners of Capri's Augusto Park, atop a steep, sheer cliff dropping to the sparkling turquoise sea beneath. The site overlooks the Faraglioni rock formation and Marina Piccola, one of Capri's two ports. A set of stairs leads up to the best vantage point from which to admire this spectacular and privileged panorama away from tourist crowds. The renovated light-filled guestrooms, featuring individual balconies, are decorated with scattered antiques and pastel-colored ceramic tiles and some have air conditioning. Breakfast is served either out on the front terrace overflowing with potted flowers or in the luminous veranda bar/dining room. Mother-daughter team Valentina and Donatella do an excellent job of caring for their guests, many of whom are regulars. Reserve well in advance. *Directions*: Take the *funicolare* cable car up to Capri center (la piazzetta). Walk to Via Emanuele, past the Quisisana hotel, down to Viale Matteotti. The hotel is to the right up a ramp, as indicated (ten minutes from the main square).

VILLA KRUPP
Hostesses: Valentina & Donatella Coppola
Viale Matteotti 12, Capri (NA) 80073, Italy
Tel: (081) 8370362 or 8377473
Fax: (081) 8376489
12 rooms with private bathrooms
Lire 200,000–260,000 double B&B
2-night minimum stay, Breakfast only
Open March to November
Some English, French & German spoken
Region: Campania

Capri has long had a reputation as an exclusive island, with prices only the elite were able to afford. However, the cost of tourism across Italy has soared, bringing other destinations more in line with Capri in terms of expense and making it relatively more affordable than it once was. Besides the many hotels, there are just a few true bed and breakfasts and Villa Vuotto is one of the best. Antonino Vuotto and his wife, a local couple both with hotel experience, opened up their centrally located, prim white home in the town of Capri, making four bedrooms down one hall available to guests. The very pleasant and airy rooms are very clean and neat, with typically tiled floors, and private baths and balconies in each. All have a full or partial view of the sea. Breakfast is not served because there are no common rooms for guests. The Villa's convenient location makes it easy to get to any of Capri's fine restaurants for breakfast, lunch, and dinner. It would be impossible to find another accommodation with such an incredible price/quality rapport. Their remarkable rate has remained virtually untouched for the past four years! *Directions*: Take the cable car up to Capri. Go through the main town square to Via Emanuele, past the Quisisana Hotel and continue to the end of the street. Turn left onto Via Certosa, then left again on Cerio. The Villa is on the corner of Campo di Teste and is marked with its original name, Villa Margherita.

VILLA VUOTTO
Hosts: Antonino Vuotto family
Via Campo di Teste 2
Capri (NA) 80073, Italy
Tel & fax: (081) 8370230
4 rooms with private bathrooms
Lire 130,000 double (no breakfast)
No meals served
Open all year
Very little English spoken
Region: Campania

Bed & Breakfast Descriptions   63

The Ombria farmhouse nestles amidst the foothills just 30 kilometers from both beautifully austere Bergamo and Lecco on Lake Como. Bed-and-breakfast/restaurant activity in this 1613 stone house began after meticulous restoration by owner Luciano Marchesin, who has now retired, leaving the business in the capable hands of the Vergani brothers, part of his staff from the beginning. An arched entryway leads into a stone courtyard with gazebo and open grill, where tables are set for summer meals. The Ombria is well-known for its exceptional restaurant where locals enjoy candlelit regional cuisine at long tables in the intimate stone-walled dining room—as long as they make reservations three months in advance! For those retiring to bed early, it would be best to avoid weekends. The spacious doubles, which accommodate up to four persons, are decorated with country antiques and wrought-iron beds. Original fireplaces, exposed beams, warm wood floors, and stone walls make them very appealing and cozy. Special attention has been given to bathrooms, which are beautifully tiled and rather luxurious. Readers give Ombria a high rating. *Directions*: From autostrada A4, exit at Dalmine and follow signs for Lecco on route 36. After Pontida, turn right at the sign for Celana and continue on to Celana, then Ombria (total 15 km).

OMBRIA
Hosts: Alberto & Giuseppe Vergani
Localita: Celana
Caprino Bergamasco
(BG) 24030, Italy
Tel & fax: (035) 781668
3 rooms with private bathrooms
Lire 100,000 per person half board
Breakfast & dinner served
Open all year
Some English spoken
Region: Lombardy

Between the cities of Bergamo and Brescia is a vast commercial area that incorporates the wine region known as Franciacorta—or "land of bubbles." The Ricci Cubastro vineyards, made up of 60 acres, are located in the heart of the area based at the foot of Lake Iseo. The family is one of the most well-known producers of top-quality (D.O.C.G.) Franciacorta brut champagne, among 12 other varieties of wine. The large and busy family estate just on the main road is made up of a complex of houses, which include the family's villa, wine cellars, and wine-tasting show room, an antiques store, and an interesting agricultural museum and library filled with ancient farm tools and wine presses. Across the street is the farmhouse, transformed into five guest apartments of various sizes (studio, one and two bedrooms), each with living area and kitchenette facilities. Rooms are simply decorated with country antiques and stenciled borders around windows and doorways. Here you have the advantage of being close to town while having views of the flat vineyards from bedroom windows. Sports facilities in the area include golf, horseback riding, and biking. This is a conveniently located accommodation for independent travelers. *Directions*: Exit at Palazzolo from the A4 autostrada and follow signs to Capriolo (4 km). Turn right before town at the sign for Ricci Cubastro and drive for another 2 km.

AZIENDA AGRICOLA RICCI CUBASTRO   New
Hosts: Ricci Cubastro family
Via Adro 37
Capriolo (BS) 25031, Italy
Tel: (030) 736094, Fax: (030) 7460558
5 apartments
Lire 80,000–180,000 daily per apartment
2-night minimum stay
No meals served
Open all year
English spoken well
Region: Lombardy

Casaprota is located halfway between Rome and Rieti in the countryside named Sabina for the mountain range. Primarily an agricultural area, it is characterized by small villages and hills covered with olive groves from which the prized olive oil comes. Paola transplanted herself here from the northernmost region of Italy, Friuli, and brought practically her entire home with her. In fact, upon entering her very inviting and cozy home, you have the feeling that you are in a chalet in the Dolomites. To the right is an intimate living area with fireplace where guests have a glass of wine before enjoying a scrumptious meal, prepared by your energetic hostess, at one long table in her dining room filled with curiosities from her world travels and overlooking the kitchen. This exposed-beamed room opens out to the *focolare*, which Paola had constructed especially for her—a typical mountain-area fireplace/stove with seating all around and decorated with antique kitchen utensils. Upstairs are three bedrooms besides her own, each with an animal theme, hardwood floors, and quilts, one with private bathroom and the other two sharing one. The exterior is a typical stone farmhouse immersed in olive groves with marvelous views of the distant mountains. *Directions*: The house is 3 km from the town of Casaprota on a country road without signs. It is best to ask for a detailed map or call when in Casaprota to be met.

CJASE ME
Hostess: Paola Marpillero
Localita: Vignanello
Casaprota (RI) 02030, Italy
Tel & fax: (0765) 85341
3 rooms, 1 with private bathroom
Lire 140,000 double B&B
Breakfast served, dinner upon request
2-night minimum stay
Open all year
English spoken well
Region: Lazio

After 20 years of managing guided tours throughout Italy, Welsh-born Maureen, along with her architect husband, Roberto, has literally brought her expertise "home" to La Torretta. Restoration work on the three-story 15th-century building, tucked away on a narrow cobblestoned street of this charming village, began four years ago. The entrance stairway leads to a large open and elegant living room with stone fireplace and 16th-century frescoes discovered during the restoration process, off which lead all seven bedrooms. Beamed rooms are individually decorated with taste and simple design, and each has an en-suite bathroom and stunning views over the rooftops of medieval Casperia. Breakfast and dinner upon request are served upstairs in the family's mansard living room with a set of enormous beams cutting across the room, open kitchen, and terrace looking up to the wooded Sabine Mountains. This virgin territory is filled with hilltop villages to explore, besides being on the border of Umbria and a 45-minute train ride from Rome. Delightful hostess Maureen and daughter, Kathleen, also a top-rated guide, customize itineraries for their guests, while Roberto specializes in ancient Roman architecture and archaeology. *Directions*: From Rome, exit at Fiano Romano from the A1 and continue in the direction of Passo Corese, Cantalupo, and Casperia. The village is closed to traffic and accessible by foot only. Cars are easily parked below on the street and luggage is handled by special vehicle.

LA TORRETTA
Hosts: Maureen & Roberto Scheda
Via Mazzini 7, Casperia (RI) 02041, Italy
Tel & fax: (0765) 63202
Cellphone: (0368) 3454914
7 rooms with private bathrooms
Lire 140,000–180,000 double B&B
2-night minimum stay
Breakfast & occasional dinner served
Open all year
English spoken fluently. Region: Lazio

Bed & Breakfast Descriptions

A stay at the Villa Aureli with Count di Serego Alighieri (descendant of Dante) and daughter Flavia can only be memorable. With its back to the town and looking out over the Italian Renaissance garden and surrounding countryside, the imposing brick villa has been standing for the past 300 years. When it was bought by the di Serego family in the 18th century, it was meticulously restored and embellished with plasterwork, decorative painted ceilings, richly painted fabrics on walls, ornately framed paintings and prints, colorful tiles from Naples, and Umbrian antiques. Left intentionally intact by the Count, who disdains overly restored historical homes, the elegant apartments for guests maintain their original ambiance. They can accommodate from four to six persons and are spacious, having numerous sitting rooms with fireplaces, although do not expect updated bathrooms or kitchens. A small swimming pool set against the villa's stone walls is a refreshing spot for dreaming. The villa serves as an ideal base from which to explore Umbria and parts of Tuscany, as well as special local itineraries prepared for guests by the Count. *Directions*: Exit from the Perugia highway at Madonna Alta and follow route 220 for Citta della Pieve. After 6 km, take the left for Castel del Piano.

VILLA AURELI
Hosts: Leonardo di Serego Alighieri family
Via Cirenei 70
Castel del Piano Umbro (PG) 06071, Italy
Tel: (075) 5140444 or (075) 5159186
Fax: (075) 5149408
2 apartments
Lire 1,650,000–2,200,000 weekly (heating extra)
No meals served
Open all year
English spoken well
Region: Umbria
www.karenbrown.com/italy/villaaureli.html

Castelfiorentino is 40 kilometers from Florence, Siena and Pisa, and although its outskirts are very commercial, it is a strategic touring base and the surrounding countryside is lovely. Massimo and Susanna continue a long tradition of making guests feel at home—their hotel in Florence has been in the family for four generations. They decided to expand their hospitality to the countryside and after major restoration of two hilltop farmhouses, opened this bed and breakfast three years ago. The completely refurbished rooms with many modern amenities (some have a kitchenette), new bathrooms, fresh landscaping, and recently installed swimming pool and tennis court give a very new feeling. Spacious bedrooms are appointed with authentic and reproduction antiques, and have colorful Sicilian ceramic tiles above beds, with matching ones in bathrooms. The former barn was converted into a small restaurant decorated with contemporary art, a kitchen with viewing window, and a common living room/library upstairs. The preparation of delectable Tuscan fare using ancestral recipes is another strong tradition and cooking lessons are happily arranged for those eager to take home family secrets. A buffet breakfast is served. The side terrace, overlooking soft hills, is where guests can both enjoy breakfast and watch the sunset in the evening. *Directions*: From Castelfiorentino turn off at signs for Renai (this can be tricky to locate) and follow signs for Locanda Country Inn Le Boscarecce (5 km).

LE BOSCARECCE
Hosts: Susanna Ballerini & Massimo Ravalli
Via Renai 19
Castelfiorentino (FI) 50051, Italy
Tel: (0571) 61280, Fax: (055) 283391
Email: info@hotelalbion.it
7 rooms with private bathrooms
Lire 240,000 double B&B
Breakfast & dinner served
Open all year
English spoken well, Region: Tuscany
www.karenbrown.com/italy/boscarecce.html

The Villa Gaidello farm has been written up on several occasions (in *Bon Appetit*, *Cuisine*, *Eating in Italy*), mostly as a result of its superb cuisine. There is nothing extravagant about hostess Paola Bini's recipes, carefully prepared by local women. Rather, the secret to her success seems to lie in the revival of basic traditional dishes using the freshest possible ingredients. Pasta is made daily (a great treat to watch) and features all the local variations on tagliatelle, pappardelle, and stricchettoni. *Reservations for dinner must be made several days in advance.* Paola is one of the pioneers in agritourism, transforming her grandmother's nearly-200-year-old farmhouse into a guesthouse and restaurant just over 25 years ago. One to five guests are accommodated in each of the eight apartments, which include kitchen and sitting room. The apartments are cozy and rustic with exposed-brick walls, country antiques, and lace curtains. The dining room, set with doilies and ceramic, is situated in the converted hayloft and overlooks the vast garden and a small pond. This is a convenient stopover just off the Bologna-Milan autostrada. *Directions*: Exit the A1 autostrada at Modena Nord (or Bologna Nord from the south). Follow Via Emilia/route 9 towards Castelfranco. Turn left on Via Costa (hospital) and follow signs to Gaidello.

VILLA GAIDELLO
Hostess: Paola Bini
Via Gaidello 18
Castelfranco Emilia (MO) 41013, Italy
Tel: (059) 926806, Fax: (059) 926620
Email: gaidello@tin.it
8 apartments
Lire 150,000–400,000 per apartment daily with breakfast
All meals served
Restaurant closed Sunday evenings & Mondays
Closed August, Credit cards: all major
Very little English spoken, Region: Emilia-Romagna
www.karenbrown.com/italy/villagaidello.html

There is no doubt that the spectacular Amalfi coast must be seen, but in high season when the traffic is unbearable and it's elbow-to-elbow down the streets of Positano, a welcome retreat is the coast farther south at Castellabate. This is a very quiet and modest resort area where the majority of summer tourists are Italians. The winding road climbs up to the medieval village of Castellabate and La Mola, the summer home of the Favilla family from Rome, is right on the road entering town. Rather nondescript from the roadside entrance, the four-story historical building (ex-olive press), perched on the cliffside, faces out to the bay. Each room takes in some angle of this formidable panorama, two having balconies and the two-bedroom suite having a terrace. With an occasional antique, the bedrooms and living room with spiral staircase are pleasantly uncluttered so as not to detract from the inspiring sea views. On a clear day the Amalfi coastline and even Capri are visible. Hostess Loredana takes care of guests, preparing cakes and bread for breakfast, which is served on a table made from the old stone press on the main terrace filled with potted flowers. It is difficult to tear oneself away from this dreamlike state to try one of the interesting itineraries with an emphasis on either nature or ancient history (temples of Paestum, Certosa, or Padula). *Directions*: 60 km from Salerno. Take the road up to the town center and La Mola is marked on the side of the gray building on the right, the first house as you enter town on Via Cilento.

LA MOLA
Host: Francesco Favilla
Via A. Cilento 2
Castellabate (SA) 84048, Italy
Tel & fax: (0974) 967053
5 rooms with private bathrooms
Lire 180,000–200,000 double B&B
Breakfast served, dinner upon request
Open March to October, Credit cards: AX, VS
Some English spoken
Region: Campania

A really unique stay involving an exceptional culinary experience can be found at the Borgo Villa a Sesta, a complete medieval stone village in the middle of the beautiful countryside of Chianti. The estate produces Chianti wines and olive oil, and offers seven lovely apartments of various sizes within the village. They are all well furnished with a mix of antiques and contain one or two bedrooms, new bathroom, living room, and fully equipped kitchen for independent travelers (no breakfast served). Four are situated in a three-story brick house overlooking the vineyards and swimming pool. What really makes the stay here so special is a meal at the nearby Ristorante Bottega del'30, an intimate eight-table restaurant, well-known for its superior cuisine—the two independent establishments work hand in hand. Bottega del'30, run by energetic and congenial hosts Franco Camelia and French-born Helene Stoquelet is sure to be memorable. They have opened a Tuscan cooking school, with both an authentic country kitchen and a fully equipped modern kitchen, which is truly impressive. A characteristic dining room with long wood table is where everyone joins together for lunch and plenty of wine after a lesson (available weekly or daily). *Directions*: From Siena on route 73 exit at Castelnuovo Berardenga. Pass the town and continue for San Gusme. Villa a Sesta is on the left 2 km after the turnoff for San Gusme.

BORGO VILLA A SESTA
Host: Oskar Sigrist
Localita: Villa a Sesta
Castelnuovo Berardenga (SI) 53019, Italy
Tel: (0577) 734064, Cellphone: (0336) 706596
Fax: (0577) 734066
7 apartments
Lire 180,000–320,000 per apartment
3-night minimum stay, 1 week July & August
Lunch with cooking school, dinner at Bottega del'30
Open all year
Some English spoken, Region: Tuscany
www.karenbrown.com/italy/villaasesta.html

While roving our way back to Umbria from the Adriatic coast through picture-perfect landscapes, we came upon the Giardino degli Ulivi bed and breakfast and were immediately intrigued. The absolutely charming accommodation is actually part of a 12th-century stone village and faces out to the rolling hills splashed with bright patches of yellow sunflowers and backed by a mountainside. The scenery per se is enough to leave one in awe, let alone Maria Pia's marvelous cuisine with its Michelin rating. The carefully restored building, left ingeniously intact, thanks to her architect husband, Sante, includes the stone-walled restaurant downstairs with its many intimate nooks, centered around the ancient wine-making press. The five bedrooms upstairs off two sitting rooms with fireplace have wrought-iron beds, antique bedside tables, and beamed ceilings. The favorite corner bedroom (at a higher rate) has a large arched window taking in the breathtaking view. While their son, Francesco, tends to the breeding of horses, daughter Raffaele assists guests with the many interesting itineraries in the area (Camerino, San Severino, Matelica, and Fariano—famous for its paper industry). A real sense of discovery is experienced in this authentic region, which has been able to keep traditions and folklore intact. *Directions*: From Castelraimondo follow route 256 towards Matelica, turning at the first left for Castel S. Maria then Castel S. Angelo.

IL GIARDINO DEGLI ULIVI
Hosts: Sante Cioccoloni family
Localita: Castel S. Angelo
Castelraimondo (MC) 62022, Italy
Tel: (0737) 642121, Fax: (0737) 640441
5 rooms with private bathrooms
Lire 130,000–220,000 double B&B
  Reduced rates for stays of 3 or more nights
All meals served
Closed 2 weeks in November
Credit cards: AX, VS
English spoken well, Region: Marches
www.karenbrown.com/italy/ilgiardino.html

Tucked away off a winding mountain road in the enchanting Siusi Alps is a typical Tyrolean farmhouse where the Jaider family has resided ever since the 15th century, traditionally running a dairy farm. Their inviting home, with its authentic ambiance of the past, is colorfully accented with green shutters and flower-laden windowboxes. Two wooden barns are connected to the residence via a stone terrace. Paula Jaider runs her home with the hotel efficiency expected by visitors to this predominantly German-speaking area. Meals are served either out on the vine-covered terrace or in the original dining room, whose charm is enhanced by the low, wood-paneled ceiling and little carved wooden chairs. Be sure to reserve dinner: the food is excellent and it is just too far to go out for a meal. Cuisine in this region has an Austrian flavor, featuring *speck* ham, meat and potatoes, and apple strudel, and regulars come from afar to this well-known restaurant. Lovely country antiques are dispersed throughout the house and the eight very nice bedrooms, which are wood-paneled from floor to ceiling and have pretty valley views (two have balconies). A real charmer and a bargain. Book in advance. *Directions*: Exit from the Bolzano-Brennero autostrada at Klausen and drive south to Ponte Gardena where you turn left across the river and first right towards Castelrotto. After 3.5 km make a sharp right for San Osvaldo and follow the narrow road for 2.5 km to the Tschotscherhof, just beyond the church.

TSCHOTSCHERHOF
Hosts: Jaider family
San Osvaldo 19
Castelrotto (BZ) 39040, Italy
Tel: (0471) 706013, Fax: (0471) 704801
8 rooms with private bathrooms
Lire 90,000 double B&B
* 59,000 per person half board*
All meals served, Open March to October
Very little English spoken (German)
Region: Trentino-Alto Adige

Il Loghetto is located 10 kilometers east of Bologna and is a combination of converted farmhouse with the efficiency and service of a small hotel. Run by Ulicia and her son, Andrea, the yellow house surrounded by a large garden and then flat fields has ten beamed bedrooms upstairs and a restaurant downstairs. There is a reception area at the entrance and also an elevator up to rooms, which are all very new with rather standard wood furniture and amenities such as television and air conditioning. The dining room with fireplace and hanging brass pots, where fresh pasta dishes and other local specialties are served, is filled with a variety of antiques collected by Andrea. Beyond is an enormous living room with arched glass doors overlooking the garden and outdoor tables, a bar, billiard table, piano, and two sitting areas. There may be minimal noise from the nearby road. Transfers are arranged to Bologna or the airport. Besides this being a convenient stopover, marvels such as Ravenna, Ferrara, and Faenza (ceramic museum) can be visited from here. *Directions*: From the ring highway of Bologna, exit at S. Vitale (N11) and continue towards Villanova. After the commercial area of Castenaso, turn left for Budrio. Il Loghetto is indicated on the left.

IL LOGHETTO
Hosts: Mazza family
Via Zenzalino Sud 3–4
Castenaso (BO) 40050, Italy
Tel: (051) 6052218, Fax: (051) 6052254
10 rooms with private bathrooms
Lire 180,000 double B&B
Restaurant closed Sunday evenings & Mondays
Closed August & January
Credit cards: MC, VS
Some English spoken
Region: Emilia-Romagna

Liguria is the sliver of a region touching France and boasting the Italian Riviera with its port towns of Portofino, Santa Margherita, San Remo, and Cinque Terre. From the busy coastal town of Sestri Levante, an 8-kilometer rough and winding road leads up a mountain to the rather remote but serene Monte Pu farm, where Aurora and Pino migrated from Milan. The three-story, peach-color brick farmhouse complex, dating from 1400, commands a marvelous sweeping view over wooded mountains and valleys down to the sea. The guestrooms, a combination of triples and quads, are simple and immaculate, with light-pine furniture and wildflower bouquets. Downstairs is the warm and airy dining room where a full country breakfast awaits guests each morning. Dinner, prepared by a local woman, is served outside in the courtyard in warmer months. The culinary emphasis is on vegetarian dishes such as risotto, soups, and salads, prepared with ingredients straight from the garden. Horses are available for riding in the forest preserves surrounding the property. Aurora and Pino take time from their busy schedule of running the farm and looking after their baby to assist guests with local itineraries. *Directions*: Exit from the Genova-Livorno autostrada at Sestri Levante and follow signs for Casarza Ligure. After town turn left for Campegli-Massaco. Take another left turn and follow Monte Pu signs for 4.5 km.

MONTE PU
Hostess: Aurora Giani
Castiglione Chiavarese (GE) 16030, Italy
Tel & fax: (0185) 408027
Email: montepu@libero.it
9 rooms, 5 with private bathrooms, 1 apartment
Lire 120,000–140,000 double B&B
* 85,000–95,000 per person half board*
50% discount for children under 8
All meals served, Open Easter to November
English spoken well
Region: Liguria
www.karenbrown.com/italy/montepu.html

Eight years ago Michela and Paolo, an enterprising host of American descent, bought and restored a small roadside hotel and transformed it into a pleasant bed and breakfast. A part of the pale-yellow house with brick trim is reserved for themselves, leaving 11 rooms for guests. With floral bedspreads and matching beds and armoires, each bedroom has its own bathroom. Downstairs to the left of the reception area is a large restaurant specializing in typical Tuscan fare. Divided by a brick archway, it has a bar and is adorned with colorful ceramic plates from Deruta. The small garden in back has a gazebo and bar set up for guests. Paolo gets very involved with his guests, helping to plan individualized itineraries covering the area between Rome and Florence (all within an hour's drive). In the evening guests and many locals come back to either a wine-tasting or cocktail hour before settling down to a meal. Although right on the road just before town, this is a strategically located bed and breakfast with easy access to the autostrada. *Directions*: Exit at Chianciano and follow signs to Chiusi. La Querce comes up quickly on the left-hand side.

LA QUERCE
Hosts: Michela & Paolo Bartolozzi
Localita: Querce al Pino 41
Chiusi (SI) 53043, Italy
Tel: (0578) 274308, Fax: (0578) 274449
11 rooms with private bathrooms
Lire 96,000–180,000 double B&B
All meals served
Restaurant closed Mondays
Open all year
Credit cards: all major
English spoken fluently
Region: Tuscany

One of our favorite bed-and-breakfast hostesses, the delightful and accommodating Stella Casolaro, started another bed and breakfast in her home after having sold the Scuderia in Badia di Passignano years ago. If you were ever one of her fortunate guests, you would understand why travelers come back and stay with her year after year. Casa Italia, 35 kilometers west of Siena, is in the lesser-known, more rugged part of the Tuscan countryside. In fact, much to the delight of husband, Carlo, who has a passion for hunting for porcini mushrooms, dense woods cover the entire area. The white 60-year-old house with encircling garden is right on the edge of the quaint village of Ciciano. Three sweet bedrooms, each with its own bathroom (two just outside the room), and a living room have been reserved for guests on the couple's first floor, while they reside on the upper floor. All rooms have a double wrought-iron bed with a variety of country antiques in keeping with the simple and old-fashioned ambiance. Son Paolo has joined in and set up a wine bar downstairs where light meals are served, accompanied by music (he plays guitar). It's like "coming home." Not to be missed are the mystic ruins of San Galgano cathedral. *Directions*: From Siena, take route 73 towards Grosseto. After Frosini, turn off right for Chiusdino, then Ciciano (45 km from the seaside). Casa Italia is right on the main street in town.

CASA ITALIA
Hosts: Stella & Carlo Casolaro
Via Massetana 5
Ciciano-Chiusdino (SI) 53010, Italy
Tel & fax: (0577) 750656
3 rooms with private bathrooms
Lire 90,000 double (no breakfast)
Light dinner served
Open all year
Some English spoken
Region: Tuscany

In the hills between Tuscany and Umbria and overlooking the Tiber and Chiana valleys, is the Nannotti family's typical farm property. Renato and Maria Teresa used to run a restaurant nearby before deciding to open a bed and breakfast and serve delicious Tuscan-Umbrian recipes at home. The two adjacent red-stone houses include five guestrooms, one apartment, and the family's private quarters. Two rooms are on the ground floor, another has an upstairs terrace, and all are decorated in a simple, pleasant country style with a mix of armoires, wrought-iron beds, and some modern pieces. Renato specializes in organic produce and makes his own honey, jams, grappa, wine, and olive oil, which are brought directly to the dining-room table or served out under the porch. Maria Teresa creates an easy, informal ambiance and young daughter Aureliana and son Ernesto both help out. Being close to the charming, historical village and having easy access to the autostrada make this a super touring location. There are also bikes, a swimming pool, hiking trails, a special spa package at nearby thermal waters, a park for children, many farm animals, fitness track, and horses to ride. *Directions*: Exit at Chiusi from the north or Fabro from the south and follow signs for Citta della Pieve. In town follow signs for Ponticelli—the bed and breakfast is well marked before this town.

MADONNA DELLE GRAZIE
Hosts: Renato Nannotti family
Via Madonna delle Grazie 6
Citta della Pieve (PG) 06062, Italy
Tel & fax: (0578) 299822, Cellphone: (0330) 880223
Email: madgrazie@ftbcc.it
5 rooms with private bathrooms, 1 apartment
Lire 160,000–190,000 double B&B
  100,000–115,000 per person half board
  1,100,000–1,400,000 apartment weekly
Breakfast & dinner served, Open all year
Some English, French & German spoken
Region: Umbria
www.karenbrown.com/italy/madonna.html

British expatriate Dawne Alstrom finally found the farmhouse property of her dreams eight years ago and immediately set about organizing major restoration work on the crumbling stone house—the ground floor was completed in record time and the final results are indeed splendid. Dawne's organizing skills learned in film production enabled her to coordinate the various artisans quite naturally, and her years of stylist experience were put to use in ingenious decorating, incorporating fireplaces and antique pieces she bought to create an authentic Italian country home. Two lovely luminous bedrooms with large bathrooms are located on the ground floor off the cozy living room with its music and reading library. The remaining three upstairs are also decorated with fine antiques and are all corner rooms with another sitting room, allowing privacy and total silence. The atmosphere is that of a continual house party and guests convene in the delightful country kitchen around an enormous table for delectable five-course dinners (80,000 lire). The vineyards out back creep right up to the pool. From here Tuscany, Umbria, and unusual "backroad" local attractions are all at your fingertips. Truly special. *Directions*: From Rome leave the A1 autostrada at Attigliano and head left towards Bomarzo, turning right towards Castiglione for 12 km. Turn left at the silos (Battisti Cereali) to the first house on the right with a small tower.

L'OMBRICOLO
Hostess: Dawne Alstrom-Viotti
Via Ombricolo
Civitella d'Agliano (VT) 01020, Italy
Tel & fax: (0761) 914735
5 rooms with private bathrooms
Lire 180,000–240,000 double B&B
Breakfast & dinner served
Open all year
Credit cards: all major
Fluent English spoken
Region: Lazio

Cortina has enjoyed a long-standing reputation as one of the most "in" resorts of the Dolomites, helped also by its center-stage location. Prominent politicians, stars of television and cinema, socialites, and nobility have vacation homes here and congregate three times a year at Christmas, Easter, and during the month of August. In town, there is a large range of accommodation available, but if you want to be part of the scene yet desire a quiet place to sleep, the Baita Fraina of the Menardi family is the perfect choice. A *baita* is a typical chalet farmhouse where home and barn are incorporated into one building. Overlooking mountains to the back and a large park for children to the front, the Fraina is primarily a well-established and esteemed restaurant cited in top restaurant guides and specializing in pastas with fresh mushrooms as well as the exquisite local *fartaies* dessert with wild-berry sauce. Three paneled and intimate dining rooms have ceramic-tiled stove heaters, lace curtains, antique kitchen tools, and dried flower arrangements. The six simply decorated bedrooms done in pinewood were added later on the top two floors. A sauna, Jacuzzi, and sun terrace are extra features of this characteristic bed and breakfast. *Directions*: Entering Cortina on route 48, turn left before town for Fraina and take the road for 1.2 km.

BAITA FRAINA
Hosts: Adolfo Menardi family
Localita: Fraina
Cortina d'Ampezzo (BL) 32043, Italy
Tel: (0436) 3634, Fax: (0436) 863761
6 rooms with private bathrooms
All meals served (restaurant closed Mondays)
Lire 150,000–220,000 double B&B
* 120,000–180,000 per person half board*
Open January to April 15, June 28 to September 23
Credit cards: MC, VS
English spoken well
Region: Veneto

Cortina is one of the most frequented spots for travelers passing through the Dolomites on their way up to Austria, or those who just want to get a taste of a mountain resort Italian-style. The multitude of ski lifts and variety of slopes along with the absolutely gorgeous scenery make it an easy winner. For shorter stays, accommodation right in town is convenient to restaurants, ski slopes, and hiking trails. The Oasi is a pleasant, recently updated bed and breakfast on the outskirts of town (easily reached by foot) and at the beginning of a pretty residential street. This former private residence dating to 1925 has ten rooms located on the ground and first floors, while the Luchetta family, original owners, reside on the top floor. New bedrooms are comfortably appointed with pinewood beds topped with fluffy comforters and soft-pea-green curtains and matching chairs. Amenities include satellite TV and phones in the rooms. A good buffet breakfast is served in the downstairs breakfast room with bay window. A small garden to the side of the house offers a restful spot. This is an efficient little hotel maintaining the warmth of a home and the Seppis are true hosts. *Directions*: The Meuble Oasi is in town on the road leaving Cortina towards Dobbiaco and well marked.

MEUBLE OASI
Hosts: Lorenza Seppi & Tranquillo Luchetta
Via Cantore 2
Cortina d'Ampezzo (BL) 32043, Italy
Tel: (0436) 862019, Fax: (0436) 879476
10 rooms with private bathrooms
Lire 120,000–250,000 double B&B
Breakfast only
Open all year
Credit cards: MC, VS
English & German spoken well
Region: Veneto

The Villa Alpina is another good choice for an efficient and moderately priced family-run bed and breakfast (or *meublé*, as they are called) right in Cortina. The inviting white stucco house with front bay windows has a large veranda on one side lined with flowerboxes where a buffet breakfast is set up for guests. Tables and umbrellas are set up outside in the summer months. Elio and his mother reside in a part of the large home, which has been just recently renovated, with the addition of an elevator up to the bedrooms. Each carpeted room is decorated individually in characteristic style using mostly wood furniture and paneling. Some have balconies in the back looking over town and up to the mountains, and all have satellite TV and telephones. There is also a comfortable sitting room with Tyrolean printed fabrics on sofas and curtains whose focus is the ceramic-tiled wood-burning stove heater so typical in this mountain area. *Directions*: Just a few minutes' walk to the pedestrian-only main street (Corso Italia) with all its famous shops. Follow signs through town to Via Roma—Villa Alpina is well marked.

VILLA ALPINA
Host: Elio Zardini
Via Roma 72
Cortina d'Ampezzo (BL) 32043, Italy
Tel: (0436) 2418, Fax: (0436) 867464
12 rooms with private bathrooms
Lire 150,000–250,000 double B&B
Breakfast only
Open all year
Credit cards: all major
English spoken well
Region: Veneto

Borgo Elena, located in the hills outside one of our favorite Tuscan towns, Cortona, belongs to Mario Baracchi, whose brother owns the gorgeous inn, Il Falconiere (listed in our Inns guide). In fact, you can reach Borgo Elena by passing through the Falconiere property (stop in for an exquisite meal) on a narrow, steep gravel road that ends at the cluster of stone houses bordered by dense chestnut woods. Here you are totally immersed in nature and complete silence, with hilltop Cortona to one side and the immense Chiana Valley spread out before you. Seven quaint apartments, each with independent entrance, are dispersed among the various stone houses, which were once the quarters for the farmhands of the Falconiere estate a century ago. Their original rustic ambiance remains while convenient modern utilities and amenities have been incorporated. The apartments, all charmingly appointed with Tuscan country pieces, accommodate from two to six persons and are all different in layout, most being on two levels. A lovely swimming pool sits higher up and takes in even more of the expansive view. The Borgo Elena is an ideal base for independent travelers who want to settle in one place for easily touring Tuscany's highlights. Jovial host, Mario, is on hand during the day to assist guests while he tends to the vast property. *Directions*: Instead of going into the center of Cortona, follow signs for Arezzo and drive past Camucia on the outskirts of town to Tavarnelle. Turn right at San Pietro a Cegliolo and drive 2 km up to Borgo Elena.

*BORGO ELENA   **New***
Host: Mario Baracchi
Localita: San Pietro a Cegliolo
Cortona (AR) 52042, Italy
Tel & fax: (0575) 604773
7 apartments
Lire 800,000–1,500,000 weekly per apartment
No meals served
Open all year
Very little English spoken
Region: Tuscany

For British couple, Scarlett and Colin, the fantasy of restoring a farmhouse in the Tuscan hills and enjoying a slower-paced life became reality when they found their dream property, Stoppiacce. Set amongst the lush green mountains separating Tuscany and Umbria beyond Cortona, the ancient stone farmhouse was meticulously restored and tastefully appointed with country antiques and matching fabrics. Within are the hosts' quarters plus three lovely guestrooms, the "Tower" room having its own independent entrance. Scarlett, an excellent cook, prepares light lunches or, by prior arrangement, dinners accompanied by top-choice local wines (85,000 lire per person). Just restored below the main house is a cozy nest for two (*Il Castagno*) with sitting room and kitchenette, terrace on the first floor, and bedroom with bathroom on the second floor. This is an ideal place for those who like to combine leisurely local touring with pure relaxation, taking advantage of the lovely swimming pool with the most incredible views over the valley. *Directions*: Exit from the A1 autostrada at Val di Chiana and follow the highway towards Perugia. Exit at the second turnoff for Cortona, pass the city, and continue for Citta del Castello on a small winding road. After 5 km turn left at Portole and call Stoppiacce for instructions on how to find the house.

STOPPIACCE
Hosts: Scarlett & Colin Campbell
Localita: San Pietro a Dame
Cortona (AR) 52044, Italy
Tel & fax: (0575) 690058
Cellphone: (0348) 2903725
3 rooms with private bathrooms, 1 house
Lire 220,000 double B&B
  Castagno: 300,000 daily, Jul & Aug 1,400,000 weekly
2-night minimum stay
Breakfast served, lunch & dinner upon request
Open April to November
Fluent English spoken, Region: Tuscany
www.karenbrown.com/italy/stoppiacce.html

The Antica Fattoria came highly recommended by several readers who stayed there in the first year it opened. It is indeed a delightful combination of pretty countryside, strategic touring position, comfortable rooms, excellent meals, and warm hospitality. Following the increasingly popular lifestyle trend of abandoning the city for a rural pace, Roman couple Alessandro and Anna left their offices to become, essentially, farmers. They bought and restored two connected stone farmhouses and incorporated seven rooms, decorated pleasantly with a characteristic country flavor, for guests. While Alessandro tends to the crops and farm animals, Anna lives out her passion for cooking, much to guests' delight. Meals are served either outside at one long table or in the transformed horse stalls below with cozy sitting area and fireplace. At times the *allegria* and good food keep guests at the table until the wee hours. A lovely swimming pool looks over the wooded hills to the valley. The busy hosts take time to assist guests with the many local itineraries and organize a wide variety of games. Perfect for families and a great base for exploring Umbria. The town of Deruta is world-famous for its painted ceramic pottery and is lined with workshops and showrooms. *Directions*: From Perugia (18 km), exit from route 3 bis at Casalina. Take the first right and follow signs to the Fattoria.

ANTICA FATTORIA DEL COLLE
Hosts: Anna & Alessandro Coluccelli
Strada Colle delle Forche 6
Deruta (PG) 06053, Italy
Tel & fax: (075) 972201
Cellphone: (0360) 343544
Email: umbia@anticafattoriadelcolle.it
7 rooms with private bathrooms
Lire 140,000 double B&B (low season only)
  130,000–150,000 per person half board (June to September)
1-week minimum stay July & August
All meals served, Open all year
English spoken well, Region: Umbria
www.karenbrown.com/italy/anticafattoriadelcolle.html

At the edge of the Mugello area north of Florence is the property of Enrico and Elisa Lippi and their growing family. The primary activity on the farm is the production of the highest-grade quality (D.O.C.G) Chianti Rufina, something that guests can observe up close as the cantinas and guests' farmhouses and main villa are closely integrated, forming a *borgo*. Independent houses have from one to three bedrooms, living room, kitchen, and small garden with sitting area. They have been freshly redone, retaining wood-beamed ceilings and some exposed brick features. Country antiques were also restored and fit in well with the general ambiance. "Rosmarino" and "Bosco," within or attached to the ancient medieval tower, are most characteristic of all apartments. Il Cavaliere is designed for longer stays and is a nice base for exploring this lesser-known part of northern Tuscany and Emilia Romagna, divided by the Apennines with their villages of medieval and even Etruscan origins. Mountain bikes can be rented, a pool is open to guests from June through September, and courses in Italian wine and olive-oil production are arranged. *Directions*: From Florence head for Pontassieve and continue to Dicomano. At 1 km before town, turn right for Frascole and follow signs to Il Cavaliere.

IL CAVALIERE
Hosts: Elisa & Enrico Lippi
Via di Frascole 27
Dicomano (FI) 50062, Italy
Tel & fax: (055) 8386340
4 apartments
Lire 650,000–2,150,000 weekly (high season)
3-night minimum stay
No meals served
Open all year
Some English, French spoken
Region: Tuscany

An excellent choice as a base for visiting the villas of Palladio and the stunning historical centers of Verona and Padova (plus being 20 minutes from Venice) is the recently opened Villa Goetzen. With a long tradition in hospitality, the local Minchio family bought the peach-colored home (dating from 1739) sitting on the Brenta Canal in town and transformed it into an elegant bed-and-breakfast accommodation. Although bordering the main road, silence reigns within. You enter the iron gates into a courtyard, where on the right is a miniature coachhouse with two of the twelve rooms. These are the favorites and most romantic, with beamed mansard ceilings, parquet floors, and canal view. All rooms are decorated with classic good taste in the selection of antique pieces, wrought-iron beds, and coordination of fabrics and individual color schemes. Immaculate bathrooms have black-and-white checked tiles. Fortunate guests can sample delectable Venetian meals prepared by Paola and her son, Massimiliano, in one of the three intimate dining rooms. Brother Cristian receives guests and attends to their needs with great charm and finesse. It would be virtually impossible to find a hotel with similar standards in Venice at this rate. *Directions*: Exit at Dolo from the A4 autostrada and go straight into town until you arrive at the canal. Turn left and follow signs for Venezia. The villa is on the right.

VILLA GOETZEN
Hosts: Minchio family
Via Matteotti 6
Dolo (VE) 30031, Italy
Tel: (041) 5102300, Fax: (041) 412600
12 rooms with private bathrooms
Lire 200,000 double B&B
All meals served
Open all year
Credit cards: all major
English spoken well
Region: Veneto

Picturesque Courmayeur, on the Italian side of the tunnel cutting through Mont Blanc into France, is a popular ski and summer resort. In the summer months comfortable temperatures and spectacular mountain scenery along with activities such as hiking, golf, horseback riding, and kayaking attract many visitors. The warm Berthod family have been offering hospitality to guests for some time, greeting them by name as they return "home" year after year. The old stone chalet and barn, squeezed between other houses in the center of the centuries-old village of Entreves, outside Courmayeur, has been restored using old and new materials. The cozy reception area maintains its original rustic flavor with flagstone floors and beams, hanging brass pots, typical locally made pine furniture, and homey touches like dried-flower arrangements and lace curtains. The 23 simply appointed rooms have been divided between two buildings and offer the amenities of a standard hotel. A hearty breakfast is the only meal served; however, half-board arrangements can be made with local restaurants for longer stays. La Grange is an efficiently run bed and breakfast right at the foot of the snow-capped Alps. *Directions*: From Aosta where the A5 autostrada ends, continue on route 26 to Courmayeur. Entreves is 5 km beyond.

LA GRANGE
Hosts: Berthod family
Fraz. Entreves
Courmayeur (AO) 11013, Italy
Tel: (0165) 869733, Fax: (0165) 869744
Email: lagrange@courmayeur.valdigne.com
23 rooms with private bathrooms
Lire 150,000–250,000 double B&B
Breakfast only
Closed May, June, October, November
Credit cards: AX, VS
English spoken well
Region: Valle d'Aosta
www.karenbrown.com/italy/lagrange.html

Casa Palmira, directly north of Florence, was originally a group of rural buildings attached to an 11th-century tower guarding the road to the Mugello area of Tuscany. Stefano and Assunta, the amiable hosts, named their bed and breakfast after the 96-year-old woman who has lived here her entire life. She represents perhaps the spirit of the place, reminding all of the basic values of simple country living. The seven bedrooms on the top floor are decorated in a fresh, simple, country style, with hardwood floors, dried and fresh flowers, patchwork quilts, botanic prints, and local country antiques. Rooms are accessed by a large open sitting area with skylights and green plants. The hosts' naturally informal style of hospitality has guests feeling so at home that you can't resist assisting as Assunta works wonders in the open kitchen. This is part of a multi-functional space incorporating kitchen, dining room, and cozy living area with wicker chairs and large fireplace. Meals based on fresh vegetables are served either here or out in the garden under the portico. Daily cooking lessons for individuals or weekly cooking courses for small groups are arranged. Transfers from train station or airport are also offered. *Directions*: Halfway between Borgo S. Lorenzo and Florence on route 302 (Via Faentina), 2 km after Olmo coming from Florence (16 km). Casa Palmira is on the right at the sign for Ristorante Feriolo. From the north leave the A1 at Barberino del Mugello.

CASA PALMIRA
Hosts: Assunta & Stefano Mattioli
Localita: Feriolo
Via Faentina
Borgo S. Lorenzo (FI) 50030, Italy
Tel & fax: (055) 8409749
7 rooms, 5 with private bathrooms
Lire 110,000–145,000 double B&B
Breakfast served, dinner upon request
Open March to December
Very little English spoken, French spoken well
Region: Tuscany

Best friends Luciano and Tommaso, refugees from city life, have over the past ten years or so transformed the 1,000-acre property, La Casella, made up of woods, rivers, and valleys, into a veritable countryside haven for vacationers. Foremost attention has been given to the 28 rooms, which are divided between three separate stone houses. The *Noci* house contains seven doubles upstairs appointed with country antiques, and a large vaulted room downstairs used for small meetings or dining. *La Terrazza*, originally a hunting lodge, has nine rooms, one with namesake terrace looking over the poplar woods. On the highest point sits *San Gregorio*, with small chapel, where guests revel in the utter silence and a spectacular 360-degree view over the entire property. The lively dining room offers delectable cuisine, whose ingredients come directly from the farm. The many sports facilities include a beautiful big swimming pool, tennis, archery, and an equestrian center where many special outings and events are organized, as well as a spa program with natural treatments. Well-marked trails lead the rider, biker, or hiker to such marvels as Todi, Orvieto, or even Perugia. *Directions*: Exit at Fabro from the Rome-Firenze A1 autostrada. Follow signs for Parrano (7 km), turning right at the Casella sign, and continue for another 7 km on a rough gravel road.

LA CASELLA
Hosts: Luciano Nenna & Tommaso Campolmi
Localita: La Casella
Ficulle (TR) 05016, Italy
Tel: (0763) 86588, Fax: (0763) 86684
Email: lacasella@tin.it
28 rooms with private bathrooms
Lire 135,000–145,000 per person half board
1-week minimum stay July & August
All meals served
Open all year
Credit cards: all major
Fluent English spoken, Region: Umbria
www.karenbrown.com/italy/lacasella.html

August brings unbearable heat and overcrowded conditions at the seaside in most parts of the country, so it is small wonder that the cooler elevations of the Alps and Dolomites have become favorite vacation spots for Italian families. These resorts offer invigoratingly fresh mountain air, numerous outdoor activities, spectacular scenery, and, best of all, the least expensive "getaways" in the country. The darling Merlhof is owned and operated by the Kompatschers, who have created four apartments within their family home in the town of Fiè. The traditional, Tyrolean-style white-and-dark-wood dwelling with barn has geraniums cascading brightly from each windowsill, and looks directly onto the Sciliar Mountain at the back. Each apartment has its own sitting room with kitchen, bedroom, and bathroom. The apartments vary in size and can accommodate from two to five people. The Merlhof is geared for families, with a swimming pool in the garden, children's play area, and table tennis. The barbeque area is a popular and sociable place to prepare an evening meal. As the Kompatschers live on the ground floor they are always on hand to offer advice on where to go and what to see in the Dolomites. This is actually a small farm property, yet within walking distance of the town. *Directions*: Exit at Bolzano Nord from the Verona-Brennero autostrada. Follow signs for Siusi and Fiè (also called Völs) and, at the main intersection, turn right and the Merlhof is the first house on your left.

MERLHOF
Hosts: Waltraud & Georg Kompatscher
Via Sciliar 9
Fiè allo Sciliar (BZ) 39050, Italy
Tel & fax: (0471) 725552
4 apartments
Lire 70,000–135,000 daily per apartment
No meals served
Open all year
No English spoken (German)
Region: Trentino-Alto Adige

The Hotel Aprile, owned by the Cantini Zucconi family for over 35 years, is located in a 15th-century Medici palace behind the Piazza Santa Maria Novella, near the train station and many fine restaurants and shops. The historical building was restored under the strict ordinance of Florence's Commission of Fine Arts. The small and charming hotel is full of delightful surprises: from 16th-century paintings and a bust of the Duke of Tuscany to the frescoed breakfast room and quiet courtyard garden. The old-fashioned reception and sitting areas are invitingly furnished with Florentine Renaissance antiques, comfy, overstuffed red armchairs, and Oriental carpets worn with time. The wallpapered bedrooms include telephones and mini bars, and feature parquet floors and high vaulted ceilings, but vary widely in their size and decor—some are too basic and modern. There are 28 doubles, all now with private bathrooms after a recent restoration. Request one of the quieter rooms at the back of the hotel, overlooking the garden. At the desk is manager Roberto Gazzini looking after guests' needs. *Directions*: Use a detailed city map to locate the hotel, three blocks north of the Duomo. There is a parking garage.

HOTEL APRILE
Hosts: Valeria Cantini Zucconi family
Via della Scala 6
Florence 50123, Italy
Tel: (055) 216237, Fax: (055) 280947
28 rooms with private bathrooms
Lire 290,000 double B&B
Breakfast only
Open all year
Credit cards: all major
English spoken well
Region: Tuscany

The relaxed and friendly Ariele Hotel has been in the Bertelloni family for the past 40 or so years. Located in a quiet residential section across from the Opera House, it is within a short walking distance to the center of town. The entrance and reception area is made up of several old-fashioned-style sitting rooms, giving an immediate sense of the private home it used to be (dating back to 14th century). These spaces include a breakfast room and wallpapered sitting room with antique reproductions, gold velvet armchairs, fireplace, and Oriental carpets on tiled floors. A pleasant side garden with white wrought-iron tables and chairs offers a shady spot for breakfast. Hidden off in a corner is an unusual independent double room. There is also space here for parking at a minimal charge. The spacious, high-ceilinged bedrooms are individually decorated using a mix of old and new furnishings and have either wood parquet or marble floors. Extra amenities include air conditioning, telephone, and satellite TV. Unfortunately, the fluorescent lighting does not help brighten up the sometimes drab color scheme. Guests can depend on the kind assistance of the staff for restaurant and itinerary suggestions. *Directions*: Between Piazza Vittorio Veneto and the River Arno. Use a detailed city map to locate the hotel.

HOTEL ARIELE
Hosts: Bertelloni family
Via Magenta 11
Florence 50123, Italy
Tel: (055) 211509, Fax: (055) 268521
40 rooms with private bathrooms
Lire 180,000–250,000 double B&B
Breakfast only
Open all year
Credit cards: MC, VS
English spoken well
Region: Tuscany

The Hotel Hermitage is a dream of a small, well-manicured hotel with efficient service and breathtaking views over the city's most famous monuments. The location could not be more central—on a small street between the Uffizzi gallery and the River Arno. Housed in a 13th-century palazzo, the fifth-floor reception area looking out to the Ponte Vecchio bridge has a cozy living-room feeling with selected antique pieces, Oriental rugs, and corner fireplace. Across the hall is the veranda-like breakfast room dotted with crisp yellow tablecloths and topped with fresh flowers where privileged guests view the tower of Palazzo Signoria. Color-coordinated, separate air-conditioned rooms, some with hydrojet baths, have scattered antiques, framed etchings of the city, and more views. However, the highlight of a stay at the Hermitage is spending time dreaming on the rooftop terrace. The view embraces not only the previously mentioned marvels of Florence, but also the famous dome of the Duomo cathedral and Giotto's tower. Guests are served a Continental breakfast under the ivy-covered pergola and among the many flower-laden vases lining its borders. Reserve well in advance. *Directions*: Consult a detailed city map. There is a parking garage in the vicinity. Call for instructions as car traffic in this part of the city is strictly limited.

HOTEL HERMITAGE
Director: Vincenzo Scarcelli
Piazza del Pesce
Florence 50122, Italy
Tel: (055) 287216, Fax: (055) 212208
Email: florence@hermitagehotel.com
29 rooms with private bathrooms
Lire 410,000 double B&B
Breakfast only
Open all year
Credit cards: MC, VS
English spoken well
Region: Tuscany
www.karenbrown.com/italy/hotelhermitage.html

The refurbished Hotel Silla is located on the left bank of the River Arno opposite Santa Croce, the famous 13th-century square and church where Michelangelo and Galileo are buried. This position offers views from some of the rooms of several of Florence's most notable architectural attractions—the Duomo, the Ponte Vecchio, and the tower of Palazzo Vecchio. Housed on the second and third floors of a lovely 15th-century palazzo with courtyard entrance, 39 new and spotless double rooms with private baths are pleasantly decorated with simple dark-wood furniture and matching bedspreads and curtains. Air conditioning and an elevator were recently added necessities. The fancy, cream-colored reception area is appointed in 17th-century Venetian style, with period furniture, chandelier, and large paintings. Breakfast is served on the splendid and spacious second-floor outdoor terrace or in the dining room overlooking the Arno. The Silla is a friendly, convenient, and quiet hotel, near the Pitti Palace, leather artisan shops, and many restaurants. It offers tourists a good value in pricey Florence. A parking garage is available. *Directions*: Refer to a detailed city map to locate the hotel.

HOTEL SILLA
Host: Gabriele Belotti
Via dei Renai 5
Florence 50125, Italy
Tel: (055) 2342888, Fax: (055) 2341437
Email: hotelsilla@tin.it
39 rooms, 30 with private bathrooms
Lire 290,000 double B&B
Breakfast only
Open all year
Credit cards: all major
English spoken well
Region: Tuscany
www.karenbrown.com/italy/hotelsilla.html

Off on a quiet side street, the Splendor manages to miss most of the city center's traffic and street noise, yet guests are still able to walk almost everywhere, since the hotel is only three blocks from the Duomo and near the Accademia museum with its *David*. The prim, centuries-old palazzo, of the pale-yellow hue characteristic of Florence, is owned and run by the Bufalini family who, starting this year, have taken over the reins from the Masoero family who ran it with loving care for the past 43 years. The hotel will remain closed until mid-March 2001 for renovation, striving to maintain the ambiance of an elegant private home, with its frescoed foyer and sitting rooms graced with portraits, chandeliers, overstuffed armchairs, and Oriental carpets. On the second and third floors arc the 31 spacious guestrooms (a few can sleep a family of four), all with air conditioning and mini bars, decorated with reproduction matching armoires and beds. Perhaps the architectural highlight is the gracious breakfast room (breakfast is a superb buffet), with high ceilings, parquet floors, and frescoed panels all around. French doors lead from this area to an outdoor terrace with white iron chairs and tables where guests may take in a lovely view of San Marco church and where afternoon beverages are served. Garage service is also available at a charge. We are anxious to see the transformation of an old favorite. *Directions*: Four blocks north of the Duomo.

HOTEL SPLENDOR
Hosts: Giacomo Bufalini family
Via San Gallo 30
Florence 50129, Italy
Tel: (055) 483427, Fax: (055) 461276
Email: info@hotelsplendor.it
31 rooms with private bathrooms
Lire 270,000–300,000 double B&B
Breakfast only
Open all year, Credit cards: all major
English spoken well
Region: Tuscany
www.karenbrown.com/italy/hotelsplendor.html

It is not hard to find accommodations in a 15th-century palace in downtown Florence—the historical center of the city has little else. The Residenza is no exception, but it features the added attraction of being situated on Florence's most elegant street, with its famous boutiques, the Tornabuoni. For the last two generations the gracious Giacalone family has owned the palazzo's top three floors and operated them as a three-star hotel. An antique mahogany elevator takes you up to the reception area, which opens onto a pretty dining room with pink tablecloths and shelves lined with a collection of bottles, vases, and ceramics. Twenty-four tastefully furnished rooms with amenities including air conditioning are divided between three floors, capped with a rooftop terrace burgeoning with flowerpots and surrounded by city views. A comfortable sitting room with high, beamed ceilings and a satellite television for guests is located on the upper floor. La Residenza is one of the few small hotels offering dinner on the premises, and Signora Gianna is justifiably proud of their reputation for serving authentic Florentine cuisine. *Directions*: Use a detailed city map to locate the hotel in the heart of Florence next to the Palazzo Strozzi.

LA RESIDENZA
Hosts: Gianna Vasile & Paolo Giacalone
Via Tornabuoni 8
Florence 50123, Italy
Tel: (055) 218684, Fax: (055) 284197
24 rooms, 20 with private bathrooms
Lire 360,000 double B&B, 230,000 without bath
Breakfast & dinner served
Open all year
Credit cards: all major
English spoken well
Region: Tuscany

La Torricella, just on the outskirts of Florence, offers travelers the advantage of staying in a Tuscan home in a quiet residential area, yet with the city easily accessible by public transportation. Marialisa and Piero recently completely restored great-grandfather's home and converted it into a comfortable and efficient lodging. They decided to offer all the trimmings of a hotel, with amenities such as satellite TVs, mini bars, and telephones in rooms, plus daily cleaning service. The terraced front of the pale-yellow villa is lined with terra-cotta vases of flowers and intoxicating wisteria vines. Upon entering the home, you pass through a small reception area with brick arches and equestrian prints into the luminous breakfast room where a buffet is served in the morning. The eight rooms are scattered about the large, pristine home on various levels and are each similarly appointed in soft-green and mustard hues with sparkling new white bathrooms. Reproduction armoires and desks and wrought-iron beds harmonize well with the brick floors and high, beamed ceilings. There is a small pool at the back of the house and Marialisa offers cooking classes, teaching secrets of genuine Tuscan dishes. The couple are devoted to the well-being of guests and as natives of the area are a rich source of information. *Directions*: From the Certosa exit of the A1, head for the center of the city, turning right at the stop light in Galuzzo at Piazza Acciaiuoli. Take Via Silvani for several blocks, turning right on Via Vecchia di Pozzolatico just before the fork in the road.

LA TORRICELLA
Hosts: Marialisa Manetti & Piero Giannozzi
Via Vecchia di Pozzolatico 25
Florence 50125, Italy
Tel: (055) 2321808, Fax: (055) 2047402
8 rooms with private bathrooms
Lire 220,000–260,000 double B&B
2-night minimum stay
Breakfast only
Open all year
English spoken well, Region: Tuscany

The country residences of wealthy Florentine families dating back to Renaissance times were all concentrated on the hills above the city. Villa Poggio San Felice is one of these, reached by way of a labyrinth of narrow (unbelievably two-way) winding roads past stone-walled gardens concealing magnificent villas. Livia inherited not only the actual property of her great-grandfather but also a long-standing tradition in the hospitality field—he was the founder of two of Florence's most prominent hotels, today called the Grand and the Excelsior. This bed and breakfast is special indeed as guests are given full run of the main part of the two-story villa with its library, gracious, portrait-lined sitting rooms, and high-ceilinged dining room. This is where a full buffet breakfast is served on round tables with blue-and-yellow plaid cloths overlooking the formal gardens through French doors. Enthusiastic Livia and her husband Lorenzo's desire was to have their guests experience the true flavor of a noble villa and consequently minimum possible modifications were made. This authentic ambiance is prevalent throughout the five bedrooms spread out on the upper floor, containing the family's original furniture. The romantic *I Sposi* honeymoon bedroom has fireplace, parquet floors, and hunter-green color scheme, while the spacious room *Nonni* features a large terrace looking out over cypress-lined hills to the famous dome of Florence's cathedral. *Directions*: Ten minutes from the center of Florence. A detailed map is provided.

VILLA POGGIO SAN FELICE
Hosts: Livia Puccinelli & Lorenzo Magnelli
Via San Matteo in Arcetri 24
Florence 50125, Italy
Tel: (055) 220016, Fax: (055) 2335388
Cellphone: (0335) 6818844
Email: ilpoggio@tin.it
5 rooms with private bathrooms
Lire 300,000–400,000 double B&B
Breakfast only, Open March 15 to December 1
English spoken well, Region: Tuscany
www.karenbrown.com/italy/sanfelice.html

On a hilltop overlooking the valley surrounding Foligno and covering over 1,000 acres is the enchanting Rocca Deli bed and breakfast, which opened its doors this year. A winding gravel road takes you up to the crest of the mountain covered with olive groves and Scotch broom where views are truly remarkable and where the silence is almost deafening. The rich history of the ancient tower here dates back to the year 1100 when it served as a watchtower, then through the centuries it was a stopping point on the pilgrims' path from the Adriatic Sea to Rome. Fabio, whose family bought the property in 1820, had the dream to see this mystic, meditative spot brought back to life by offering hospitality to travelers. Inside the wrought-iron gates, the first house attached to the original stone walls holds four bedrooms on two floors, reached by a spiral staircase and appointed with appropriate antiques. Within these medieval walls, immaculate bathrooms with characteristic Deruta tiles were added for each room. The fifth bedroom is in an adjacent house next to the remains of the original tower, with typical Umbrian wrought-iron bed and fireplace. Informative hostess Silvia serves guests breakfast or dinner in the charmingly authentic taverna with long wood tables or out in the panoramic garden. The family also owns the Le Due Torri on the other side of Spello, which offers very comfortable apartments for weekly stays. *Directions*: From Spoleto to Foligno, exit for Macereta and head for Carpello and La Rocca—follow the road to the end.

ROCCA DELI   New
Hosts: Fabio Ciri family
Localita: Scandolaro di Foligno
Foligno (PG) 06034, Italy
Tel: (0742) 651249, Fax: (0742) 270273
5 rooms with private bathrooms
Lire 120,000–160,000 double B&B
2-night minimum stay
Breakfast, dinner upon request
Open all year
Some English, French spoken, Region: Umbria

The bed-and-breakfast boom of the last decade in Italy has brought about a vast variety of accommodation from classic, in-home hospitality to places with many amenities that more resemble small hotels. Il Torrino brings us back to the more traditional example, with four bedrooms offered within the hostess's home. The large, old-fashioned family home of Signora Cesarina's grandparents is located in the Montechiari hills between Florence and Pisa east-west and between Volterra and Lucca north-south—a prime touring location. Here you will not find standardized rooms all decorated alike, but rather individual rooms filled with the family's personal belongings, heirloom furniture, and the authentic feeling of a Tuscan home. With her children grown and residing in various parts of the world, the very sweet hostess, Cesarina Campinotti, opened her home to travelers and welcomes guests in the downstairs living room, upstairs breakfast room where an abundant meal is served, or out in the garden with its small above-ground swimming pool. A separate two-person garden apartment with kitchenette has glass doors looking out to the tree-lined patio with glimpses of the surrounding countryside beyond. The four bedrooms with living room and kitchen can also be rented separately. Here you are in the center of Tuscany and there is a golf course 12 kilometers away. *Directions*: From Forcoli follow signs for Montechiari and Montacchita, continuing past Montacchita up to group of houses (5 km). Il Torrino has the black iron gate and no sign.

*IL TORRINO   **New***
Hostess: Cesarina Campinotti
Localita: Montechiari
Forcoli (PI) 56030, Italy
Tel & fax: (0587) 629181
4 rooms with private bathrooms, 1 apartment
Lire 180,000 double B&B
* Lire 150,000 apartment daily, without breakfast*
Breakfast only, Open all year
Very little English spoken
Region: Tuscany

Staying in the Albani hills just 7 kilometers south of Rome is an excellent alternative to the higher-priced accommodations in the city—the area offers easy public transportation, proximity to both airports, and picturesque towns, lakes, and gardens. Frascati is most well-known for its wine and many restaurants, which Romans invade on weekends. The Hotel Flora stands out among the choice of smaller hotels. Formerly a private residence, the turn-of-the-century gray-and-white pristine villa has a courtyard and surrounding garden where breakfast is served in the summer months. The best rooms, a variety of doubles, junior suites, and suites, spacious, with terraces and high ceilings, are on the upper floors, while the rest are in a newer building next door. The polished decor throughout is neoclassical, with black-and-white marble floors and bathrooms, and antique furnishings, and the guestrooms include many amenities as well as air conditioning. Top-floor rooms have balconies with nice views. To the right of the reception area is a comfortable lounge and bar. Sightseeing in the vicinity includes lakes Nemi and Albano, the gardens of Ninfa and Villa Aldobrandini, and Rocca di Papa. A shuttle service is now available for transfers to and from airports and the metro station (80,000 lire per person). *Directions*: Exit from Rome's GRA ring road at Via Tuscolana and continue straight to Frascati. Hotel signs are posted in the town.

HOTEL FLORA
Owner: Giannandrea Barbante
Viale Vittorio Veneto 8
Frascati (RM) 00044, Italy
Tel: (06) 9416110, Fax: (06) 9416546
Email: info@hotel-flora.it
32 rooms with private bathrooms
Lire 225,000–260,000 double B&B
Breakfast only
Open all year, Credit cards: all major
English spoken well
Region: Lazio
www.karenbrown.com/italy/flora.html

On the border of Umbria and the Marches regions, within reach of the unforgettably romantic towns of Spoleto, Todi, Assisi, and Perugia, is Francesco Rambotti's 18th-century stone farmhouse, beautifully situated atop a hill overlooking the peaceful countryside. Aside from wine-producing grapes, the farm raises deer, sheep, and mountain goats, which roam freely on the property. The University of Perugia conducts research here as a model of farm activity perfectly in tune with the conservation of the environment. The farm reopened in September 1999 after extensive renovation due to earthquake damage. Thirteen rooms, divided between two farmhouses, some with exposed stone walls, are rustically done with antique country furnishings from the area. Alternatively, two two-bedroom apartments with bath and kitchenette are offered for longer stays. The tavern-like dining room has a fireplace, exposed-beamed ceiling, long wood tables, and walls lined with wine casks. Hearty regional fare is served here, complemented by the farm's own wine. They produce natural creams and cosmetics at the farm using soil that is said to have been used in ancient times. This is an inexpensive and family-oriented base from which to explore the many "must-see" destinations of Umbria. *Directions*: From the Spoleto-Foligno road, turn right at La Valle 7 km after Nocera.

VILLA DELLA CUPA
Hosts: Franco Rambotti family
Via Colle di Nocera Umbra 141
Gaifana (PG) 06020, Italy
Tel: (0742) 810329, Fax: (0742) 810666
13 rooms with private bathrooms, 2 apartments
Lire 90,000 double B&B
  75,000 per person half board
All meals served
Open all year, Credit cards: AX
English spoken well
Region: Umbria

The Castello di Tornano, a strategically situated hilltop tower dating back almost 1,000 years, has a 360-degree vista of the surrounding valley and has been of great historical significance in the seemingly endless territorial battles between Siena and Florence. The current owners are the Selvolini family, whose lovely daughters, Fabiola and Barbara, opened the wine estate to guests more than ten years ago. (Patricia is now Barbara's partner.) Weekly stays begin with meeting other guests around the exquisite pool cut into the rock and spanned by a bridge. Eight simply appointed apartments, with a mix of new and, at last look, rather worn furniture, are situated in a stone farmhouse in front of the tower. Each has a living area, kitchen, one or two bedrooms, and garden. The living room in the villa is one of the common areas where guests can gather together. The *pièce de résistance*, however, is the three-floor apartment within the monumental tower, sparsely furnished with the family's antiques and featuring two bedrooms, three living rooms with fireplace, dining room, kitchen, and tower-top terrace with a view not easily forgotten. Meals can be taken at the restaurant on the property. Tennis courts are also available. The sisters may not always be present as they commute from Florence. *Directions*: At 19 km from Siena take route 408 towards Gaiole. A sign for Tornano to the right is indicated 5 km before Gaiole.

CASTELLO DI TORNANO
Hosts: Patricia & Barbara Selvolini
Localita: Gaiole
Gaiole in Chianti (SI) 53013, Italy
Tel: (0577) 746067, winter (055) 6580918
Fax: (0577) 746094, winter: (055) 6580103
9 apartments
Lire 800,000–4,000,000 (tower) weekly
Trattoria on premises
Closed mid-Jan to mid-Feb
Credit cards: all major
English spoken very well, Region: Tuscany

The heel of Italy offers a wealth of natural beauty but, because of its remoteness, few really charming places to stay. The Masseria Lo Prieno is run by the delightful Castriota family, whose crops are representative of the staples of the Apulia region, and include olives, almonds, fruits, and grains. Spartan accommodations are offered in bungalows scattered among the pine woods and palms on the family property. Each mini guesthouse includes one bedroom, kitchenette, bathroom, and an eating area containing basic necessities. Nine simply decorated rooms with bathrooms are now available within a newly constructed house on the property. What were formerly animal stalls have been converted into a large dining space rustically decorated with antique farm tools and brass pots. Along with warm hospitality, the family makes the kitchen's offerings a top priority and it is the food that makes the stay here special. For an exquisite and authentic traditional meal, the restaurant here is incomparable. Both Maria Grazia, the energetic daughter who runs the show, and her charming mother take pride in demonstrating how local specialties are prepared. This is a budget choice for touring this area. *Directions*: From Taranto take N174 to Galatone, then follow signs for Secli. Turn right on Via Gramsci, then left on Via San Luca. Follow signs for Lo Prieno. 80 km from Brindisi.

MASSERIA LO PRIENO
Hosts: Francesco Castriota family
Localita: Contrada Orelle
Galatone (LE) 73044, Italy
Tel & fax: (0833) 865443 or 865898
Fax: (0833) 861879, Cellphone: (0335) 8432610
5 bungalows, 9 rooms with private bathrooms
Lire 120,000 double B&B
* 90,000 per person half board*
3-night minimum stay, Breakfast & dinner served
Open April to September, Handicap facilities
Some English spoken
Region: Apulia

On the extreme outskirts of the Florence, the Fattoressa offers a location for dual exploration of both city and Tuscan countryside. One of the many marvelous attractions of Florence is how the countryside comes right up to the doors of the city. Just behind the magnificent Certosa monastery is situated the 15th-century stone farmhouse of the delightfully congenial Fusi-Borgioli family. They have transformed the farmer's quarters into guest accommodations: four sweetly simple bedrooms plus two triples, each with its own spotless bathroom. Angiolina and Amelio, who have tended to this piece of land for many years, treat their guests like family and, as a result, enjoy receiving some of them year after year. Daughters-in-law Laura and Katia, who speak English, have been a great help in assisting guests with local itineraries. Visitors take meals *en famille* at long tables in the cozy, rustic dining room with a large stone fireplace (lire 60,000). Here Angiolina proudly serves authentic Florentine specialties using ingredients from her own fruit orchard and vegetable garden. *Directions*: Entering Florence from the Certosa exit off the Siena superstrada, turn left one street after the Certosa Convent stoplight onto Volterrana. After the bridge, turn right behind the building. The house is just on the left.

LA FATTORESSA
Hosts: Angiolina Fusi & Amelio Borgioli
Via Volterrana 58
Galluzzo (FI) 50124, Italy
Tel & fax: (055) 2048418
6 rooms with private bathrooms
Lire 160,000 double B&B
Breakfast & dinner served upon request
Open all year
English, French, & German spoken
Region: Tuscany

Casa Mezzuola is part of a small group of farmhouses atop a hill 3 kilometers outside Greve. The land was divided into separate smaller properties. Friendly hosts, Riccardo, an antique and jewelry dealer, Nicoletta, and their two girls live in the main house while hospitality is offered within three apartments for two to four persons in the adjacent stables and *fienile* where the hay was once stored. The stone walls, beams, and original brick openings to allow air into the barn were all preserved in the tower-like construction housing two of the apartments. A two-story apartment has a tiled kitchen/living area on one floor and bedroom and bathroom on the next floor, while the snug studio apartment crowns the top of the tower. They are all nicely furnished with colorful rugs, local country furniture, satellite TV, and fully equipped kitchens. Breakfast is served within the apartments or outside under one of the pergola terraces. Just below the apartments is a swimming pool bordered on one side by a stone wall and enjoying the expansive vistas, as well as bikes for guests' use. This is a convenient base for travelers in the heart of Chianti. Greve has a full program of festivals, concerts, and events, especially during the summer. *Directions*: Entering Greve from the north (Florence), turn right at the first stop light. Follow signs for Mezzuola, Cologne, not Montefioralle. After 3 km of unpaved, bumpy road, you will come across the marked property.

CASA MEZZUOLA
Hosts: Riccardo Franconeri family
Via S. Cresci 30
Greve in Chianti (FI) 50022, Italy
Tel & fax: (055) 8544885
Email: angelica@ftbcc.it
3 apartments
Lire 160,000–230,000 daily per apartment
3-night minimum stay, weekly June to September
Breakfast served, dinner upon request
Open all year
English spoken well, Region: Tuscany
www.karenbrown.com/italy/mezzuola.html

In the northern reaches of Lazio, bordering Umbria and Tuscany, is the stately, 17th-century castle of the noble Mancini Caterini family. Antonello and Cristina, a gracious and sociable couple, decided to transfer their young family from Rome and reside permanently on the vast wooded property, overseeing the agricultural activity as once did Antonello's great-grandfather, Cardinal and chief advisor to the Pope in 1848. They have done an admirable job of restoring the large, ivy-covered farmhouse just below the family's residence and creating four charming apartments plus eight bedrooms for guests. The bi-level apartments maintain their original rustic flavor and are cheerfully decorated with antique armoires and dressers, country fabrics for curtains and bedspreads, and wrought-iron beds. Accommodation in low season and for shorter stays is offered in the *Granaio* 1 and 2, with four bedrooms on each floor and individual living rooms, which can also be used as separate apartments. On the ground floor you find outdoor and indoor eating areas, billiard room, and game room overlooking a lovely swimming pool. Activities including tennis, horseback riding, wine itineraries, and boat rides and sailing on nearby Lake Bolsena, besides exploration of the many interesting ancient Etruscan towns in this very beautiful countryside. *Directions*: From the A1 autostrada exit at Orvieto and follow signs first for Bolsena then Castel S. Giorgio-S. Lorenzo Nuovo-Grotte di Castro. Just past town turn right at the *Castello* sign.

CASTELLO DI S. CRISTINA   New
Hosts: Cristina & Antonello Mancini Caterini
Grotte di Castro (VT) 01025, Italy
Tel & fax: (0763) 78011
Cellphone: (0339) 8605166
8 rooms with private bathrooms, 4 apartments
Lire 140,000–180,000 double B&B
* Lire 950,000–3,600,000 weekly per apartment*
2-night minimum stay, 1 week high season
Breakfast only, Open all year
English spoken fluently, Region: Lazio

An outstanding alternative to the city hotels of Venice is the perfectly charming Gargan bed and breakfast situated in the countryside just 30 kilometers from Venice. The Calzavara family renovated the family's expansive 17th-century country house and opened the restaurant and guestrooms, offering four sweetly decorated bedrooms each with its own bathroom on the top floor plus two suites consisting of bedroom, sitting room, and bathroom. Signora Antonia, son Alessandro who looks after the farm, and his wife Nicoletta enjoy making their guests feel as "at home" as possible by having fresh flowers in the cozy, antique-filled bedrooms. The downstairs sitting and dining rooms display the family's country antiques as well as a large fireplace and nice touches such as lace curtains and paintings. Guests are treated to a full breakfast of home-baked cakes and exceptional four-course dinners prepared especially for guests by Signora Antonia herself, using all ingredients from the farm. The Gargan is an ideal choice in this area, being a short drive from such marvels as Padova, Venice, Treviso, Vicenza, Verona, and Palladian villas plus many smaller medieval villages. *Directions*: From Venice take route 245 to Scorze, turning right for Montebelluna at the stoplight 1 km after town. After the town of S. Ambrogio turn left at the stoplight. Turn right at the church in Levada up to the house.

GARGAN
Hosts: Calzavara family
Via Marco Polo 2
Levada di Piombino Dese (PD) 35017, Italy
Tel: (049) 9350308, Fax: (049) 9350016
Email: gargan@gargan.it
4 rooms, 2 suites, all with private bathrooms
Lire 110,000–150,000 double B&B
* 95,000–115,000 per person half board*
All meals served
Open all year
Some English spoken
Region: Veneto
www.karenbrown.com/italy/gargan.html

When Lois Martin, a retired language professor, spotted the lovely restored farmhouse at San Martino, she knew it literally had her name on it and immediately purchased it. She has been running a bed and breakfast for the past five years and offers travelers all possible amenities of home. The house is completely open to guests, from the upstairs cozy living room with large stone fireplace, which divides the four bedrooms to the downstairs country kitchen and eating area. A full breakfast is served either outside on the patio or in the kitchen with its impressive display of Deruta ceramics. One bedroom with king mattress is joined by a bathroom to a small room with twin beds, ideal for a family. The other two doubles each has a bathroom, with one being en suite. Besides a swimming pool overlooking the wooded hills and valley, other extras are satellite TV, American washer and dryer, bikes, guest bathrobes, and dinner upon request, served out on the back porch where tobacco was once hung to dry. Being right on the border of Umbria and Tuscany, towns such as Gubbio, Perugia, Cortona, Assisi, Deruta, and Lake Trasimeno are all easily accessible, plus an itinerary including ten local castles. The entire house can also be rented weekly for a group of eight persons. *Directions*: From Lisciano square, pass the bar and turn left for San Martino, continue for 2 km and take a right up the hill at the sign for San Martino for just over 1.5 km to the house.

CASA SAN MARTINO
Hostess: Lois Martin
Localita: San Martino 19
Lisciano Niccone (PG) 06060, Italy
Tel: (075) 844288, Fax: (075) 844422
4 rooms, 3 with private bathrooms
Lire 280,000 double B&B
* 6,000,000 house weekly*
3-night minimum stay
Breakfast served, dinner upon request
Open all year
English spoken fluently, Region: Umbria
www.karenbrown.com/italy/casasanmartino.html

Lucca is decidedly one of the loveliest cities of Italy with its historical churches and circular piazzas interspersed among beautiful shops featuring original storefronts and signage. Besides the well-known summer Puccini Festival (this is his birthplace), there are antiques markets, artisan fairs, and some of the most beautiful formal gardens and villas in Italy surrounding the city. In March the villas and gardens open for a special tour when the area's famed flower, the camellia (tree size), is in bloom. Over the years we have patiently awaited the arrival of a charming place to stay within the city walls and this year we were rewarded with the Corte degli Angeli. The Bonino family, already very familiar with the hospitality business with a successful hotel in Forte dei Marmi, took over a private residence in the very heart of Lucca and created six spacious bedrooms with guests' comfort in mind. The ground-floor reception area includes a cozy dining room with fireplace where an abundant buffet breakfast is served, if not in your own room. Bedrooms on the upper two floors are reached by an elevator, and all follow a specific flower theme, with pastel-colored walls giving an overall fresh feeling. Complementing the well-put-together decor are antique dressers, parquet floors, and amenities such as air conditioning, Jacuzzi tubs, mini bars, TVs, and Internet access. *Directions*: In the pedestrian-only center of Lucca near the famous Piazza Anfiteatro. Private garage parking can be arranged.

ALLA CORTE DEGLI ANGELI   **New**
Host: Pietro Bonino
Via degli Angeli 23
Lucca 55100, Italy
Tel: (0583) 469204, Fax: (0583) 991989
6 rooms with private bathrooms
Lire 300,000 double B&B
Breakfast only
Open all year, Credit cards: MC, VS
Some English spoken
Region: Tuscany

For those seeking a base for exploring the hilltowns of Tuscany while sojourning in very characteristic accommodation with a rich historical past, the Lucignanello is a sublime choice. Imagine residing in one of the cluster of stone houses that make up the quaint village immersed in the type of picture-perfect and timeless Tuscan landscapes seen in Renaissance paintings. The illustrious Piccolomini family still owns the 15th-century property and offers the possibility of living out a dream common to many lovers of Italy. Five two-bedroom houses have been masterfully restored so as not to disturb the original architectural features, while ensuring modern facilities. The irregularly-shaped interiors are filled with lovely antiques, Oriental carpets, beautifully tiled bathrooms, kitchens with travertine counters, and all but one have large fireplaces. High above the village is a pool set among olive trees with inspiring views. Guests are self-sufficient and no meals are served (although breakfast ingredients including fresh rolls and cakes are supplied), but Signora Simonetta lives in the village and is on hand for endless exploration suggestions in the area. A separate five-bedroom farmhouse with private swimming pool down the road is rented out by the week. Country charm exudes from every little corner and the ambiance is so authentic you will feel almost Tuscan before you leave! Weekly stays only. *Directions*: From San Quirico go towards Siena and take the first turnoff right to San Giovanni d'Asso. Two km before town, turn right for Lucignano d'Asso and travel 2 km up to the hamlet.

LUCIGNANELLO BANDINI
Hostess: Simonetta Lippi
Localita: Lucignano d'Asso
S. Giovanni d'Asso (SI) 53020, Italy
Tel: (0577) 803068, Fax: (0577) 803082
6 apartments, 1 villa
Lire 2,800,000–8,400,000 weekly per apartment
  8,000,000 villa weekly
No meals served
Open all year, Credit cards: MC, VS
English spoken well, Region: Tuscany

The Luz family of Luino recently refurbished another home, creating a second, more economical accommodation just 2 kilometers up the road from their hotel on Lake Maggiore. The Colmegna is run by their young and energetic daughter Lara and caters well to families—in fact, there is no charge for children under 4. The two pale-yellow buildings run right along the waterfront bordered by an old stone port. There are several terraces for dining outdoors and another with a lawn for sunning or relaxing and enjoying the view. Beyond this is a gorgeous shaded park with romantic trails, tall trees, and wildflowers at one of the prettiest points of the lake. Simply appointed bedrooms are all situated lakeside on the two floors and accommodate from two to four persons. Swimming, sailing, and windsurfing sports can be arranged. Luino is famous for its open market on Wednesdays, a long-standing tradition since 1541. Within touring distance are the lakes of Lugano and Como, the ferry from Laveno across Lake Maggiore, and the Swiss border. *Directions*: Luino is halfway up the lake on the eastern side near the Swiss border. Heading north, Colmegna is on the left-hand side of the main road just past the town of Luino.

CAMIN HOTEL COLMEGNA
Hostess: Lara Luz
Localita: Colmegna
Luino (VA) 21016, Italy
Tel: (0332) 510855, Fax: (0332) 537226
25 rooms with private bathrooms
Lire 170,000–205,000 double B&B
Breakfast & dinner served
Open March to November
Credit cards: all major
English spoken well
Region: Lombardy

The noble Albertario family have four large countryside properties in Umbria and Tuscany that they have opened up to accommodate travelers. Macciangrosso, bordered by ancient cypress trees, is the most beautiful, with its hilltop position overlooking the sweeping valley. The large stone villa, which has been added on to at various times throughout its long history (15th-century origins), belonged to the noble Piccolomini ancestors. You enter through the side gate, walk over a large patio looking onto the delightful rose garden, and climb an external stairway up to the six bedrooms. These are all accessed by a main living room, more like a museum with its rare antique pieces and gilded frame paintings. Bedrooms, each with a small bathroom, are simpler, appointed with wrought-iron beds and coordinated bedspreads and curtains. Other common living areas are the transformed cantina and dining and game rooms. The swimming pool is bordered by a stone wall from the Etruscan period and a tennis court is nearby. Ten apartments of various sizes are in the rest of the home and in a nearby house next to the chapel. Close to the thermal spas, Macciangrosso is on the edge of Umbria and Tuscany, offering easy access to the highlights of both regions. *Directions*: From Chiusi drive 3 km towards Chianciano. Turn right at the grocery store and go 1.5 km to the house.

MACCIANGROSSO
Hosts: Sonia & Luigi Albertario
Localita: Macciano
Chiusi (SI) 53044, Italy
Tel & fax: (0578) 274198 or 21459
Email: melograno@kou.net
6 rooms with private bathrooms, 10 apartments
Lire 250,000 double B&B (heating extra)
* 800,000–1,900,000 weekly per apartment*
3-night minimum stay, 1 week for apartments
Breakfast only, Closed November
English & French spoken well
Region: Tuscany
www.karenbrown.com/italy/macciangrosso.html

Ca'delle Rondini opened its doors first as a restaurant and then four years ago as a bed and breakfast establishment. The typical rectangular-shaped, pale-yellow farmhouse with incorporated barn, built in 1800, faces out to the main road in town and at the back to acres of flat fields, fruit orchards, and horse stables. In a section of the long house live gregarious host Ilo and his brother Alessandro, who helps Mamma in the kitchen with the creation of delectable local fare whose ingredients come directly from the farm. Entering the lofty restaurant with fireplace, gray-stone floors, beamed ceilings, and large arched windows, one has the sense of being part of a truly authentic local gathering place—especially for Sunday lunch. Guests sit down in one of the two dining rooms and are offered a variety of inventive antipasti served on cutting boards. The comfortable rooms upstairs and one below (with access for the handicapped) all have telephone and air conditioning, and are very pleasantly appointed in typical country style with mansard beamed ceilings, pinewood floors, and country antiques. Outings by bike or horseback are arranged in the nearby nature park reserve. Ilo can suggest many original itineraries, including a tour of Venice's abandoned islands on a friend's boat. Ca'delle Rondini is a great base for visiting Venice, Padova, Treviso, Verona, and Vicenza. Public transportation takes you to and from Piazzale Roma in Venice in 45 minutes. *Directions*: Ca'delle Rondini is in the town of Maerne, just 10 km from Venice and northwest of Mestre.

CA'DELLE RONDINI
Hosts: Silvestri family
Via Ca' Rossa 26
Maerne (VE) 30030, Italy
Tel & fax: (041) 641114
6 rooms with private bathrooms
Lire 165,000 double B&B
All meals served for guests, Restaurant open Thurs to Sun
Open all year, Credit cards: MC, VS
No English spoken, Region: Veneto
www.karenbrown.com/italy/rondini.html

It would be difficult for anyone with a passion for the outdoors to resist the challenge offered Federico when he inherited the 1,000-plus-acre estate of his great-grandfather in the wilderness of Maremma. He and his energetic wife from Verona, Elisabetta, plunged in and in two years made this dream come true. The results are notable and very ambitious, with the complete restoration of four stone farmhouses scattered about the vast property comprised of wooded hills, olive groves, and cultivated fields of grain and sunflowers. Guests first arrive at the imposing 1850s main villa, which houses the reception office and three of the twenty-four apartments. Comfortable apartments divided among the various farmhouses are nicely furnished with country pieces old and new and can accommodate from two to ten persons. Guests have the use of three swimming pools, mountain bikes, sauna, exercise, and game rooms, Jacuzzi, and massage therapy. They convene at *Podernovo* where Tuscan meals are served in the exposed stone dining room with fireplace, or out on the patio looking out over the valley and up to austere Massa Marittima. The Etruscan towns of Massa Marittima, Volterra, Vetulonia, and Populonia are waiting to be explored and you are also close to the seaside. The summer months offer a rich musical program of operas and classical concerts in the main piazza and villas. *Directions*: Drive for 2 km on the gravel road from Massa Marittima where signs are indicated for Montebamboli.

TENUTA IL CICALINO
Hosts: Elisabetta & Federico Vecchioni
Localita: Cicalino
Massa Marittima (GR) 58024, Italy
Tel: (0566) 902031, Cellphone: (0347) 6444130
Fax: (0566) 904896
Email: cicalino@cometanet.it
24 apartments
Lire 65,000–80,000 per person B&B
Breakfast & dinner served, Closed February
Some English spoken, Region: Tuscany
www.karenbrown.com/italy/cicalino.html

The La Biancarda bed and breakfast is the beautiful country home of the Florio family of Ancona, overlooking the colorful hilly countryside. Just south of Ancona begins one of the prettiest coastlines of the eastern Adriatic shores with a combination of seaside villages, hilly countryside, and dramatic mountains cascading into the sea. Signora Giovanna had the salmon-colored farmhouse dating to 1760 restored 15 years ago to provide her family with a relaxing country retreat, and adorned it with many of the family's precious antiques. The impressive, stone-walled living room upstairs with enormous fireplace, plus cozy library and billiard room are all open to guests. Six guest bedrooms include an apartment with sitting room. A real treat is waking up to breakfast in the delightful country kitchen with fireplace, long family table, beamed ceilings, and collection of hanging brass pots. Exquisite dinners based on fresh fish and local produce and wines can also be arranged. Outdoor activities in the area include golf, tennis, horseback riding, and swimming (beaches are ten minutes away). The historical towns of Macereto, Loreto, and Urbino are nearby. *Directions*: From the A14 autostrada, exit at Ancona Sud and follow signs for Numana. Keep on this road for several kilometers to Coppo, turning left onto a dirt road just after the bar—follow it to the end.

LA BIANCARDA
Hosts: Giovanna Florio & family
Via Biancarda 129
Coppo di Sirolo, Massignano (AN) 60125, Italy
Mailing address: Viale della Vittoria 44B
Ancona 60100, Italy
Tel & fax: (071) 280053, Tel & fax (winter): (071) 34331
6 rooms, 5 with private bathrooms
Lire 170,000–190,000 double B&B
  220,000-300,000 apartment weekly only
2-night minimum stay
Breakfast served, dinner upon request, Open May to Oct 15
English spoken well, Region: Marches

The simple and economical Oasi Verde ("green oasis") is just that: a convenient roadside stop for those traveling between Umbria and the Marches region. Carla and Andrea Rossi inherited the sprawling 200-year-old stone farmhouse and surrounding land, ideally located midway between Perugia and Gubbio (a not-to-be-missed medieval stone village set high up in the hillside), and decided to convert it to a bed and breakfast and restaurant. The eight rooms in the main house, each with own bathroom, have been decorated like model room number 3, with its original beamed ceiling and country-antique bed and armoire. White-tiled floors may be out of character, but give a sense of cleanliness nonetheless. Another wing of the complex houses three simply furnished suites (two bedrooms and a bathroom) for longer stays, perfect for a family of four. An additional ten rooms, each with separate ground-floor entrance, are found in a wing renovated within the last few years. The windows at the back of the house open out to green hills with alternating patches of woods and sunflower fields. Facilities tempting you to linger for a while include a swimming pool, bikes available for rent, and a horseback riding school. *Directions*: From Perugia on route 298 after 25 km, you find the bed and breakfast on the left-hand side, at Mengara, 10 km before Gubbio.

OASI VERDE MENGARA
Hosts: Andrea & Carla Rossi
Località: Mengara 1
Scritto (PG) 06020, Italy
Tel: (075) 9227004 or (0336) 633534
Fax: (075) 920049
18 rooms with private bathrooms, 3 suites
Lire 90,000–110,000 double B&B
  70,000–85,000 per person half board (no beverages)
3-night minimum stay (high season)
All meals served
Open March to November, Credit cards: MC, VS
Very little English spoken
Region: Umbria

Florentine sisters Francesca and Beatrice Baccetti eagerly accepted the challenge of converting the family's country home and vineyards into an efficient bed and breakfast. Restoration work began immediately on the two adjacent stone buildings dating back to 1400. All original architectural features were preserved, leaving the five guestrooms and eleven apartments (for two to four people) with terra-cotta brick floors, wood-beamed ceilings, mansard roofs, and many with generous views over the tranquil Tuscan countryside. The very comfortable and tidy rooms are furnished with good reproductions in country style and feel almost hotel-like with their telephones and modern bathrooms. A beautiful swimming pool with hydro-massage, tennis court, billiards room, and nearby horse stables are at the guests' disposal, although finding enough to do is hardly a problem with Florence only 18 kilometers away and practically all of Tuscany at one's fingertips. Breakfast is served at wood tables in the stone-walled dining room or out on the terrace. Readers give Salvadonica a high rating for service and warm hospitality. *Directions*: From Florence take the superstrada toward Siena for 20 km, exiting at San Casciano Nord. Follow signs for town, turning left at the sign for Mercatale. Salvadonica is on this road and well marked.

SALVADONICA
Hosts: Francesca & Beatrice Baccetti
Via Grevigiana 82
Mercatale Val di Pesa (FI) 50024, Italy
Tel: (055) 8218039, Fax: (055) 8218043
Email: salvadonica@tin.it
5 rooms with private bathrooms, 11 apartments
Lire 180,000–195,000 double B&B
  220,000–435,000 daily per apartment B&B
1-week minimum stay high season (May to Oct)
Breakfast only, Open March to November 10
Credit cards: all major
English spoken very well, Region: Tuscany
www.karenbrown.com/italy/salvadonica.html

In an industrial city where the word "charm" is practically nonexistent, the Hotel Regina, although not inexpensive, came as a pleasant surprise among the rather nondescript choice of modern hotels in Milan. For those flying in and out of Milan, with a desire to catch a glimpse of the city center (and newly restored *Last Supper* of Da Vinci—by advance reservation only), this is an ideal selection. The attractive, typically 18th-century façade and entrance invite guests into a luminous reception area converted from the original courtyard with stone columns, arches, marble floors, large plants, and a small corner bar with sitting area and tables. Completely refurbished rooms (non-smoking upon request) include all modern amenities and are very quiet, being set off the street. Decorated comfortably and uniformly with identical furniture, warmth is given to rooms with soft-pastel-colored walls, parquet floors, and scattered Oriental rugs. A full buffet breakfast is served below and is included in the room rate. Manager Michela is helpful in satisfying guests' requests and bicycles are available for visting the city's historical center. Linate airport is easily reached by cab in 20 minutes, while the Malpensa airport can be reached by bus from the train station. *Directions*: Via Correnti is just off the Via Torino, which leads to Milan's famous cathedral and shopping area, and is between the Basilicas of San Lorenzo and San Ambrogio.

HOTEL REGINA
Hostess: Michela Barberi
Via Cesare Correnti 13
Milan 20123, Italy
Tel: (02) 58106913, Fax: (02) 58107033
Email: info@hotelregina.it
43 rooms with private bathrooms
Lire 390,000–410,000 double B&B
Breakfast only
Open all year, Credit cards: all major
English spoken well, Region: Lombardy
www.karenbrown.com/italy/hotelregina.html

Bed & Breakfast Descriptions

I Girasoli opened its doors with all the characteristics of a countryside bed and breakfast—a well-restored country house with seven nicely appointed bedrooms surrounded by fields of sunflowers. Over the years its popularity as one of the best restaurants in the area grew and today, although it is still a bed and breakfast, travelers come from afar for a meal based on inventive regional dishes. A comfy living room and three luminous dining rooms downstairs are appointed with polished country flair and feature scattered antiques and stenciled borders. One room actually looks onto the busy kitchen area for mealtime entertainment. In summer months lighter meals of salads, barbecued meats, and a long list of delectable pizzas are served outside in the lush garden around a lovely heated pool. Air-conditioned bedrooms feature exposed brick walls, beamed ceilings, and pretty floral fabrics and have amenities such as TVs, telephones, and mini bars. There are also tennis courts and a park for children. For exploring the lesser-known countryside, or just a stopover on the way up or down the coast, this is the place. *Directions*: Exit at Riccione from the A14 and follow signs for Cattolica and then Morciano. Pass back over the tollway and take the second right at Via Ca'Rastelli. Follow signs for I Girasoli.

I GIRASOLI
Host: Marco Minitti
Via Ca'Rastelli 13
Misano Monte (RN) 47046, Italy
Tel & fax: (0541) 610724
7 rooms with private bathrooms
Lire 230,000 double B&B
All meals served
Open all year
Credit cards: all major
English spoken well
Region: Emilia Romagna

On the same road as the Godiolo bed and breakfast, a more independent self-catering type of accommodation is offered at the 13th-century Castello di Modanella. It is a sprawling stone complex complete with towers and turrets, many separate houses where the farmers of the vast wine estate once lived, a church, and even a school. The castle is in a constant state of restoration and along the way 33 rental apartments for two to nine persons have been incorporated in various sections. Some apartments can be found in the old schoolhouse just outside the castle walls on two floors with one, two, or three bedrooms, bathrooms, kitchen, and living room. They maintain a true rustic flavor with original beams, mansard ceilings, worn brick floors, stone walls, and a mix of old and new wood furniture. All have lovely views over the countryside. Other comfortable apartments are located in four separate houses on the vast property. Although currently there are no accommodations in the castle itself, it is worth a visit with its arched entrance, iron gates, stone courtyard, and clock tower. The estate is under the direction of Gabriella Cerretti who assists guests with their every need. Guests also enjoy sports facilities such as tennis courts, two swimming pools, and two lakes for fishing. *Directions*: Travel for 30 km from Siena on route 326 towards the autostrada, then turn left at the sign for the Castello, opposite Serre di Rapolano.

CASTELLO DI MODANELLA
Hostess: Gabriella Cerretti
Serre di Rapolano (SI) 53040, Italy
Tel: (0577) 704604, Fax: (0577) 704740
33 apartments
Lire 161,000–503,000 daily per apartment
2-night minimum stay
No meals served
Open all year
Some English spoken
Region: Tuscany

Just 20 kilometers from Siena, at the foot of Chianti is the Godiolo stone farmhouse with its double loggia and cupola dating back to 1350. Red geraniums cascade from every one of the balconies and terra-cotta urns. While retired Signor Giuliano tends to the acres of vineyards and wine production, gracious Signora Bianca dedicates her time to making their guests feel very much at home. What used to be the children's rooms are now four charming guestrooms with nice, homey touches such as embroidered linen sheets, dried flower arrangements, and heirloom furnishings. Breakfast in the typical tiled kitchen consists of homemade baked goods to which guests help themselves. Signora, with her Roman-Tuscan origins, is an excellent cook and guests can treat themselves to a delightful dinner with the family upon request. Downstairs is a large informal living and game room for guests. Nearby are the thermal baths of Rapolano where massages, mud baths, and other spa services are available—true relaxation—and the stark and fascinating crater-like landscapes (Crete Sienese) south between Rapolano and Montalcino. *Directions*: Exit from the A1 autostrada at Val di Chiana and head towards Siena on route 326 towards Serre di Rapolano, but turn right up to Godiolo rather than left into town.

GODIOLO
Hosts: Giuliano & Bianca Perinelli
Localita: Modanella
Serre di Rapolano (SI) 53040, Italy
Tel & fax: (0577) 704304
4 rooms with private bathrooms
Lire 250,000 double B&B
Breakfast only
Open all year
Some English spoken
Region: Tuscany

While many agritourism farms are run by transplanted urbanites, many are still owned and operated by farmers whose families have worked the land for generations. Such is the case with Onofrio Contento and his family, proprietors of Masseria Curatori, not far from the city of Monopoli and the Adriatic Sea, where, for five generations, the family has produced olives, almonds, and cattle. Inside the main coral-color house are modest and immaculate quarters for guests, consisting presently of a large three-bedroom apartment with kitchen and living room on the second floor, plus a double with private bath on the ground floor. Old and new family furniture has been combined to decorate the rooms. The view is pleasingly pastoral, overlooking olive-tree-studded hills. Four apartments for two to four persons were built several years ago in a nearby one-story building overlooking a lovely stone-walled garden and fruit orchard. Breakfast and extra meals are taken together with the hospitable family in their dining room. Horseback riding can be arranged for guests. Curatori is an excellent base from which to visit the highlights of this unique region of Italy. *Directions*: 40 km from Brindisi. Take coastal route N16, exiting at Monopoli-San Francesco da Paola. Take the road back across the highway and then the first left. Follow Via Conchia up to the pink house.

MASSERIA CURATORI
Hosts: Onofrio Contento family
Contrada Cristo delle Zolle 227
Monopoli (BA) 70043, Italy
Tel & fax: (080) 777472
5 apartments, 1 room with private bathroom
Lire 110,000 double B&B
  80,000 per person half board
2-night minimum stay
All meals served
Open all year
Very little English spoken
Region: Apulia

A well-kept secret among off-the-main-road travelers is the countryside north of Rome known as "Sabina" after the mountain range. It is unusual that agritourism has not developed close to Rome compared to what has occurred around Florence, but locals are beginning to wake up. Ancestors of the Gabutti family—adopted Romans—came from this area and the principal palazzos in both medieval towns of Casperia and Montasola, plus a large farm with olive groves, have been in the family for generations. One of the daughters, Letizia, decided to leave a law career in Rome to work on restoration of these properties and offer hospitality in the form of apartments. Guests began arriving four years ago and were comfortably situated in quaint Montasola. Spacious apartments include one or two bedrooms, living room, kitchen, and bathrooms, all well decorated with the family's own antiques. Characteristic architectural features have been preserved, and two apartments have terraces with a breathtaking panoramic view (our favorite is the mansard *Le Stelle*). There is something very special indeed about being a "resident" of an intact medieval village with its narrow stone alleyways. Guests can lounge under the shady trees of a stone-walled garden close by. Other charming villages dot the area, Umbria is at a short distance, and Rome is just a 45-minute train ride away. *Directions*: Arrangements to be met should be made at the time of reservation.

MONTEPIANO
Hostess: Maria Letizia Gabbuti
Via dei Casalini 8
Montasola (RI) 02045, Italy
Tel & fax: (0765) 63252
4 apartments
Lire 160,000–330,000 daily per apartment
2-night minimum stay
No meals served
Open all year
Some English spoken
Region: Lazio

As you travel southwest toward Florence through the foothills of the Appenines, the scenery transforms itself dramatically from the flatlands of the *padana* into soft green hills textured with alternating fields of wheat and grapevines. From Bologna, the Tenuta Bonzara farm and vineyard is a half-hour drive up a road that winds through scented pine forest, arriving at a group of houses owned by several farming families. The wine estate is owned by Dottor Lambertini of Bologna, and is run by warm-hearted Mario and his family, whose main responsibility is overseeing the wine production. Guest accommodation on the estate consists of two small houses containing two apartments, each with one or two bedrooms, bathroom, kitchenette, and sitting room—the nicest are the one-bedroom apartments in the older house with small corner fireplaces, red-brick floors and beamed ceilings, rustically furnished with simple pinewood pieces. A trattoria on the premises serves meals, and a museum has been set up in the old barn displaying antique farm tools, carts, and agricultural machines. A tennis court is available, and participation in the grape harvesting is encouraged. *Directions*: Take the Bologna/Casalecchio exit from the A1 autostrada and continue to Gesso, Rivabella, Calderino, Monte San Giovanni, and left up the hill to San Chierlo.

TENUTA BONZARA
Host: Dottor Francesco Lambertini
Via San Chierlo 37
Monte San Pietro (BO) 40050, Italy
Tel: (051) 6768324, Fax: (051) 225772
4 apartments
Lire 730,000–880,000 weekly
2-night minimum stay in low season
Trattoria on premises (dinner only)
Open May to October
Some English spoken
Region: Emilia-Romagna

Lucca, one of our favorite Italian cities, is well situated near Pisa, with the beautiful Valdera countryside to the south, the Apuane mountain range to the north, the seaside 20 kilometers away, and many splendid villas and famous gardens scattered in the vicinity. The city, however, is directly surrounded by a heavily commercial area until you get to the wine country around the charming hilltop town of Montecarlo, 15 kilometers east of town. This medieval stone village with fortress walls has several restaurants and cafés, its own theatre where Puccini was known to put on operas, and many olive-oil-producing farms and wineries close by. In past centuries, it was the stopping point for pilgrims making their way to Assisi. Silvia Moncini left her hometown of Montecatini where her parents have a prominent hotel to reopen the Antica Casa bed and breakfast with her husband Francesco and small child. The family resides across the street and in the early morning the perfume of fresh bread comes wafting up to the eight small rooms on the two upper floors. All but two have en-suite bathrooms and are simply appointed with wrought-iron beds, floral bedspreads, and painted stencil borders, which go well with the beamed ceilings. Breakfast is served either out on the patio where you can observe the daily life of the locals, or in the miniature breakfast room to the left of the reception and living room area. *Directions*: From the A11 autostrada, take the Altopascio exit. Head towards Pescia (3 km) and turn left for Montecarlo for another 2 km.

ANTICA CASA DEI RASSICURATI   *New*
Hosts: Silvia & Francesco Moncini
Via della Collegiata 2
Montecarlo (LU) 55015, Italy
Tel: (0583) 228901, Fax: (0583) 22498
8 rooms with private bathrooms
Lire 120,000 double B&B
Breakfast only
Open all year
Some English spoken
Region: Tuscany

Within the same quaint village as the previous listing is an alternative kind of accommodation that allows the traveler to stay in one of Montecarlo's private, historical homes. The large building on the main street of town with Pompeiian-red worn façade (a color that is predominant in the interior) dates back to the 1500s and its foundation was part of the original walls of the castle. Gracious hostess Bianca's desire was to bring back life to the ancient, antique-filled home by offering unique accommodation to travelers. Even though space would allow it, she has made no alterations or added extra rooms, preferring to keep the original architectural features of her ancestral home intact. Limited accommodation, therefore, is offered either within an enormous double bedroom with en-suite bathroom overlooking the street, or in a family suite incorporating three sleeping areas (separate double bedroom plus two sleeping alcoves for an additional three people), bathroom, and grand hall with French windows looking out over the terraced garden. Guests can relax in this lovely garden, which overlooks the countryside extending out towards Lucca. Breakfast is served in the formal dining room with antique tapestries or in the absolutely charming country kitchen with open fireplace and French plates adorning the walls. Take a step back in time in this castle-like home filled with precious antiques and paintings. *Directions*: From the A11 autostrada, take the Altopascio exit. Head towards Pescia (3 km) and turn left for Montecarlo for another 2 km.

CASA SATTI   New
Hostess: Bianca Satti Tori
Via Roma 31
Montecarlo (LU) 55015, Italy
Tel: (0583) 22347, Fax: (0583) 22007
1 room with private bathroom, 1 suite
Lire 220,000–400,000 double & suite B&B
Breakfast only
Open April to November 15
English spoken well
Region: Tuscany

The scenic approach to the Fattoria di Vibio passes through lush green hills, by picturesque farms, and is highlighted by a romantic view of the quaint town of Todi, 20 kilometers away. Two handsome brothers from Rome run this top-drawer bed and breakfast consisting of several recently restored stone houses. The houses sit side by side and share between them 13 double rooms with private baths. Common areas for guests include a cozy, country-style living room with fireplace, games room, and country kitchen. The accommodations are enhanced by preserved architectural features such as terra-cotta floors and exposed-beam ceilings, and typical Umbrian handicrafts such as wrought-iron beds, renovated antiques, and Deruta ceramics. On the assumption that guests may find it difficult to leave this haven, the hosts offer half board plus lunch and snacks, along with a beautiful swimming pool, tennis, hiking, horseback riding, fishing, and biking. Signora Gabriella, with a passion for cooking, gets all the richly deserved credit for the marvelous meals served either poolside or on the panoramic terrace. *Directions*: From either Todi or Orvieto follow route S448 until the turnoff for Vibio at the sign for Prodo-Quadro and follow the well-marked dirt road for 10 km up to the farmhouse.

FATTORIA DI VIBIO
Hosts: Giuseppe & Filippo Saladini
Localita: Buchella-Doglio
Montecastello di Vibio (PG) 06057, Italy
Tel: (075) 8749607, Fax: (075) 8780014
Email: info@fattoriadivibio.com
13 rooms with private bathrooms
Lire 110,000–150,000 per person half board
2-night minimum stay, 1 week August
All meals served
Open March to December
Credit cards: AX, VS
Very little English spoken
Region: Umbria
www.karenbrown.com/italy/fattoriadivibio.html

Surprisingly, one of the least visited regions in Italy is the Marches, an area rich in culture, nature, and history bordering on the Adriatic. Just 15 kilometers from the coast in the heart of this gentle, hilly countryside, is the Campana farm, run by 10 families of professionals and artists who came here from Milan in search of an alternative lifestyle. The farm, made up of four pale-peach stone houses dating from 1700, has been restored with great care and taste, making space for private quarters, a refined restaurant, wine cellar, studio, music room, and, for guests, eleven rooms, a few large enough for a family of four. Some have lovely terraces looking across vineyard-covered hills to the distant sea, and are decorated with a combination of old and new furnishings. Others are situated within a separate two-story, recently renovated farmhouse. Drawing on the considerable pool of available talent, an unusual variety of activities is offered—from courses in theater and photography to workshops in crafting leather, silk, and wool dying with plant extracts. A swimming pool and tennis courts were recently added, as well as bikes for local touring. *Directions*: From Ancona go south on the A14 autostrada, exit at Pedaso and continue south to Cupramarittima, then turn right at the sign for Carassai. After 6.5 km, turn right for Montefiore, then left after 1.5 km at the small sign for La Campana.

LA CAMPANA
Hosts: Co-op Agricola
Via Menocchia 39
Montefiore dell'Aso (AP) 63010, Italy
Tel: (0734) 939012, Fax: (0734) 938229
11 rooms with private bathrooms
Lire 153,000–217,000 double B&B
* 84,000–115,000 per person half board*
Breakfast & dinner served
Open all year
Credit cards: MC, VS
English spoken well
Region: Marches

La Loggia, built in 1427, was one of the Medici estates during the centuries they ruled over Florence and surrounding territories. Owner Giulio Baruffaldi, weary of urban life in Milan, transplanted himself and his wife here and succeeded in reviving the estate's splendor while respecting its past, enhancing its architectural beauty while giving utmost attention to comforts and warmth. Their informal yet refined hospitality is reflected in the care given to the decor of the apartments, each containing one to three bedrooms, living room, kitchen, some with fireplace, and many lovely antiques and original paintings from the Baruffaldis' own art collection. In fact, many important bronze and ceramic sculptures by international artists are displayed throughout the gardens of the villa. Four double rooms have been added some having a fireplace, or hydro-massage bath and steam room. Apart from just basking in the pure romance and tranquillity of this place, you can enjoy a swimming pool, horseback riding, and nearby tennis and golf facilities. Other activities include the occasional cooking or wine-tasting lesson, and impromptu dinners in the cellar. The hosts and their absolutely charming guest assistant, Ivana, seem to exist merely to pamper their guests' every whim. *Directions*: Leave the Florence-Siena autostrada after San Casciano at Bargino. Turn right at the end of the ramp, then left for Montefiridolfi (3.5 km). La Loggia is just before town.

FATTORIA LA LOGGIA
Hosts: Giulio Baruffaldi & Cuca Roaldi
Via Collina, Montefiridolfi
San Casciano Val di Pesa (FI) 50020, Italy
Tel: (055) 8244288, Fax: (055) 8241283
Email: fatlaloggia@ftbcc.it
11 apartments, 4 rooms with private bathrooms
Lire 180,000–380,000 double B&B
  250,000–900,000 daily per apartment
Occasional dinner & wine tastings, Open all year
Fluent English spoken
Region: Tuscany
www.karenbrown.com/italy/laloggia.html

Just opposite the lovely Fattoria La Loggia is a newly opened bed and breakfast that was actually one of the farmhouses belonging to the vast vineyard property. Gracious Signora Nadia fell in love with the ancient house and decided to retire here after having the entire place restored, leaving the ground floor for herself and the guests' breakfast room while the upstairs has four convertible apartments for travelers. The two adjoining apartments to the right (yellow and blue color schemes) can become a three-bedroom apartment with three colourful bathrooms, living room, kitchen, and large fireplace. The two one-bedroom apartments in green hues can be rented separately or adjoined as well. Rooms have a clean, country feeling to them with antique armoires, simple wrought-iron beds blending in nicely with stone walls, wood-beamed mansard ceilings and brick floors so typical in Tuscany. A swimming pool is expected to be completed by April 2001. This is a very easy base from which to visit most of the region's highlights besides being only 20 minutes from Florence and 30 from Siena. *Directions*: Exit at Bargino from the Florence-Siena highway and turn right and then immediately left at the sign for Montefiridolfi. After 3 km look for a stone house with large arched windows on the left side of the road before town.

MACINELLO   New
Hostess: Nadia Ciuffelli
Via Collina 9, Montefiridolfi
San Casciano Val di Pesa (FI) 50020, Italy
Tel & fax: (055) 8244459
4 apartments
Lire 150,000–400,000 daily per apartment B&B
3-night minimum stay
Breakfast only
Open all year
No English spoken
Region: Tuscany

Bed & Breakfast Descriptions

Poggio Miravalle is a peaceful and panoramic haven located atop a hill between the regions of Umbria and Tuscany. Reserved hostesses Rita and Mara have developed the hospitality end of their farm business (organic olive oil and wine) over the past years and today offer accommodation within five apartments, all but one inside the main restored stone farmhouse. Firm believers in the healing benefits of country living, they wish to offer an oasis of silence for true lovers of nature, defined as "ecotourists." Each apartment (among them four named Sun, Moon, Earth, and Sky) has an independent entrance through French doors overlooking the garden and can comfortably accommodate from two to five guests. Pleasantly decorated with a mix of old and new country-style furniture, they include living area and kitchenette. The barn has been transformed into a common area where breakfast and an occasional dinner are served and nearby is a swimming pool taking advantage of the most scenic and breezy spot overlooking the sweeping valley. Rita and Mara are full of interesting itinerary suggestions following gastronomic, cultural, recreational, or nature themes. *Directions*: Exit from the A1 autostrada at Fabro and travel towards Citta della Pieve. At S. Lorenzo (before Monteleone) turn right for Miravalle (1.5 km).

POGGIO MIRAVALLE
Hostesses: Rita Trincia & Mara Romer
Localita: Cornieto 2
Monteleone d'Orvieto (TR) 05017, Italy
Tel & fax: (0763) 835309
Cellphone: (0333) 5254620
5 apartments
Lire 100,000–180,000 daily per apt (2 persons)
Breakfast served (extra charge)
Open March 15 to October 30
English spoken well
Region: Umbria

One result of increasing interest in the singular attractions of the Maremma, or southern Tuscany, is the opening or expansion of several noteworthy places to stay. The Villa Acquaviva, once owned by nobility, has been a small family hotel for the past 11 years. The ambitious proprietors, Serafino and Valentina, completed extensive remodeling to include eight guestrooms named for and painted in the colors of local wildflowers. The bedrooms all have private baths and are decorated with country antiques and wrought-iron beds. The charming breakfast room has sky-blue tablecloths and looks out through arched windows to a lush flower garden with alternating palms and umbrella pines, and on to a view over the gently rolling landscape up to the village of Montemerano—a quaint, medieval town with excellent restaurants and artisan shops. Breakfast of homemade cakes, breads, and jams can be taken inside or out on the patio. There are ten newer, additional rooms in a stone farmhouse on the property plus eight in another, joined together by a glassed-in reception area. These are our favorites, with beautiful local antiques and colorful matching fabrics adorning beds and windows. The farmhouses have their own spacious breakfast room and living area downstairs. A swimming pool in the garden with bar service and tennis courts are attractive features of the complex. *Directions*: From Rome, take the Aurelia road, exiting at Vulci. Follow signs for Manciano, then for Montemerano. About 1½ hours from Rome.

VILLA ACQUAVIVA
Hosts: Valentina di Virginio & Serafino d'Ascenzi
Localita: Acquaviva
Montemerano (GR) 58050, Italy
Tel: (0564) 602890, Fax: (0564) 602895
26 rooms with private bathrooms
Lire 150,00–250,000 double B&B
  300,000 suite
3-night minimum stay in high season
Breakfast only, Open all year
English & French spoken well, Region: Tuscany

The Fontanelle country house sits in the heart of the Maremma area of Tuscany where, besides being pleasant and well run, it fills a need for the growing interest in this off-the-beaten-track destination. Signor Perna and his two lovely daughters, originally from Rome, searched and found this peaceful haven from the stress of city life, promptly transferring themselves and undertaking major restoration work. Looking over a soft green valley up to the nearby village of Montemerano, the stone farmhouse with its rusty-red shutters offers four comfortable rooms with spotless private bathrooms. The converted barn houses five rooms while the last room is in a separate cottage set in the woods. Sunlight pours into the front veranda-like breakfast room where coffee and cakes are taken together with other guests at one large table. The Pernas assist guests in planning local itineraries including visits to artisan workshops. With due notice, guests can find a wonderfully prepared dinner awaiting them under the ivy-covered pergola in the rose garden. The property is part of a reserve where deer, wild boar, and various types of wildlife can be observed. *Directions*: From Rome, take the A12 autostrada. Continue north on Aurelia route 1, turning off at Vulci after Montalto. Follow signs for Manciano then Montemerano. Turn left at the bed-and-breakfast sign before town and follow the dirt road for 1 km.

LE FONTANELLE
Hosts: Daniela & Cristina Perna
Localita: Poderi di Montemerano
Montemerano (GR) 58050, Italy
Tel & fax: (0564) 602762
10 rooms with private bathrooms
Lire 140,000 double B&B
Breakfast served, dinner upon request
Open all year
Some English spoken
Region: Tuscany

A pleasant alternative to a countryside bed and breakfast is one right in the historical center of the marvelously preserved medieval town of Montepulciano. Most famous for its prized Rosso di Montepulciano wines, its striking charm of the past rivals that of its hilltop neighbors, Pienza and Montalcino. Cinzia Caroti not long ago converted her father's law offices, housed on the first floor of a 16th-century palazzo on the main street of town, into a bed and breakfast. The street is lined with shops and restaurants and is off limits to cars, which adds much to its medieval aura. One flight of wide stairs takes you up to L'Agnolo's reception area. There are three bedrooms off this area and another two off the frescoed dining room with wrought-iron chandelier. The spacious, high-ceilinged rooms have a subdued ambiance, with wrought-iron beds, family antiques, and new white-tiled bathrooms. Better lighting could be used to show off lovely original frescoed ceilings and painted borders. A classic breakfast of cappuccino and fresh croissants is served in the coffee shop below the home, making one feel like a true local resident. Cinzia lives next door and is present throughout the day to assist guests and make suggestions from the many sightseeing possibilities in this rich area of Tuscany, bordering Umbria. *Directions*: Park your car in a nearby lot (north or east lot) outside the village walls and follow Via di Gracciano running north-south to the middle. There is a small gold plaque "L'Agnolo" at the door.

L'AGNOLO
Hostess: Cinzia Caroti
Via di Gracciano nel Corso 63
Montepulciano (SI) 53045, Italy
Tel & fax: (0578) 757095 or 717070
Cellphone: (0339) 2254813
5 rooms with private bathrooms
Lire 150,000–200,000 double B&B
Breakfast only
Open all year
Very little English spoken
Region: Tuscany

Signora Novella and her family, warm and gregarious hosts, have been welcoming guests for over 15 years, ever since they moved to Emilia-Romagna from the south. Having agricultural experience, they were able to set up a farm, with Novella, a retired schoolteacher, overseeing the kitchen. She is an excellent cook and guests return time and time again for her handmade pasta, joining the family at the long wood table in their rustic dining room with its hanging brass pots and ox harnesses. Guest accommodations have been transferred from upstairs in the white 18th-century farmhouse (one room remains) to the horse stalls, which have been converted into seven simple double rooms with private baths all on one level. The rooms are immaculate, if rather plain, with basic modern furnishings. Guests tend to their own rooms and are even apt to help clear the table in the very informal *en famille* atmosphere at Le Radici. The sea, just 15 kilometers away, can be seen in the distance, and several medieval towns and castles dot the hills in the surrounding countryside. "Must-sees" include Ravenna, Ferrara, and ceramic center, Faenza. A unique experience, best enjoyed if you speak some Italian. *Directions*: On route 9 from Rimini to Cesana, follow signs for Calisese and after town continue for Casale-Sorrivoli. Before Casale turn left on Via Casale then left again at the sign Le Radici-Via Golano. Total of 12 km from Cesana.

LE RADICI
Hostesses: Alessandra & Novella Piangatelli
Localita: Montenovo
Via Golano 808, Montiano (FO) 47020, Italy
Tel & fax: (0547) 327001
7 rooms with private bathrooms
Lire 90,000 per person half board
Breakfast & dinner served
Open March to December, Handicap facilities
Some English & French spoken
Region: Emilia-Romagna

In the northern Piedmont region, leading into the foothills of the Alps, is the peaceful countryside where Piercarlo Novarese, Il Mompolino's cordial host, decided to establish his inn and equestrian center. Run more like a small hotel, the Mompolino has sixteen guestrooms divided between two mustard-color buildings. Each room has a private bath and balcony, and is complemented with rustic furnishings. The larger suites feature sitting rooms and are the nicest, furnished with the occasional antique. A large, open dining room serves breakfast, lunch, and dinner, and boasts delectable regional dishes skillfully prepared by local women. Il Mompolino makes an ideal stopover on the way to the Alps, the lake region, or Milan. It also provides an appealing spot to relax for a few days between more demanding tourist destinations. Sports activities abound, including horseback riding, tennis, swimming, and a gym with sauna. A variety of horseback-riding lessons is offered at the equestrian center, as are mounted excursions into the adjacent national park. Perhaps a good idea between bowls of pasta! *Directions*: Take the Carisio exit from the Milan-Turin A4 autostrada. From Carisio Mompolino is 7 km and well marked.

IL MOMPOLINO
Host: Piercarlo Novarese
Localita: Mompolino
Mottalciata (VC) 13030, Italy
Tel: (0161) 857668 or 669, Fax: (0161) 857667
16 rooms with private bathrooms
2 apartments
Lire 115,000–135,000 double B&B
All meals served
Restaurant closed Mondays
Open all year
Credit cards: all major
Very little English spoken
Region: Piedmont

Right next door to the Grazia farm is the very similar property of the Lignana family. Again, a long, straight road takes you off the busy coastal Aurelia highway back to the 200-plus-acre farm and hunting reserve looking out to the distant sea and Mount Argentario. Gracious Signora Marcella and husband Giuseppe live in the ivy-covered ancient stone tower and attached villa, while guests reside within seven comfortable self-catering apartments in a converted barn down the road. Spacious apartments have two bedrooms and two bathrooms, living/dining area, and kitchenette. Some apartments have the bedrooms on a second floor, while others have them split between the main floor and an open loft space. They are nicely appointed in a clean and easy style, with fresh white walls, smart plaid cushions on built-in sofas, framed prints, wicker furniture, and wrought-iron beds. The farm produces wheat, sunflowers, peaches, and vegetables as well as raising typical Maremman cattle. For nature lovers, the area is full of marvelous expeditions on foot or bike, including the WWF oasis, National Park of Uccellina, various forts on Mount Argentario with their spectacular views, and the islands of Giglio and Giannutri, not to mention the thermal spa of Saturnia. *Directions*: From Rome take the Aurelia Highway 1 and turn right down the road at the sign "Piante-Vivaio" (after the turnoff for Ansedonia). From the north you must exit at Ansedonia and return to the highway heading towards Grosseto. It is 140 km from Rome's Fiumicino airport.

*IL CASALONE   **New***
Hosts: Marcella & Giuseppe Lignana
S.S. Aurelia sud km 140.5
Orbetello Scalo (GR) 58016, Italy
Tel: (0564) 862160, Fax: (0564) 866308
7 apartments
Lire 300,000 daily per apartment
  (plus 50,000 linen charge)
2-night minimum stay, 1 week July & August
No meals served, Open all year
English spoken well, Region: Tuscany

The expansive Grazia farm is uniquely located at 3 kilometers from the sea. Gracious and warm hostess, Signora Maria Grazia, divides her time between Rome and the 300-acre property she inherited from her grandfather. The long cypress-lined driveway takes you away from the busy Aurelia road past grazing horses up to the spacious, rust-hued edifice with its arched loggia. The hosts' home, office, three guest apartments, farmhands' quarters, and horse stables are all housed within the complex, which is encased by superb country and peeks of the sea in all directions. From here one can enjoy touring Etruscan territory: Tuscania, Tarquinia, Sovana, Sorano, and the fascinating Roman ruins of Cosa, or stay by the coast on the beaches of Feniglia on the promontory of Argentario. Comfortably modest accommodations, including breakfast basket, living area, and kitchen, pleasantly decorated with homey touches, are offered within three apartments for two to four persons. Maria Grazia can suggest a myriad of local restaurants specializing in seafood or local country fare. Tennis and horseback riding lessons are available. Altogether a delightful combination. *Directions*: Take the coastal Aurelia road from Rome and after the Ansedonia exit turn right into an unmarked driveway **immediately** after the Pitorsino restaurant.

GRAZIA
Hosts: Maria Grazia Cantore family
Via Aurelia, km 140.1
Orbetello Scalo (GR) 58016, Italy
Tel & fax: (0564) 881182 or (06) 483945
3 apartments
Lire 160,000–250,000 per apartment daily*
*Includes breakfast
3-night minimum stay
Breakfast served, Open all year
English & French spoken well
Region: Tuscany
www.karenbrown.com/italy/grazia.html

The location of La Chiocciola bed and breakfast, minutes from the main tollway from Rome to Florence and on the border of the Lazio and Umbria regions, is ideal. Added bonuses are the warm hospitality, deliciously prepared regional meals, and lovely country-style bedrooms. Roberto and Maria Cristina from Rome bought the stone farmhouse dating back to 1400 several years ago and began restoration work while living in the newer house next door. The results of their efforts are four perfectly neat and spotless bedrooms in each of the two houses, a living room area for guests, and a large rustic dining room with outdoor veranda. Obvious care and attention has been put into the decorating of the air-conditioned bedrooms with wrought-iron canopy beds, crisp, white linen curtains, and botanical prints. The 50-acre property with fruit orchards and vineyards is part of the Tiber river valley and woods. There are bicycles and a swimming pool for guests' use. Innumerable day trips and itineraries of special interest are offered in the area of Umbria and Lazio and it's a 40-minute train ride to Rome. *Directions*: From Rome or Florence on the A1 autostrada, exit at Orte and turn immediately left, passing under the tollway. Go in the direction of Amelia and repass over the tollway, taking the first left towards Penna in Teverina. La Chiocciola is 5 km along this road.

LA CHIOCCIOLA
Hosts: Roberto & Maria Cristina de Fonseca Pimentel
Localita: Seripola
Orte (VT) 01028, Italy
Tel: (0761) 402734, Fax: (0761) 490254
8 rooms with private bathrooms
Lire 170,000 double B&B
  115,000 per person half board
All meals served
Open all year, Credit cards: MC, VS
English & French spoken well
Region: Lazio
www.karenbrown.com/italy/lachiocciola.html

A very high rating goes to the Locanda Rosati on the border of Umbria and Lazio, and just steps away from Tuscany. Giampiero and sister, Alba, with their respective spouses, Luisa and Paolo, sold their cheese production business in Lucca and returned to Orvieto to transform the family farmhouse into a bed and breakfast. The results are splendid and guests, taking priority over the agricultural activity in this instance, are treated with extra-special care. The downstairs common areas include two cozy living rooms with fireplace and a large stone-walled dining room divided by a brick archway leading down to the "tufo" stone cellar. Seven bedrooms upstairs (one with access and bathroom for the handicapped) have been decorated with an animal theme evident in the carvings on bedboards and lamps. Two more bedrooms (formally the family's private quarters) were added for guests on the top floor with mansard ceilings, leaving the entire home to the bed and breakfast business. Although right on the road, most rooms face the countryside to the back where a large open lawn space leads to the inviting swimming pool. Paolo delights guests with his appetizing pastas, soups, and homemade breads. *Directions*: Exit from the A1 autostrada at Orvieto and follow signs for Viterbo-Bolsena. Skirt town and continue towards Bolsena for about 8 km on route 71. After a series of sharp curves, the *locanda* comes up on the right.

LOCANDA ROSATI
Hosts: Rosati family
Localita: Buonviaggio 22
Orvieto (TR) 05018, Italy
Tel & fax: (0763) 217314
Email: locandarosati@pn.iTnet.it
9 rooms with private bathrooms
Lire 160,000–200,000 double B&B
  120,000–140,000 per person half board
Closed January & February, Handicap facilities
Very little English spoken, Region: Umbria
www.karenbrown.com/italy/locandarosati.html

A convenient stopover while heading either north or south along the main artery—A1 autostrada—is the Villa Ciconia inn. Located below the historical center of Orvieto, in the newer commercial outskirts, the property maintains its tranquil setting thanks to the fortress of trees protecting the 16th-century stone villa. The first floor includes reception area, breakfast room, and two large high-ceilinged dining rooms. These latter, with their somber gray-stone fireplaces, tapestries, heavy dark-wood beams, and subdued-color frescoes depicting allegorical motifs and landscapes, give the place a medieval castle's air. The ten air-conditioned bedrooms on the second floor are appointed either in appropriate style, with antique chests and wrought-iron beds, or with more contemporary furnishings (lower rates) and all the amenities of the four-star hotel that this is. Most rooms are quiet and look out onto the 8 acres of woods behind the villa. There are also two enormous beamed sitting rooms on this floor for guests. The restaurant has a solid reputation for creating excellent Umbrian specialties. Manager Luigi Falcone is always on hand to assist guests. *Directions*: Exiting from the autostrada, turn right towards Orvieto and right again where marked Arezzo, Perugia, passing under the tollway. The Ciconia is just after the river on the left-hand side of the road.

VILLA CICONIA
Hosts: Petrangeli family
Via dei Tigli 69
Orvieto (TR) 05019, Italy
Tel: (0763) 305582, Fax: (0763) 302077
Email: villaciconia@libero.it
10 rooms with private bathrooms
Lire 234,000–278,000 double B&B
All meals served
Restaurant closed Mondays
Open all year, Credit cards: all major
English & French spoken well
Region: Umbria
www.karenbrown.com/italy/villaciconia.html

Claudia Spatola does a great job of running single-handedly a bed and breakfast in the complex of stone houses known as Borgo Spante, which dates back to the 15th century and has been in her family since 1752. Consisting of a main villa, connecting farmers' houses, chapel, barns, swimming pool, and garden, it is isolated in 500 acres of woods and hills, yet only 16 kilometers from Orvieto and not far from Assisi, Todi, and Perugia. Guests stay in a combination of rooms and apartments in the former farmers' quarters with their irregular-sized rooms, sloping worn-brick floors, and rustic country furnishings—very charming in its way. Authentically Umbrian meals, prepared by local women, are served in the dining room with long wood tables and fireplace. A larger dining area has been added in the former barn, along with four additional mini-apartments—simply and characteristically decorated. Memorable evenings are spent in the garden or poolside conversing with other guests or listening to an impromptu concert. *Directions*: From the A1 autostrada exit at Orvieto and follow signs for Arezzo on route 71. After 7 km, turn right at Morrano and proceed for 12 km to the sign for Spante. Turn left and continue for 2 km.

BORGO SPANTE
Hostess: Claudia Spatola
Localita: Ospedaletto
San Venanzo (TR) 05010, Italy
Tel: (075) 8709134, Fax: (075) 8709201
5 rooms with private bathrooms
8 apartments
Lire 120,000 per person half board
2-night minimum stay
Breakfast & dinner served
Open all year
Some English spoken
Region: Umbria

The Belfiore farm property certainly stands out among a very bland choice of bed and breakfasts in the area between the well-preserved Renaissance city of Ferrara and Ravenna with its extraordinary mosaics. The flat countryside is characterized by marshland and the National Delta del Po Park, a paradise for birdwatchers and bikers, where many excursions are organized. The Bertelli sisters, Fiorenza and Daniella, from Ferrara sold their hotels at the seaside and transformed their farm into a country restaurant with ten bedrooms on the upper two floors. They are identically appointed with rustic wood beds painted with a floral motif and matching armoires. Guests can feel right at home in the spacious living room with antiques and enormous open fireplace. The restaurant, where locals come for excellent local fare based on organically produced fruits and vegetables, is divided among several beamed dining rooms and guests are invited into the kitchen for a demonstration of making various types of pastas and breads. Italian lessons are also offered free of charge. A neat garden surrounds the simple rectangular-shaped house with burgundy shutters and a swimming pool sits invitingly in one corner. It is an easy day trip to Venice. *Directions*: Exit from the Ferrara-Comacchio highway at Ostellato and pass through the rather nondescript town to the tall bell tower at the corner of Via Pioppa and follow signs to Belfiore.

BELFIORE
Hosts: Tullio Bertelli family
Via Pioppa 27
Ostellato (FE) 44020, Italy
Tel: (0533) 681164, Fax: (0533) 681172
Email: agriturismobelfiore@libero.it
10 rooms with private bathrooms
Lire 150,000 double B&B
* 130,000 per person half board*
Breakfast served, Restaurant open Thursdays to Sundays
Open all year, Credit cards: MC, VS
Some English spoken, Region: Emilia-Romagna
www.karenbrown.com/italy/belfiore.html

Lo Spagnulo is an excellent example of how the *masseria* farms of Apulia functioned in the 1600s. They were self-sufficient agricultural production centers, described as "factories," which included the proprietor's villa, housing for farmers, common dining area, church, administrative offices, animal shelters, and work areas. The Spagnulo still cultivates animals, fresh produce, almonds, and olives. Fortress-like in appearance, its white-stone exterior leads inside to a courtyard garden, off which the guest quarters are located. These vary in size and shape, many comprising two or three bedrooms, living/eating area, and kitchen. Featuring the vaulted ceilings, exposed beams, terra-cotta floors and stone walls of the original building, the rooms display charm despite the somewhat spartan furnishings. These accommodations are recommended over the nondescript rooms that have been added in a modern building nearby. The stalls have been converted into a restaurant for guests, serving typical local dishes family-style. Proprietor Livino Massari, a professor, and his family are present on weekends and during the summer. *Directions*: Heading south on route 379, exit at Marina di Ostuni. Follow signs to Rosa Marina, turning left at the sign for the farm.

MASSERIA LO SPAGNULO
Host: Livino Massari
Localita: Rosa Marina-Contrada Spagnulo
Ostuni (BR) 72017, Italy
Tel: (0831) 350209, Fax: (0831) 333756
26 apartments
Lire 130,000 double B&B
* 85,000 per person half board*
Weekly only July & August
All meals served
Open all year, Credit cards: AX, VS
Handicap facilities
English spoken well, Region: Apulia

With her children grown and traveling around the world, Christine, an expatriate from England, decided to offer hospitality to travelers in her country home. Situated an hour north of Rome by train or car, the pretty countryside home made of typical local tufo brick is a short distance from the ancient village of Otricoli with its ancient Roman origins. It is one of many villages centered in the Tiber river valley, historically an important area for trade and commerce with Rome. A long wing off the main house, reserved for guests, offers three beamed bedrooms decorated with country furniture and overlooking the garden and hills. An order-as-you-like breakfast is served either in the kitchen or out on the patio. The cozy living room with open fireplace invites guests to relax after a day in the city. Being at the edge of Umbria and Lazio, she can suggest a myriad of local itineraries and destinations, known and not so well-known, as well as town festivals throughout the region and concentrated in the months of May and June. This is a very informal, at-home accommodation just 7 kilometers from the main Rome-Florence autostrada. *Directions*: Exit at Magliano Sabina and turn left for Otricoli-Terni. Turn off for Otricoli and take the first road to the right—Strada Crepafico. Gates to Casa Spence are on the corner.

CASA SPENCE
Hostess: Christine Spence
Strada Crepafico 29
Otricoli (TR) 05030, Italy
Tel & fax: (0744) 719758
3 rooms, 1 with private bathroom
Lire 135,000 double B&B
  125,000 without private bath
Breakfast only, Open all year
Fluent English spoken
Region: Umbria

Paciano, situated on the border of Umbria and Tuscany, south of Lake Trasimeno, is a perfectly intact medieval village, once named the most ideal village in Italy. It is here that young Luigi Buitoni, of the famous pasta-producing family, decided to put to use his refined culinary skills, organizing daily cooking lessons. His darling wife Caterina oversees the rest and accompanies lucky guests on her own backroads itinerary. The old olive-oil press building, part of the family's 12th-century residence in town, now serves as a restaurant with bed and breakfast accommodation upstairs. Seven sweet bedrooms are decorated in country style, each with its own color scheme noted in the rich fabrics of the bedspreads and curtains. (Ask for one of the larger ones.) The palazzo was ingeniously restored preserving all original architectural features while adding an extra floor and converting arched doorways to closets. The upstairs sitting room is inviting with a collection of eclectic antiques, floral tapestry armchairs, fresh flowers, and crystal bottles lining shelves. A full buffet breakfast is served and a swimming pool has been added this year just across the way. A large part of the marvelous attached medieval tower is rented weekly. *Directions*: Exit at Chiusi-Chianciano from the A1 autostrada; take the road towards Trasimeno and Perugia and turn right to Paciano where indicated.

LOCANDA DELLA ROCCA
Hosts: Caterina & Luigi Buitoni
Viale Roma 4
Paciano (PG) 06060, Italy
Tel: (075) 830236, Fax: (075) 830155
Email: l.buitoni@flashnet.it
7 rooms with private bathrooms, 1 apartment, 1 suite
Lire 190,000 double B&B
* 420,000 daily per suite*
Breakfast & dinner served
Open March to December, Credit cards: MC, VS
English spoken well, Region: Umbria
www.karenbrown.com/italy/locandadellarocca.html

45 kilometers south of the Amalfi coast is the archaeological site of Paestum with its three well-preserved Greek temples, a major tourist attraction. The area is surrounded by unattractive commercial strips and much new construction, very common in the south of Italy, although farther south are the lovely Cilento National Park and coastline. The Seliano farm is an oasis of peace and tranquillity very near the sea. Baroness Cecilia and her two sons, Ettore and Massimiliano, and Dutch manager, Nicola, are wonderful hosts and make the managing of this busy farm, the horseback riding center, restaurant, and bed and breakfast look like a delightful game. The emphasis here is on the preparation of meals using local recipes and their own produce, including fresh mozzarella, most famous in this area. In fact, the Baroness conducts week-long cooking classes including excursions to local cultural and gastronomic highlights. Pleasantly decorated rooms with tiled floors and family antiques are situated in the farmhouse or adjacent yellow house, with two comfortable living rooms for guests. Truly delectable meals are served out on the covered terrace or in the former stables, a long dining/living room with fireplace and historic paintings. There is an inviting swimming pool for guests. *Directions*: Exit from the A3 autostrada at Eboli (less traffic than Battipaglia) and head for Paestum. Turn right off the main road (S.S.18) at Paestum and after 1 km turn into the driveway marked Seliano. Pass the main villa (uninhabited) to the main gate and entrance.

SELIANO
Hostess: Baroness Cecilia Bellelli Baratta
Localita: Seliano
Paestum (SA) 84063, Italy
Tel: (0828) 724544, Fax: (0828) 723634
14 rooms with private bathrooms
Lire 120,000–200,000 double B&B
Breakfast & dinner served
Open all year, Credit cards: MC,VS
English spoken well, Region: Campania

We look all over for bed and breakfasts that radiate a natural sort of charm like that of Fagiolari, just outside Panzano. Cordial hostess Giulietta has seemingly unintentionally created a haven for travelers just by letting her home be a home. The unique stone farmhouse on three levels is brimming with character and has been restored with total respect for its innate simplicity using stone, terra-cotta brick, and chestnut wood beams. Entering the front door into the cozy living room with large fireplace, I was impressed by the refreshingly authentic ambiance of this Tuscan home. Two bedrooms are just off this room, the larger having an en-suite bathroom of stone and travertine. The main house and former barn, where you find two other good-sized bedrooms, are united by a connecting roof, left open in the middle to allow for an enormous fig tree. Giulietta and her son live in the rest of the house, with a workshop where she creates terrra-cotta appliqués. Bedrooms hold lovely antiques, book-lined shelves, collections of framed drawings and artwork, embroidered linens, and views of her delightful garden and cypress-lined paths. An adorable one-bedroom house on the property with a bookcase dividing the kitchen and living area is rented out weekly. *Directions*: From the piazza of Panzano follow Fagiolari signs, taking the road for Mercatale and turning off to the left almost immediately at the small wooden sign "Fagiolari." Take the gravel road to the end.

FAGIOLARI
Hostess: Giulietta Giovanonni
Case Sparse 25
Panzano in Chianti (FI) 50020, Italy
Tel & fax: (055) 852351, Cellphone: (0335) 6124988
Email: info@fagiolari.it
4 rooms with private bathrooms, 1 apartment/house
Lire 140,000–180,000 double B&B
* 1,100,000 house weekly*
Breakfast, dinner upon request
Open all year, Credit cards: MC, VS
Some English spoken, Region: Tuscany
www.karenbrown.com/italy/fagiolari.html

As you wind your way up a steep unpaved road through thick woods, you will no doubt wonder as we did how English couple Sonia and Edward ever found the secluded 70-acre property set above the Sieve river valley to the east of Florence. Upon arrival you will be greeted and rewarded with a glass of fresh spring water from the fountain "shower" (*la doccia*). It is understandable that long ago the farmhouse was originally a farm for the monks of the local abbey—the views are inspirational and the positions of both the house and the swimming pool take full advantage of the expansive panorama encompassing the Rufina wine valley nature reserve. Original features remain intact after a complete restoration of the house that created a variety of high-level accommodation in the form of four bedrooms, three suites with individual kitchenettes, and two attached houses with two bedrooms each for weekly stays. The perfectly charming home is filled with lovely antiques (local and imported from England), rare queen- or king-sized beds, and beautiful linens and tiled bathrooms. Guests can wander about the many common rooms and have a glass of wine in front of a spectacular sunset while Edward works Mediterranean wonders in the kitchen. Prepare to be pampered. *Directions*: 40 minutes from Florence, 5 km from Pelago. Detailed directions are supplied at the time of reservation.

LA DOCCIA
Hosts: Sonia & Edward Mayhew
Localita: Paterno, Ristonchi 19/20
Pelago (FI) 50060, Italy
Tel: (055) 8361387, Fax: (055) 8361388
Email: info@ ladocciawelcomes.com
4 rooms with private bathrooms, 3 suites, 2 apts
Lire 200,000–255,000 double B&B
  1,335,000–2,000,000 weekly per apartment
2-night minimum stay
Breakfast served, dinner upon request
Open all year, Credit cards: all major
Fluent English spoken, Region: Tuscany
www.karenbrown.com/italy/doccia.html

Ideally located at the edge of Chianti and just 20 minutes from the main A1 autostrada, the Fattoria Montelucci property is made up of over 1200 acres of woods, olive groves, vineyards, and pastures. In the heart of this working farm sits the pale-yellow villa with its 12 guestrooms, each decorated in simple country style with eyelet curtains, wrought-iron beds, and antique chests. Downstairs are several common sitting rooms including billiard and music rooms. A luminous, beamed dining room, where a buffet breakfast is served, opens out to a large terrace looking over the breathtaking wooded hills. Other meals are served next door in the converted olive mill, with its original press, stone fireplace, and arched windows looking out over the same spectacular view. A typical Tuscan meal in this marvelous setting is alone worth the visit. Host Stefano's true passion is revealed at the riding stables, with its 30 horses, indoor/outdoor rings, and jumping course, offering lessons and country outings. A lovely new swimming pool has just been completed. Nearby are the two ancient cities of Arezzo and Cortona. *Directions*: Exit the autostrada at Valdarno and follow signs for Montevarchi-Arezzo. Follow route 69 for Arezzo until you reach Pergine Valdarno where there are signs for the Fattoria (5 km).

FATTORIA MONTELUCCI
Host: Stefano Balzanelli
Localita: Le Ville
Via Montelucci 24
Pergine Valdarno (AR) 52020, Italy
Tel: (0575) 896525, Fax: (0575) 896315
12 rooms with private bathrooms, 5 apartments
Lire 170,000–210,000 double B&B
 130,000–170,000 per person half board
 800,000–1,800,000 weekly per apartment
All meals served
Open March to October, Credit cards: MC, VS
English spoken well, Region: Tuscany

The southernmost, "heel-side" of Italy's boot-shaped peninsula, known as Puglia, presents another facet of the country's many-sided culture. It is a land with spectacular coastlines, villages with distinct Greek and Turkish influence, endless lines of olive groves, fields of wildflowers, and a rich history of art including baroque (Bari's Santa Nicola church is exquisite). All of this plus delectable cuisine and a warm and open people await in Puglia (Apulia), as does the Masseria Salamina, a 16th-century fortified farmhouse between Bari and Brindisi covering 100 acres of land and producing primarily olive oil. The driveway leads to the sand-colored castle with turreted tower with expansive vistas sweeping to the sea. The seven suites, each with a separate entrance and decorated with reproductions and wicker furniture, are found through the courtyard. Host Gianvincenzo and family live in the main wing and run their *masseria* with hotel efficiency and service. A large lofty restaurant with terra-cotta floors provides all meals for guests. Eight additional apartments are available for longer stays and in the low season a fascinating week-long organized stay including Mediterranean cooking lessons and local excursions for small groups is arranged. *Directions*: From the S.S.16 exit at Pezze di Greco. Just before town take the first right for 1 km to the *masseria*.

MASSERIA SALAMINA
Host: Gianvincenzo de Miccolis Angelini
Pezze di Greco (BR) 72010, Italy
Tel: (080) 4897307, Fax: (080) 4898582
7 suites with private bathrooms, 8 apartments
Lire 140,000–180,000 double B&B
* 100,000–120,000 per person half board*
1-week minimum stay July & August
All meals served
Open all year, Credit cards: MC, VS
Some English spoken
Region: Apulia

The most striking images of southern Tuscany are in the Orcia Valley—enchanting landscapes with soft, rolling hills topped with rows of cypress trees silhouetted against the sky. This alternating with the area called *le crete Senesi*—barren hills made of clay and resembling moon craters—makes for fascinating scenery. Le Traverse, at 4 kilometers from Pienza, is submersed in this soothingly peaceful countryside to which your gracious hosts, Pinuccia and Enrico, retired from Milan. Their charming home has been very tastefully restored and all the right touches (such as terry bathrobes and the finest-quality bedlinens) added to make guests feel right at home. The stone farmhouse with front courtyard is divided between the couple's own quarters, rooms for their visiting children, and an apartment for guests with independent entrance. The other two bedrooms are situated in the one-level converted barn nearby and are enhanced with the family's country antiques and prints. Huge terra-cotta vases overflowing with geraniums, trailing roses, and azalea plants dot the 50-acre property. Olive oil is produced as well as jams using homegrown fruit. The intimacy of the place with its three rooms makes you feel like a true houseguest and the area is chock-full of delightful day trips. *Directions*: From Pienza (circular piazza) follow signs for Monticchiello. After 3.3 km turn left on an unpaved road up to a group of cypress trees and the entrance to the house.

LE TRAVERSE
Hostess: Pinuccia Barbier Meroni
Localita: Le Traverse
Pienza (SI) 53026, Italy
Tel & fax: (0578) 748198
Cellphone: (0360) 575158
3 rooms with private bathrooms
Lire 220,000 double B&B
2-night minimum stay
Breakfast only
Closed November 15 to 30 & January 15 to 30
English, French spoken very well, Region: Tuscany

Right along the road connecting the hilltowns of Pienza and Montepulciano is the conveniently positioned farm of Felice and Giulia, transplanted from their hometowns in the regions of Marches and Campania respectively. The 18th-century stone farmhouse forms a U with inner courtyard from which you gain access to the breakfast room/bar, stone-walled restaurant with large dividing arch, living room, and upstairs bedrooms divided on both sides. Bedrooms are luminous and spacious, with immaculate bathrooms, pretty bedspreads, and country furniture. The bedrooms on the right side overlook the hilly countryside, swimming pool, and the 100-acre property of woods and fields, which produces its own wine and olive oil. Ancient Pienza can be seen at a distance. The real treat here is Giulia's cooking using the farm's own fresh produce. She has a flair for combining local traditional recipes with her own personal inventions, having homemade pastas as her base. Hard-working Felice relaxes and jokes with guests, often ending the evening playing the guitar. This is an easy-access touring base for the endless itineraries available, including Siena Montalcino and tours of the d'Orcia wine valley, and a great value. *Directions*: Exit from the autostrada at Chiusi and follow signs for Montepulciano, then Pienza. After a total of 25 km, well before Pienza, the iron gates of the Santo Pietro are on the left.

SANTO PIETRO
Hosts: Felice d'Angelo & Giulia Scala
Strada Statale 126, No. 29
Pienza (SI) 53026, Italy
Tel & fax: (0578) 748410
9 rooms with private bathrooms
Lire 120,000 per person half board
3-night minimum stay
Breakfast & dinner served
Open all year
Some English spoken, Region: Tuscany
www.karenbrown.com/italy/santopietro.html

La Piccola Pieve is situated several kilometers south of the ancient fortified town of Colle Val d'Elsa with its many crystal factories. The ancient house of Silvana Ravanelli, dating back to 1200, is actually the core of a cluster of stone houses. Stairs overflowing with cascading geraniums lead up to the front door of her cozy home, which the warm and gracious hostess practically hands over to her guests. A large, antique-filled living room with open stone staircase, fireplace, paintings, Oriental carpets, silver collection, and family photographs puts one immediately at ease. Two lovely bedrooms with one bathroom (perfect for families or two couples) are found down a small corridor to the left of this room, while the other two rooms upstairs are at opposite ends of another comfortable beamed sitting room. The air-conditioned bedrooms as well as bathrooms are quite spacious and elegantly appointed with parquet floors and antique beds. Breakfast of homemade cakes is served at the dining table in the inviting open kitchen with hanging brass pots and exposed brick arches. A wonderful surprise is the expansive garden and lawn with gazebo backdropped by hills. The advantages—location, ambiance, rate—are many in Silvana's warm and charming home in central Tuscany. *Directions*: From Colle take 541 south to Gracciano and right after the public park, take the small gravel road to a group of houses, taking the first right at the driveway.

LA PICCOLA PIEVE
Hostess: Silvana Ravanelli
Localita: Pieve a Elsa 92
Colle Val d'Elsa (SI) 53034, Italy
Tel & fax: (0577) 929745
4 rooms, 2 with private bathrooms
Lire 170,000 double B&B
3-night minimum stay
Breakfast only
Open March to November
Very little English spoken, some French
Region: Tuscany

As more and more Italians reclaim family property in the countryside or buy and restore their own abandoned castles, people such as the Baccheschi family are moving into more affordable, lesser-known areas. They left behind a successful fashion business to come to the quiet southern part of Tuscany where they bought the ruins of a 13th-century stone castle/ex-convent and are in the process of ambitiously putting its pieces back together to form their own private residence and rooms for guests. In the meantime, two adjacent stunning stone guesthouses are available. The smaller one, *I Sassi*, has one bedroom, a large bathroom, and glassed-in living room taking in the sumptuous view of virgin territory. *La Chiesina* has a kitchen and spacious living room with intarsia parquet flooring, two bedrooms, and two bathrooms. They are sophisticatedly appointed with family antiques and colonial pieces from Indonesia, and are worthy of an article in *Architectural Digest*. The travertine swimming pool hangs on the edge of the manicured garden, which drops down into untamed landscapes. This is a unique property for those really wanting to get away from it all. *Directions*: From the Grosseto-Siena highway 223, exit at Paganico. After 3 km turn right for Sasso d'Ombrone, and right again for Poggi del Sasso. In town watch for street sign Via de Vicarello on the right and follow the dirt road, keeping left at the fork for 7.5 km to the gray iron gate on the right.

CASTELLO DI VICARELLO
Hosts: Aurora & Carlo Baccheschi Berti
Via di Vicarello 1
Poggi del Sasso (SI) 58043, Italy
Tel & fax: (0564) 990718
Cellphone: (0337) 307656
2 houses
Lire 380,000–780,000 daily per house
3-night minimum stay, 1 week July & August
Breakfast, lunch & dinner upon request
Open all year
English spoken well
Region: Tuscany

The picturesque countryside dotted with medieval hilltowns north of Rome called Sabina is finally getting some recognition after centuries of being just a sleepy rural area. Bed and breakfasts are springing up right and left and at long last the tourist, inexplicably foreign to this lovely area so close to the capital city, has the opportunity to explore this virgin territory with its ancient traditions still in practice. Maria Vittoria, the warm and enthusiastic hostess of "Wonderland," as her bed and breakfast translates, is another newcomer to Sabina. She offers a very comfortable level of accommodation in her own home set down below the main road outside of town and facing out to an impressive panorama of hills covered with olive groves and distant mountains. Four bedrooms are found in the main house, elegantly appointed with precious antiques, paintings, and various collections from Maria Vittoria's worldwide travels. Some have terraces from which you can watch sunsets over the magnificent valley. Two other independent suites have been built into the hillside in front of the home. These are both adorable "nests," one having a loft bedroom with sitting area and kitchenette below. A homemade breakfast is served on the front patio. *Directions*: From the Rome-Rieti Via Salaria (route 4), turn off left for Poggio Nativo and continue on the main road 42 for 5 km. There is an iron gate to the house on the right-hand side before Santa Maria.

PAESE DELLE MERAVIGLIE
Hostess: Maria Vittoria Toniolo
Via Mirtense Km 5
Poggio Nativo (RI) 02030, Italy
Tel & fax: (0765) 872599
6 rooms with private bathrooms
Lire 140,000 double B&B
2-night minimum stay
Breakfast only
Open all year
English spoken well
Region: Lazio

After welcoming many Karen Brown travelers to their previous home—the Podere Capretto—the Zito family, from the States, happily started up another bed and breakfast in a lesser-known area of Tuscany, south of the stunning Etruscan town of Volterra. Their new home was actually that of the priest of the adjacent church, dating to the 1600s. The front entrance hall filled with potted plants leads to the dining and living room furnished with a variety of antiques and a grand piano. Upstairs are two guest bedrooms, one with private bathroom, appointed with the family's antique beds and armoires. Between the two rooms is a cozy sitting room with video library off which are Rose and Alfred's bedroom and that of their son, David. The garden surrounding the house and looking on to the woods has been restored to its original state following the replanting of shrubs and flowers. Also available for weekly stays is a separate house within the nearby medieval stone village of San Dalmazio. It has been renovated almost entirely by Alfred and David, keeping intact all characteristic features such as beams and sloping brick floors. Residents of Italy for over 10 years, the Zitos are a rich source of information for Tuscan itineraries. David also manages the weekly rental of another lovely 12-bedroom villa just across the street from the bed and breakfast. *Directions*: Take route 68 at Cecina from the coast highway route 1 to Pomarance and call to be met. The house is out of town at S. Ippolito.

CASA ZITO
Hosts: Zito family
Localita: S. Ippolito
Pomarance (PI) 56045, Italy
Tel & fax: (0588) 67789
2 rooms, 1 with private bathroom, 1 apartment
Lire 130,000 double B&B
* 900,000 weekly per apartment*
Breakfast served, dinner upon request
Open all year
Fluent English spoken, Region: Tuscany
www.karenbrown.com/italy/zito.html

Forty-five kilometers northeast of Florence, in a beautiful, hilly area of Tuscany, lies the Rufina Valley, famous for its robust red wine. Crowning a wooded slope is one of the many residences of the noble Galeotti-Ottieri family. The interior of the 15th-century main villa, once a convent, reveals spacious high-ceilinged halls with frescoes depicting family history. The family has also restored several stone farmhouses on the vast property, one of which is the Locanda Praticino (run by son Enrico and Antonella) whose upper floor contains seven lovely, simple double rooms with countryside views down one long hall, each named after its color scheme. Downstairs is a large rustic dining and living room with vaulted ceiling, enormous stone fireplace, worn brick floors, and casual country furniture. Full country-fresh Tuscan meals are only 25,000 lire. The addition of a swimming pool and tennis courts, plus enchanting landscape, makes it difficult to tear oneself away for touring. In order to retain the characteristic flavor of a sojourn in farmers' quarters, the properties have an intentionally unrestored, natural air to them. Available for longer stays are five very tastefully decorated apartments (two in the main house). The Petrognano is a tranquil spot where guests may enjoy the gracious hospitality of this historically important Florentine family. *Directions*: From Florence head toward Pontassieve. Continue to Rufina, turning right at Castiglioni-Pomino. Follow the winding road to the property, marked just before Pomino (12 km from Pontassieve).

FATTORIA DI PETROGNANO
Hosts: Cecilia Galeotti-Ottieri family
Localita: Pomino
Rufina (FI) 50060, Italy
Tel: (055) 8318812 or 8318867
Fax: (055) 242918
7 rooms with private bathrooms, 5 apartments
Lire 130,000 double B&B
All meals served, Open March to October
English & French spoken well
Region: Tuscany

Annabella and Cesare Taticchi, daughters, and 11 grandchildren warmly welcome guests to their corn, sunflower, and horse-breeding farm above Perugia, a rambling villa owned by the family since 1600. The former farmer's quarters near the main house contain a breakfast room and guestrooms with wood-beamed ceilings and brick floors, furnished in simple country style. Additional rooms are within the villa. Ceramic bathroom tile (and lamps), handmade by their talented daughter, depicts horses, ducks, roses, butterflies, and the like, for which the rooms are named. The main villa's dramatic entrance foyer with arched stairway leads up to a glassed-in veranda overlooking a neglected garden and woods through which the River Tiber flows. Annabella serves her specialties in the old-style dining room with chandelier and frescoes. Time stands still in the original library/billiard room and the two living rooms with piano, Oriental carpets, and period paintings. Horses are available for lessons in the indoor/outdoor ring or excursions in the area. Week-long courses with special all-inclusive rates are available in cooking, ceramics, and riding. Il Covone is a busy and informal place for families. *Directions*: Take route E45 from Perugia, exiting at Ponte Pattoli. Turn right at the T-junction and continue for 1 km. The farm is just after the tennis/sport complex.

IL COVONE
Hosts: Annabella & Cesare Taticchi
Strada della Fratticiola 2
Ponte Pattoli (PG) 06085, Italy
Tel: (075) 694140, Fax: (075) 694503
10 rooms with private bathrooms
Lire 130,000–150,000 double B&B
  100,000–120,000 per person half board
2-night minimum stay
Breakfast & dinner served
Open all year, Credit cards: all major
English spoken well
Region: Umbria

Gennarino a Mare is primarily a restaurant—one of the best known in Ponza both for its seafood specialties and its prime location right on the waterfront. It even has a large deck that stretches out over the water, built upon wooden pilings. Gennarino a Mare is a favorite place to dine, especially in summer when boats of all shapes and sizes dock at the adjacent pier and the merry yacht set comes to eat and drink. The restaurant has hosted many of the world's rich and famous, so there's no telling who might be sitting at the next table. It is no wonder the restaurant is so popular: as you enjoy dinner, you can watch the reflection of the fishing boats shimmering in the water and, behind them, the gaily painted houses of Ponza stepping up the hill like brightly painted blocks. The property's gracious owner, Francesco Silvestri, was born right in the same house where the restaurant now stands—his parents lived here and ran a small *pension*. The 12 simple bedrooms, located on the floors above the restaurant, are all decorated similarly with colorful matching drapes and bedspreads setting off white walls. Although small, each room has its own little step-out balcony with a romantic view. Remember, Gennarino a Mare is basically a restaurant, but a real winner for a simple, reasonably priced place to stay in Ponza. *Directions*: Take either the ferry or hydrofoil from Anzio to Ponza. The hotel is on the opposite side of the port, so it is best to take a taxi if you have luggage.

GENNARINO A MARE
Hosts: Tilla & Francesco Silvestri
Via Dante, 64
Isola di Ponza (LT) 04027, Italy
Tel: (0771) 80071, Fax: (0771) 80140
12 rooms with private bathrooms
Lire 220,000–360,000 double B&B
All meals served
Open all year
Credit cards: all major
English spoken well
Region: Lazio

The Vecchio Convento is a real gem, offering quality accommodation for a moderate price. Its several dining rooms are brimming with rustic country charm and serve delicious meals prepared from local produce. There are 20 guestrooms tastefully decorated with antiques—most have private bathrooms. The town of Portico di Romagna is like the inn, inviting yet unpretentious—an old village surrounded by wooded hills and clear mountain streams. A stroll through medieval pathways, which twist down between the weathered stone houses leads you to an ancient stone bridge gracefully arching over a rushing stream. The inn, too, is old, but was not (as you might expect from its name) originally a convent. According to its gracious owner, Marisa Raggi, it was named for a restaurant located in a convent that she and her husband, Giovanni (the chef) used to operate—when they moved here they kept the original name. The restaurant (closed Wednesdays) is still their primary focus, as its fine, fresh cuisine reflects. Italian lessons are also organized. *Directions*: Because of the winding, two-lane mountain highway that leads to the village, it takes about two hours to drive the 75 km from Florence. The inn is located 34 km southwest of the town of Forli.

ALBERGO AL VECCHIO CONVENTO
Hosts: Marisa Raggi & Giovanni Cameli
Via Roma 7
Portico di Romagna (FO) 47010, Italy
Tel: (0543) 967053, Fax: (0543) 967157
20 rooms, 15 with private bathrooms
Lire 170,000 double B&B
All meals served (except Wednesdays)
Open all year
Credit cards: all major
Some English spoken
Region: Emilia-Romagna

On the outskirts of historical Mantova sits the Villa Schiarino, one of the magnificent estates formerly belonging to the Gonzaga family, once among the most powerful nobility in Lombardy. The very cordial Lena Eliseo family, the present owners, have taken on the enormous task of restoring the 15th-century palace room by room. With high vaulted ceilings, completely frescoed rooms, wrought-iron chandeliers, and original terra-cotta floors, the seemingly endless parade of rooms reveals one delight after another. Besides being a museum, the villa is also used for large parties, weddings, and business meetings, and guestrooms will be available when a restoration project is completed sometime in 2001. Surrounding the villa are small houses, once inhabited by farmhands, which are now available to travelers on a daily or weekly basis. The three modest but spacious and comfortable apartments are appointed with a mixture of antique and contemporary furniture and can accommodate up to four persons. Each apartment has its own living area and one includes a kitchenette. This location is the ideal spot to base yourself while exploring less-touristy Ferrara, Cremona, Verona, and Mantua, which are filled with medieval and Renaissance buildings (Palazzo del Te and Palazzo Ducale are "must sees"). *Directions*: From Mantova take route N62 north past the church and turn left on Via Gramsci. Follow it for 1 km to the villa.

VILLA SCHIARINO LENA
Hosts: Giuseppe Lena Eliseo family
Via Santa Maddalena 7
Porto Mantovano (MN) 46047, Italy
Tel: (0376) 398238, Fax: (0376) 393238
3 apartments
Lire 170,000–200,000 daily per apartment B&B
Breakfast only
Open mid-March to October
English spoken well
Region: Lombardy

For those travelers wishing to explore the lesser-known Marches region, or about to embark on a ferry to Greece, the unique Fortino hotel offers comfortable and relaxing accommodations. Five kilometers along the coast from the city of Ancona, the hotel boasts a beachfront location. Originally a fortress, the vantage point it affords must have been considered strategic by Napoleon in 1811, when he ordered it constructed. Fifteen guestrooms, four suites, and a restaurant are housed within the low white, stone structure while the remaining 15 rooms are in a new building nearby. The restaurant specializes in fresh seafood dishes and looks so directly out to sea, it gives the impression of being on a ship. At the heart of the fort is a courtyard, complete with cannons, where breakfast is served, and a separate building contains a bar and a spacious living room with fireplace, decorated in neoclassic style. Rich period antiques appoint the three lovely suites, while simpler wicker furniture is found in the double rooms. Just two steps away is the beach, and up on the roof of the one-story fort is a deck with a spectacular coastal view. A swimming pool is also available for guests. *Directions*: From Ancona, follow signs for Camerano. Take a left at Portonovo, heading down to the sea. Watch for signs indicating the hotel's entrance.

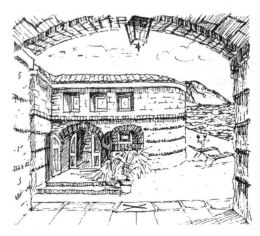

FORTINO NAPOLEONICO
Hosts: Amleto Roscioni family
Via Poggio
Portonovo (AN) 60020, Italy
Tel: (071) 801450, Fax: (071) 801454
30 rooms, 4 suites all with private bathrooms
Lire 280,000–330,000 double B&B
All meals served
Open all year
Credit cards: all major
English spoken well
Region: Marches

High above the strip of shore holding the Fortino Napoleonico hotel sits the Hotel Emilia, owned by the Fiorini Dubbini family. Grandmother Emilia opened a small restaurant right on the beach over 50 years ago, gaining an excellent reputation for fresh seafood dishes. That successful undertaking was followed by the hotel which, not surprisingly, has a restaurant known for seafood specialties and now a second restaurant on the beach. It is surrounded by an extensive lawn sweeping to the edge of a cliff, which drops 150 meters straight down to the sea below. Truly breathtaking views of Mount Conero and the dramatic, rugged coast can be enjoyed from this point as well as from any of the guestrooms. Although the hotel has a rather stark and modern exterior, interiors are softened by wicker couches topped by plump, yellow floral-print pillows, paintings, and flower bouquets. The all-white rooms are basic but comfortable, with wicker and rattan beds and clean, tiled bathrooms. This is traditionally a summer resort with beach, swimming pool, and tennis available on the premises, plus a nearby golf course, although it is lovely also in fall and winter months. Art shows and concerts are held here annually and enthusiastic owner Maurizio also has a quaint bar/trattoria down the road featuring jazz music. *Directions*: Exit at Ancona Sud off autostrada A14 and follow signs for Camerano, then Portonovo. Watch for signs for the hotel's entrance.

HOTEL EMILIA
Host: Maurizio Fiorini
Localita: Poggio di Portonovo
Portonovo (AN) 60020, Italy
Tel: (071) 801145, Fax: (071) 801330
Email: info@hotelemilia.com
27 rooms with private bathrooms, 3 suites
Lire 250,000–350,000 double B&B
All meals served
Open all year, Credit cards: all major
Handicap facilities
English spoken well, Region: Marches
www.karenbrown.com/italy/hotelemilia.html

Accommodation of all levels is available in Positano's many hotels: from five-star luxury to simple bed and breakfasts like Casa Cosenza, with its sunny yellow façade. Sitting snug against the cliff side, halfway down to the beach, it is reached by descending one of the variety of stairways found in this unique seaside town. The front arched entranceway, lined with terra-cotta pots overflowing with colorful local flora, leads to an enormous tiled terrace overlooking the pastel-color houses of Positano and the dramatic coastline. Seven guestrooms on the second floor, each with private bathroom and balcony, enjoy the same breathtaking panorama. The residence dates back 200 years, as evidenced by the typical cupola ceilings in each room, originally designed to keep rooms cool and airy. Rooms have bright, tiled floors and are simply and sweetly decorated with old-fashioned armoires, desks, and beds. Room 7 (at a slightly higher rate), although smaller and with an older bathroom, has a lovely large terrace, as do two newly added suites behind the main house that can accommodate three to four persons. A Continental breakfast is served on the terrace. The helpful, very friendly Cosenza family assures visitors of a pleasant stay. A ferry leaves Positano beach every morning in summer months for the island of Capri. *Directions*: Park your car in a garage in town and ask for directions for the *scalinatella* stairway where there are signs to Casa Cosenza. Remember to pack light!

CASA COSENZA
Hosts: Salvatore Cosenza family
Via Trara Genoino 18
Positano (SA) 84017, Italy
Tel & fax: (089) 875063
Email: casacosenza@divinacostiera.it
9 rooms with private bathrooms
Lire 240,000–350,000 double B&B
3-night minimum stay in high season
Breakfast only, Open all year
Very little English spoken
Region: Campania
www.karenbrown.com/italy/casacosenza.html

The spectacular Amalfi coast offers a wide variety of accommodation, yet few as special as La Fenice—as fantastic as the mythological bird for which it is named. Guests leave their cars on the main road and climb the arbored steps to discover the idyllic white villa hidden amid the lush Mediterranean vegetation. The incredibly hospitable proprietors, Costantino and Angela, heartily welcome new arrivals on the shady front terrace, where breakfast is served each clement morning, accompanied by classical music. Seven luminous bedrooms, three with terrace and marvelous sea views, the others with lateral sea or garden view, are simply decorated with scattered antiques in a wing off the family's home. Eight more rooms, most with terraces, reached by *many* steps down from the road, are built separately into the side of the cliff and have colorful, tiled floors and similar furnishings. Descending yet *more* steps (always surrounded by incredible coastal views), you'll come across the curved sea-water pool and Jacuzzi carved against the rock (open June to October), where a fresh Mediterranean lunch is served, at an extra cost, during summer months, prepared primarily with home-grown ingredients. A fishing boat picks up guests on the beach for a delightful tour of the coast and lunch on board. This property may have few amenities in rooms, but is a natural wonder, cascading down to the sea and a small private beach. *Directions*: Located on the coastal highway south of Positano in the direction of Amalfi. Two curves after town, watch for gates on the right.

LA FENICE
Hosts: Angela & Costantino Mandara
Via Marconi 4
Positano (SA) 84017, Italy
Tel: (089) 875513, Fax: (089) 811309
15 rooms with private bathrooms
Lire 200,000 double B&B
Breakfast & lunch served (extra charge for lunch)
Open all year
Some English spoken, Region: Campania
www.karenbrown.com/italy/lafenice.html

Villa Rosa opened its doors four years ago after some restoration work by local couple Virginia and Franco who own a clothing store and ceramic store in town (the house has always been in Virginia's family). The 150-year-old villa, built into the cliffside and hidden behind bougainvillea vines high above the road right in town, is on three levels. Taking the stairs up to the middle level, you find the reception area and large common living room where guests are greeted. The twelve rooms are spread over all three floors, each having access to the large front terraces which are divided by plants and grapevine-covered pergolas for privacy. Picturesque views of Positano's colorful houses and the spectacular coastline are enjoyed from any point. Breakfast is served either in rooms or out on individual terraces adorned with large terra-cotta vases laden with cascading pink and red geraniums, in sharp contrast with pure white walls. Bedrooms maintain original tiles and vaulted ceilings and are furnished with simple antiques, while bathrooms display typical yellow and blue hand-painted tiles from Vietri. Air conditioning is an exceptional amenity offered along with satellite TV and mini bar. Easy day trips include Amalfi, Ravello, and the ruins of Pompeii, Paestum, or Herculum. The Caldieros have just opened a second bed and breakfast, Villa La Tartana, down by the beach. *Directions*: Following the main road through town, you find Villa Rosa almost at the end just before the famous Sirenuse Hotel. Parking is possible in a nearby public garage only.

VILLA ROSA
Hosts: Virginia & Franco Caldiero
Via C. Colombo 127
Positano (SA) 84017, Italy
Tel: (089) 811955, Fax: (089) 812112
12 rooms with private bathrooms
Lire 190,000–210,000 double B&B
Breakfast only
Open March to October
Some English spoken, Region: Campania
www.karenbrown.com/italy/villarosa.html

From the moment you enter the grand foyer of Villa Rucellai looking out over the classical Italian Renaissance garden of this 16th-century country villa, all sense of time and place is lost. The Rucellais' devotion to their estate (in the family since 1759) is apparent, as is their warm and enthusiastic hospitality. Guests are given the run of the charming old home: from the cozy bedrooms, varying in size and decor (ask for the largest); antique-filled library; and spacious living room with fireplace, worn floral sofas, and family portraits to the country kitchen and breakfast room overlooking a long and narrow 14th-century pool right in front of the entrance to the house, where guests are served *en famille* at a long wooden table. Members of the family enjoy suggesting itineraries of particular interest for their guests, as well as cultural events such as art courses, concerts, and art exhibits. The Villa Rucellai serves as an excellent base from which to visit Florence, Siena, Lucca, and Pisa. The development of the city of Prato has crept up to the doors of the villa, so be advised that this is not a countryside setting. *Directions*: From Florence take the A11 autostrada, exiting at Prato Est. Turn right on Viale della Repubblica, then left on Borgo Valsugana, following signs for Trattoria La Fontana, and proceed on Via di Canneto for 1.5 km up to the Villa.

VILLA RUCELLAI DI CANNETO
Hosts: Giovanna Rucellai Pique family
Via di Canneto 16
Prato (FI) 59100, Italy
Tel & fax: (0574) 460392
11 rooms with private bathrooms
Lire 160,000 double B&B
Breakfast only
Open all year
Fluent English spoken
Region: Tuscany

One option (among at least 20 possibilities) for in-home accommodations in the Radda area is at the home of a gregarious Florentine couple, Giuliana and Enis Vergelli, whose stone house sits on a long, winding road, just before the castle/village of Volpaia. The guest quarters are actually found in another stone house a few steps away in the quaint 14th-century village. The wood-shuttered residence can be rented entirely or as two separate apartments. One apartment is just like a doll house, comprised of a mini living area with minuscule fireplace, kitchenette, and a ladder staircase leading up to the bedroom and bath—an absolutely adorable love nest for two. The other apartment, also on two floors, has a good-sized living room with kitchen, bathroom, and two bedrooms, simply and very comfortably furnished. Giuliana also offers accommodation in a bedroom with bathroom, garden, and separate entrance in her own home. Guests are welcome to wander through the Vergellis' garden and enjoy the terrace with sweeping views over Chianti country. Giuliana adores pampering her guests and appears now and then with jams, honey, or a freshly made soup. *Directions*: Driving through the town of Radda, turn right at signs for Volpaia castle. Go uphill for several kilometers to the first house before entering town, marked Vergelli.

AZIENDA AGRICOLA VERGELLI
Hosts: Enis & Giuliana Vergelli
Localita: Volpaia
Radda in Chianti (SI) 53017, Italy
Tel & fax: (0577) 738382
2 apartments, 1 room with private bathroom
Lire 115,000 double (no breakfast)
  135,000 apartment for 2 persons daily
  200,000 apartment for 4 persons daily
No meals served
Open all year
No English spoken
Region: Tuscany

Weary of life in the intense financial world of Milan, Guido and Martina packed up and headed for the hills of Chianti and the "good life" that attracts so many there. After a long search they chose the scenic property where La Locanda now stands, primarily for its magnificent position facing out to medieval Volpaia and an endless panorama filled with layers of virgin hills. The results of their meticulous restoration of three simple stone farmhouses are formidable and today fortunate guests can share in their dream. Its remote location among woods and olive groves guarantees total silence and tranquillity and the comfortable, decorator-perfect common rooms and luminous colors harmonize divinely with this idyllic setting. An understated elegance permeates the six bedrooms and suite divided among one of the two-story farmhouses. They are tastefully appointed with antiques and smart plaid curtains, and four have the advantage of the views. Breakfast and occasional dinner are served out on the terrace above the swimming pool whose borderless edge spills into the landscape. Guido and Martina, natural and gregarious hosts, exude a contagious enthusiasm for their new surroundings. *Directions*: From Radda follow signs for Firenze and turn right for Volpaia. Continue on the unpaved road for another 3.8 km after Volpaia village, following signs to La Locanda/Montanino.

LA LOCANDA
Hosts: Guido & Martina Bevilacqua
Localita: Montanino
Radda in Chianti (SI) 53017, Italy
Tel & fax: (0577) 738833
Email: info@lalocanda.it
6 rooms, 1 suite, all with private bathrooms
Lire 350,000–400,000 double B&B
Breakfast served, dinner upon request
Open mid-March to mid-January
Credit cards: all major
English spoken well
Region: Tuscany
www.karenbrown.com/italy/lalocanda.html

For its combination of idyllic location, charming ambiance, and delightful hosts, the Podere Terreno is an example of the best in Italian bed and breakfasts, with Sylvie and Roberto, a Franco-Italian couple, along with gregarious son, Francesco, dedicating themselves to pampering their guests. The 400-year-old house is surrounded by terra-cotta flower vases, a grapevine-covered pergola, a small lake, and sweeping panoramas of the Chianti countryside. Within are seven sweet double bedrooms with very small bath, each decorated differently with country antiques and the family's personal possessions; a wine cellar loaded with the proprietors' own Chianti Classico; and a billiard room/library. Guests convene in the main room of the house around the massive stone fireplace on comfortable floral sofas for hors d'oeuvres before sitting down to a sumptuous candlelit dinner prepared by your hosts. This is a cozy, stone-walled room, filled with country antiques, brass pots, and dried-flower bouquets hanging from the exposed beams, and shelves lined with bottles of wine—quite delightful. *Directions*: From Greve follow signs to Panzano, then go left for Radda and on to Lucarelli. After 3 km turn right at Volpaia. After 5 km, turn right at the sign for Podere Terreno.

PODERE TERRENO
Hosts: Marie Sylvie Haniez & Roberto Melosi
Via della Volpaia
Radda in Chianti (SI) 53017, Italy
Tel & fax: (0577) 738312
Email: podereterreno@chiantinet.it
7 rooms with private bathrooms
Lire 170,000 per person half board
2-night minimum stay
Breakfast & dinner served
Open all year, Credit cards: MC, VS
English spoken very well
Region: Tuscany
www.karenbrown.com/italy/podereterreno.html

Both Radda and Greve are excellent bases from which to explore scenic Chianti wine country with its regal castles and stone villages, in addition to Siena, Florence, and San Gimignano. Radda in particular offers a myriad of possibilities for accommodation, including many private homes with rooms or apartments. The Val delle Corti is the home and vineyard property of gracious hostess Eli Bianchi and her son Roberto where they produce a high-quality Chianti wine. The cozy pale-stone house with white shutters tops a hill overlooking the quaint town. The hosts, who moved here over 25 years ago from Milan, are extremely active in community affairs and are a superb source for area information. Guests have a quarter of their stone farmhouse: a rustic two-bedroom apartment on the upper floor with a separate entrance, a large bathroom, kitchen, and living room with fireplace, all furnished simply with family belongings. The second accommodation is a lovely separate little house, just recently completed, with a large open kitchen and living space looking out to the vineyards, and two bedrooms, one bathroom on the first floor. Meals can be taken at one of the excellent restaurants right in nearby Radda. *Directions*: Equidistant from Florence and Siena off the N222 Chianti road. Before entering Radda, turn right toward Lecchi-San Sano, then take the first left at Val delle Corti.

PODERE VAL DELLE CORTI
Hosts: Eli & Roberto Bianchi
Localita: La Croce
Radda in Chianti (SI) 53017, Italy
Tel: (0577) 738215, Fax: (0577) 739521
Email: gbianchi@chiantinet.it
2 apartments
US $700 per week
Open Easter to October
English spoken very well
Region: Tuscany
www.karenbrown.com/italy/poderevaldellecorti.html

In the very heart of Chianti between Radda, Castellina, and Vagliagli sits the Pornanino farm surrounded by 65 acres of wooded hills and olive groves. Delightful and amiable hosts, Franco and Lia invite one family at a time to share their little piece of Tuscany. They are part of the increasing breed of "neo-farmers" migrating from major cities (Milan in this instance) in search of a slower-paced lifestyle where basic values of life are emphasized in everyday living. Franco has taken on the role of producer of top-quality olive oil with great passion and even conducts small seminars and tastings on the subject. The adorable stone guesthouse overlooking the main house, barn, and chapel consists of a large living area with fireplace, open kitchen, two double and one single bedrooms, and two bathrooms. It is appointed with the same warm country style as their own home, with country fabrics and furniture complementing beamed ceilings and brick floors. A large arched window looks out to the terrace and pergola. Guests can also take advantage of the lovely swimming pool. The Lombardis are part of a group of family and friends offering similar rentals in the area. *Directions*: The farm is located 9 km south of Radda and 4 km north of Vagliagli on route 102 but the turnoff is not marked, so it is best to call ahead. 18 km from Siena and 54 km from Florence.

PORNANINO
Hosts: Lia & Franco Lombardi
Localita: Pornanino 72
Radda in Chianti (SI) 53017, Italy
Tel: (0577) 738658, Fax: (0577) 738794
1 guesthouse
Lire 1,300,000–1,800,000* weekly 2 to 4 persons
  *Heating extra
No meals served, Open all year
English spoken well
Region: Tuscany

On the opposite side of town from the Podere Val delle Corti live Lele Bianchi Vitali and her family, who offer a two-bedroom apartment in a stone tower dating from 1832. This unique accommodation, perfect for a family of four, has an enchanting view of Radda and the countryside. The three-story tower has terra-cotta floors and beamed ceilings, a living room/kitchenette on the ground floor, one bedroom and a bath on the second floor, and a second bedroom on top. Furnishings are simple and in keeping with tower's rustic features. A small olive grove separates the tower from the Vitalis' lovely home, where a swimming pool awaits road-weary guests and a double bedroom with bathroom is offered. Lele is a vivacious hostess who divides her time between guests, a small in-house weaving business, and helping out her son and daughter-in-law, a young and ambitious couple who converted a farmhouse into the most authentic regional restaurant in town—Le Vigne. A half-board meal plan can be arranged for guests of the tower. *Directions*: From either Siena or Florence, follow signs for Radda off the spectacular Strada del Chianti N222. Go through town until you reach the hotel/restaurant Villa Miranda (not recommended), after which turn right at the sign for Canvalle and follow the dirt road up to the tower.

TORRE CANVALLE
Hosts: General Enrico & Lele Bianchi Vitali
Localita: La Villa
Radda in Chianti (SI) 53017, Italy
Tel & fax: (0577) 738321
1 apartment, 1 room with private bathroom
US $100 double B&B
  US $700 weekly
Half board available at Le Vigne restaurant
Open all year
English spoken very well
Region: Tuscany

Nicoletta Innocenti is the delightful owner and hostess of La Palazzina, one of our favorite bed and breakfasts. The stately 18th-century villa has 12 lovely guestrooms appointed with antiques, each having its own cool pastel color scheme. The large double dining room with checked black-and-white tiled floors looks out to the garden and expansive lawns. A swimming pool hugs the side of the hill overlooking sweeping panoramas. Two of the three apartments within a 17th-century stone farmhouse, *Colombaio*, have two double bedrooms each, living area with kitchenette, fireplace, and bathroom. The third dwelling is a studio apartment for two persons. They are rustically furnished with local antiques and offer gorgeous views over the Orcia Valley. The lovely Villa Fonte Emerosa, appointed with period antiques, has two bedrooms, two bathrooms, large living rooms with fireplace, garden, and swimming pool and faces out to the mountains. The 18th-century farmhouse, Casa di Terra, is set among the vineyards and includes three bedrooms, kitchen, living, and dining room. This southeast corner of Tuscany offers a rich variety of sites to explore, from the Amiata Mountains for nature lovers, to the hilltowns of Montepulciano, Pienza, and Montalcino for art, food, and wine lovers, to Chianciano for thermal baths. *Directions*: From Florence on the A1 autostrada, exit at Chiusi and drive towards Sarteano on route 478, turning left for Radicofani. After 14 km turn left for Celle Sul Rigo then right at the sign for La Palazzina.

LA PALAZZINA
Hosts: Innocenti family
Localita: Le Vigne
Radicofani (SI) 53040, Italy
Tel: (0578) 55771, Fax: (0578) 53553
12 rooms with private bathrooms, 3 apartments, 2 houses
Lire 180,000–250,000 double B&B
* 400,000–950,000 weekly per apartment*
* 300,000,000–500,000,000 weekly per house*
Breakfast served, Open all year, Credit cards: all major
English spoken well, Region: Tuscany
www.karenbrown.com/italy/palazzina.html

The Villa Maria is perhaps best known for its absolutely delightful terrace restaurant, which has a bird's-eye view of the magnificent coast. Whereas most of Ravello's hotels capture the southern view, the Villa Maria features the equally lovely vista to the north. The Villa Maria is two minutes by foot from the main square on the path winding to the Villa Cimbrone. After parking in the square (or at the Hotel Giordano), look for signs for the Villa Maria, perched on the cliffs to your right. The building is a romantic old villa with a garden stretching to the side where tables and chairs are set, a favorite place to dine while enjoying the superb view. Inside, there is a cozy dining room overlooking the garden. The bedrooms are air conditioned and furnished with antique pieces including brass beds. The bathrooms were remodeled a year or so ago and some even have Jacuzzi tubs. The hotel is owned by Vincenzo Palumbo whose staff speak excellent English and go out of their way to assist guests. Vincenzo also owns the nearby more modern Hotel Giordano, which has a heated pool that you can use. Guests at the Villa Maria enjoy a wonderful view and location in a charming villa with a fine restaurant. *Directions*: Ravello is about 6 km north of Amalfi on a small road heading north from the highway.

VILLA MARIA
Host: Vincenzo Palumbo
Via San Chiara 2
Ravello (SA) 84010, Italy
Tel: (089) 857255, Fax: (089) 857071
17 rooms with private bathrooms, 2 apartments
Lire 300,000–380,000 double B&B
  190,000–230,000 per person half board*
  *Required in high season, June to September
All meals served
Open all year, Credit cards: all major
English spoken very well
Region: Campania

Bed & Breakfast Descriptions   179

Ravenna is a splendid small city boasting one of the world's most prized collections of Byzantine mosaics housed within eight of its churches, basilicas, and mausoleums. The city comes alive in the summer months with a full program of theater, opera, and outdoor concerts, and even evening opening hours of churches to view the mosaics by night. There are lovely shops and the historical center of Ravenna is quiet since most residents get around by bicycle. Since we found bed and breakfast possibilities in the surrounding area to be much too spartan, the Hotel Diana with its yellow façade, in the center of Ravenna, is the best accommodation choice. A very friendly staff welcomes you into the luminous reception area with various sofas and armchairs arranged around a faux-marble fireplace, and a small patio outside. A buffet breakfast is served downstairs and an elevator takes you up to the second and third floors where the renovated bedrooms are located. These are rather standard but pleasant, with cream-colored walls and bedspreads, carpeting, and reproduction furniture. All have satellite television, air conditioning, and nice new bathrooms. The recommended superior doubles afford more space and have hydromassage bathtubs. Within a drive of an hour or less are Venice, Padua, Rovigo, Ferrara, Bologna, and the ancient ceramic center of Faenza. *Directions*: Follow signs for city center (*Centro*) then follow yellow hotel signs. Near the San Vitale Basilica.

HOTEL DIANA
Manager: Filippo Donati
Via G. Rossi 47
Ravenna 48100, Italy
Tel: (0544) 39119 or 39009, Fax: (0544) 30001
33 rooms with private bathrooms
Lire 204,000 double B&B
Breakfast only
Open all year, Credit cards: all major
English spoken well
Region: Emilia-Romagna

Bed & Breakfast Descriptions

The lesser-known area of Tuscany south of Siena makes a delightful discovery and the variety of landscapes within an 8-kilometer drive provides one of the most fascinating excursions in the region. Besides the charming hilltowns of Montepulciano, Pienza, and Montalcino, there are the abbeys of Monte Oliveto and Sant'Antimo, plus the thermal baths of Bagno Vignoni. A perfect base in this richly historical and natural area is the magnificent castle of the Aluffi Pentini family, theirs for the past 400 years or so and practically a village in itself. The family resides in the upper reaches of the castle while guests are accommodated in several separate farmer's houses divided into a combination of apartments with one or two bedrooms, living room and kitchenette, plus six simply and characteristically appointed bedrooms with country furniture. Rooms facing out have absolutely breathtaking views over the virgin valley. Downstairs is the dining room with wood tables covered with cheery checked cloths, where breakfast and dinner are served using homegrown products. A common space for guests is the old granary, converted into a large cozy reading room with fireplace. A fairy-tale-like place. *Directions:* The castle is well marked at 5 km from San Quirico d'Orcia. Ripa d'Orcia is marked on most maps.

CASTELLO DI RIPA D'ORCIA
Hosts: Aluffi Pentini family
Localita: Ripa d'Orcia
Via della Contea 1/16
San Quirico d'Orcia (SI) 53023, Italy
Tel: (0577) 897376, Fax: (0577) 898038
7 apartments, 6 rooms with private bathrooms
Lire 190,000–230,000 double B&B
* 890,000–1,490,000 weekly per apartment*
2-night minimum stay (rooms)
Breakfast & dinner served (except Mondays)
Open March to November, Credit cards: MC, VS
English spoken well, Region: Tuscany

With passion and determination, Daniela and her architect husband, Piero, brought back to life the family's ancient property with total respect for its 9th-century origins. This very special place has a rich historical past and a Romanesque church within the home where concerts are held. A nature lover's paradise, the complex of stone houses is surrounded by lush vegetation, vineyards, woods, and olive groves from which the family's prestigious olive oil comes, and the perfume of lavender and jasmine is divinely intoxicating. Hospitality is offered within six apartments attached to the main house accommodating from two to five persons, impeccably decorated with the family's refined antiques, which live harmoniously with their perfectly preserved centuries-old environment. The dwellings feature living room with fireplace, balconies taking in either the sweeping countryside views down to the sea or out to the woods and a 200-year-old oak tree, wrought-iron beds, and original paintings by Daniela's father, a renowned fresco painter. Daniela, a world traveler, is a hostess *par excellence* and her contagious enthusiasm makes a stay at Caminino nothing less than splendidly memorable. Besides Siena and Montalcino, there are plenty of off-the-beaten-track sights to see and bikes can be rented. The farm also produces wine and honey, which guests can purchase. *Directions*: From Grosseto take Aurelia route 1 north and exit at Braccagni. Continue straight towards Montemassi and before town turn right for Caminino (listed on most maps) and Roccatederighi. After 1 km turn right at the gate for Caminino.

FATTORIA DI CAMININO
Hosts: Daniela Locatelli & Piero Marrucchi
Via Provinciale di Peruzzo
Roccatederighi (GR) 58028, Italy
Tel: (0564) 569737 or (055) 214898, Fax: (055) 2675819
Email: caminino@caminino.com
6 apartments, Lire 160,000–380,000 daily per apartment
2-night minimum stay low season, 1 week June to September
Breakfast & dinner upon request, Open all year
English spoken well, Region: Tuscany
www.karenbrown.com/italy/caminino.html

Tuscany is the most visited region in Italy—mostly between Siena and Florence—but it nonetheless contains many other treasures off the beaten track. Heading west from Florence toward the coast are the lovely towns of Lucca and Pisa, and just north of them is the beautifully scenic area known as Garfagnana, which features two nature reserves and the Apuan Alps. Here in the northernmost tip of Tuscany is evidence of how Italian culture varies not only from one region to another, but within a region itself. In the heart of these mountains, the genial Coletti family runs a lively local restaurant in the village and cultivates cereals, wild berries, and chestnuts on the farm. Hospitality is offered within seven very simple double rooms with a mountain-cabin feeling, having pinewood floors and ceilings, in a restored three-story building within the stone village of Roggio. Most have a balcony and all have modern bathrooms. Meals, including breakfast, are taken around the corner at the family restaurant where Gemma Coletti prepares her special lasagna and polenta with porcini mushrooms, among other local specialties. A budget choice for nature lovers and climbers, and a way to see a slice of village life. *Directions*: From Lucca, take route 445 toward Castelnuovo and on to Vagli di Sotto then right for Roggio. Take a winding road up to Roggio, where a sign indicates the Coletti restaurant in the village.

LA FONTANELLA
Hosts: Gemma & Severino Coletti
Localita: Vagli Sotto
Roggio (LU) 55100, Italy
Tel: (0583) 649179, Fax: none
7 rooms with private bathrooms
Lire 60,000 double
All meals served
Closed Christmas
Very little English spoken
Region: Tuscany
www.karenbrown.com/italy/lafontanella.html

A delightful alternative to our other accommodations in Rome is Casa Stefazio, the only true in-home bed and breakfast. The location and setting are as perfect as the dedication and warm hospitality offered by Stefania and Orazio in their large, ivy-covered suburban home, just 30 minutes from the city center, surrounded by several acres of manicured garden and utter silence. On the lower level, with a separate entrance, are one bedroom and two spacious suites (with sauna) accommodating a family of four, each with its own immaculate bathroom, satellite TV, air conditioning, and mini bar. The main areas include living room, large American-style kitchen, where the Azzolas work wonders, and eating area overlooking the expansive lawn and distant woods. Dinner is served on request under the pergola. Their style, in both decorating and easy entertaining, has obviously been influenced by their yearly winter sojourn in the States, which they adore. Sports activities such as horseback riding, tennis, golf, and swimming are easily arranged. The hosts also organize excursions for groups of friends throughout Italy. Highly recommended by readers. *Directions*: Located north of Rome just outside the circular highway around the city (GRA), close to the tollway north to Florence and south to Naples. Call one day ahead for detailed directions.

CASA STEFAZIO
Hosts: Stefania & Orazio Azzola
Via della Marcigliana 553
Rome 00138, Italy
Tel: (06) 87120042, Fax: (06) 87120012
Email: casastefazio@hotmail.com
1 room, 2 suites with private bathrooms
US $200 double B&B
  US $230–$250 suite
Breakfast served, dinner upon request
Open mid-March to December
English spoken very well, Region: Lazio
www.karenbrown.com/italy/casastefazio.html

It is truly refreshing to have found such an efficiently and professionally run, friendly, and well-priced accommodation as the Hotel Celio in a central area of Rome, not overrun by tourists. Just around the corner from the Colosseum, the Celio is part of an authentic Roman neighborhood. The restored façade of the turn-of-the-century building, along with the redone interiors, makes a pleasing first impression of this accommodation with its ancient Roman theme. Brothers Roberto and Marcello, also owners of the Santo Stefano in Venice (see listing), are most attentive to guests' comfort and needs. The small entrance leads to a cozy reception/sitting area and bar with large lit paintings, giving the immediate feeling of being in more of a private home rather than a hotel. Eighteen bedrooms of varying dimensions are each named after the famous artist whose fresco reproduction adorns the wall over the bed. A luxurious "penthouse" suite has a Jacuzzi bathtub and two private rooftop terraces with a view of the Colosseum. Marble halls lead to guestrooms traditionally decorated with rich fabrics in royal blue and yellow, antiques, and gilded framed paintings. Each has a small, but very updated and well-equipped bathroom with mosaic tiles. Breakfast is served in rooms or in the courtyard. Other extras include private garage facilities, air conditioning, and, above all, silence, a rarity in Rome. The Celio combines personal attention and intimacy with the amenities of a four-star hotel. *Directions:* Two blocks east of the Colosseum.

HOTEL CELIO
Hosts: Quatrini family
Via S.S. Quattro 35/C
Rome 00184, Italy
Tel: (06) 70495333, Fax: (06) 7096377
18 rooms with private bathrooms
Lire 270,000–420,000 double B&B
* 500,00–1,000,000 penthouse suite*
Breakfast only
Open all year, Credit cards: all major
English spoken well, Region: Lazio

Bed & Breakfast Descriptions

The Due Torri, a good example of a small and charming city hotel, dates to the early 1800s and is tucked away on a tiny, narrow cobblestone street in the historical heart of Rome very near the Navona square with its Bernini fountains. The 26 rather petite bedrooms are decorated with care, featuring newly tiled bathrooms, period antiques, and matching burgundy drapes and bedspreads. Many amenities are offered, including elevator and air conditioning, which provides welcome relief on Roman hot summer days. The elegant reception and contained sitting area have Oriental carpets, pieced marble floors, brocaded draperies, gilt-framed mirrors and paintings, and red velvet chairs accenting the cream-colored walls. The fifth-floor mansard rooms have small terraces and fourth-floor rooms have balconies with enchanting views over typical tiled rooftops and terraces. A buffet breakfast is served in a windowless rooms made cheery with painted borders and paintings. Super hostess Cinzia (owner also of the Fontanella Borghese, separate listing) and her courteous staff are incredibly helpful at arranging everything from advance ticketing for museums to transfers and restaurant and itinerary suggestions. Due Torri is a popular little hotel so be sure to reserve well in advance. *Directions*: Use a detailed city map to locate the hotel, north of Navona Square in a maze of winding streets.

HOTEL DUE TORRI
Owner: Cinzia Pighini Giordani
Vicolo del Leonetto 23
Rome 00186, Italy
Tel: (06) 6876983 or 6875765
Fax: (06) 6865442
26 rooms with private bathrooms
Lire 320,000–380,000 double B&B
Breakfast only
Open all year, Credit cards: all major
English spoken well, Region: Lazio
www.karenbrown.com/italy/duetorri.html

Many hotels in Rome can boast panoramic views over the city, but few have such a close-up view of a world-famous monument as the Fontana Hotel. Located directly on the square containing the magnificent Trevi fountain, the Fontana's windows look out on to its gushing waters, where you can practically toss a coin from your room. The sleek black-and-white breakfast room with wrought-iron chairs and tables is situated on the top floor of the 14th-century building, giving a bird's-eye view over the square from an enormous picture window. The small rooms are sweetly done with pastel-floral wallpaper, bedspreads, and white curtains and vary in size and decor. Bathrooms were incorporated into each room later, and are quite small. Narrow, vaulted-ceilinged halls leading to the guestrooms are adorned with antique prints of Rome. A very gradual updating of rooms is in progress and the initial results are splendid. Signora Elena and her staff at the desk attend to guests' every need. The noise commonly associated with a city hotel is not a problem here as the square is closed to traffic, although loud voices of tourists lingering into the early hours can be a problem in the summer when the fountain closes at midnight. There is a supplement for air conditioning in rooms without a fountain view. *Directions*: Use a detailed city map to locate the hotel in the Piazza di Trevi off the Via Tritone.

FONTANA HOTEL
Hostess: Elena Daneo
Piazza di Trevi 96
Rome 00187, Italy
Tel: (06) 6786113 or 6791056, Fax: (06) 6790024
27 rooms with private bathrooms
Lire 350,000–450,000 double B&B
Breakfast only
Open all year
Credit cards: all major
English spoken well
Region: Lazio

The many travelers who have enjoyed staying at the Due Torri hotel can now experience the same charismatic hospitality given by Cinzia in her more recently opened accommodation very close by. The hotel has the same name as the triangular-shaped piazza where it is located, directly in front of the imposing Palazzo Borghese leading to the Spanish Steps. The enormous doors of the 17th-century building open up to a courtyard where you take the elevator up to the fourth floor. The small lobby has a sitting corner and a sweeping spiral staircase up to additional rooms on the next floor. Guestrooms have sparkling new bathrooms and modern amenities such as satellite TV and air conditioning, and are appointed with either an antique desk or armoire, green or blue matching bedspreads and draperies, and antique prints of Rome. An effort was made to preserve the original gray-marble floors in some rooms, while parquet flooring was put in the others. Most have a view on a narrow and very characteristic cobblestone street, or on the inner courtyard, offering rare silence. The reception area leads to the breakfast room with marble floors and matching faux-marble doorways. Cinzia oversees every detail in both hotels and the secret to her success is that she obviously has guests' comfort foremost in mind. Even extra assistance such as securing advance reservations to certain museums is offered. *Directions*: Consult a city map.

HOTEL FONTANELLA BORGHESE
Owner: Cinzia Pighini Giordani
Largo Fontanella Borghese 84
Rome 00186, Italy
Tel: (06) 68809504, Fax: (06) 6861295
29 rooms with private bathrooms
Lire 330,000–380,000 double B&B
Breakfast only
Open all year
Credit cards: all major
English spoken well
Region: Lazio
www.karenbrown.com/italy/fontanellaborghese.html

The Locarno Hotel is centrally located on the corner of a rather busy street, only two blocks from bustling Popolo Square. Its downtown location makes noise unavoidable, so it is advisable to request a room away from the street, even though the installation of thermal windows has helped. Even with the extensive renovations it has undergone, the hotel, dating from 1925, retains the art-deco flavor it had originally. The red-carpeted reception area leads to a cozy bar and long, mirrored sitting room lined with cushioned banquettes and café tables. There is also a side patio with shady canvas umbrellas where guests can have breakfast in warm weather, if not in the new and cheery breakfast room looking out to the patio. Another fabulous addition is the opening of the rooftop garden where you can gaze over Rome's tiled roofs and terraces to St. Peter's dome and Villa Borghese park. The comfortable rooms (regular and superior doubles), decorated with antiques, gold-framed mirrors, and pretty floral wallpaper, are air-conditioned. Two apartments (no kitchen) are offered to guests in the building directly across the street. The Locarno features such extras as a parking garage and free use of bicycles with which you might tour the Villa Borghese park. It is no wonder that this has always been a favorite among artists and writers. Reserve well in advance. *Directions*: Use a detailed city map to locate the hotel one block east of the River Tiber at Flaminia square sign.

HOTEL LOCARNO
Hostess: Caterina Valente
Via della Penna 22
Rome 00186, Italy
Tel: (06) 3610841 or (06) 3610842, Fax: (06) 3215249
Email: info@hotellocarno.com
48 rooms, 2 suites with private bathrooms, 2 apartments
Lire 385,000–420,000 double B&B
Breakfast only
Open all year, Credit cards: all major
Handicap facilities
English spoken well, Region: Lazio
www.karenbrown.com/italy/hotellocarno.html

Trastevere, literally translated as "across the Tiber," is the most delightful and authentically Roman neighborhood of the city's historic center. Tourists flock here to stroll down the narrow cobblestone streets, visit artisans' shops, dine in one of the many excellent sidewalk trattorias, or just to watch the daily life of locals. What pleasure to have discovered the new Hotel Santa Maria, the first accommodation to speak of in the area, which promises to be a winner. Native Romans Paolo and Valentina had the ingenious idea of transforming a plot of open land between the jumble of ancient apartment buildings into a unique one-story hotel with rooms looking out to two courtyards with orange trees. Taking advantage of his experience in architectural studies, Paolo designed the complex himself then supervised the construction, which took four years to complete. The couple welcomes travelers as private houseguests, serving a buffet breakfast with freshly baked cakes either out in the courtyard or in the breakfast room/wine bar. Before going out for dinner in one of many nearby favorite restaurants, guests enjoy a glass of wine with nibbles from a nearby bakery. Contained rooms each with its own entrance to the outside are identically decorated in pale-yellow, with a splash of color on matching bedspreads and curtains, and amenities such as air conditioning, mini bar, and TV. *Directions*: In the heart of Trastevere just behind the famous Piazza Santa Maria, on the tiny Vicolo del Piede. Garage parking available.

HOTEL SANTA MARIA   New
Hosts: Paolo & Valentina Vetere
Vicolo del Piede 2
Rome 00153, Italy
Tel:(06) 5894626, Fax: (06) 5894815
18 rooms with private bathrooms
Lire 220,000–330,000 double B&B
Breakfast only
Open all year, Credit cards: all major
Handicap facilities
English spoken well, Region: Lazio

A welcome addition to the group of family-run city hotels is the Venezia, efficiently run and owned by brother and sister team, Patrizia and Francesco. Although hotels near train stations are generally less desirable, the area around Rome's Termini station has experienced dramatically positive changes, thanks to the city's mayor—there is a high concentration of hotels and offices within refurbished turn-of-the-century-style buildings. Although the Venezia has 61 rooms, it has the feeling of a small and friendly place the moment you enter its doors. Patrizia and Francesco inherited the hotel from their parents and are intent on maintaining their reputable tradition in hospitality. Their mother's passion for collecting antiques such as Orientals rugs and rich period paintings is evident throughout the spacious sitting rooms. A buffet breakfast is served in a room with peach tablecloths and fresh flowers topping tables. Upstairs the spotless rooms are decorated uniformly in white and rose hues with Venetian glass chandeliers, and offer all modern amenities. Patrizia has purposely decorated predominantly with white (even bedspreads), so that any sign of dirt can be spotted immediately. The corner rooms are the most spacious and those on the top floor have small balconies. Centrally located, the hotel is a 15-minute walk to Rome's historical center. In the exact same style is the family's nearby, newly-opened, 26-room Hotel Columbia with its lovely rooftop terrace. *Directions*: Consult a detailed city map—the hotel is to the right of the station.

HOTEL VENEZIA
Hosts: Patrizia & Francesco Diletti
Via Varese 18
Rome 00185, Italy
Tel: (06) 4457101, Fax: (06) 4957687
Email: info@hotelvenezia.com
61 rooms with private bathrooms
Lire 238,000–266,000 double B&B
Breakfast only
Open all year, Credit cards: MC, VS
English spoken well, Region: Lazio
www.karenbrown.com/italy/venezia.html

Behind the city gates of Porta Pinciana, whose ancient walls lead from the Via Veneto, is tranquil, tree-lined Via Nomentana, once a luxurious residential street. Many elegant pastel-colored villas remain (including that of Mussolini), but most have been converted into embassy-owned apartments over the years. The Villa del Parco has been transformed into a lovely and quiet hotel with a bed-and-breakfast feel to it. A flower-edged driveway leads to the villa, passing by tables set up for breakfast in the small front garden. When you enter the pleasant lobby scattered with antiques and comfy sofas, you feel that you've arrived home. Three cozy sitting rooms invite guests to sit and relax. All of the 30 guestrooms, each with private bath, have been renovated and vary greatly in size and decor, which tends to be a mixture of old and new furnishings. Request one of the larger rooms facing out the back of the hotel just in case the street noise might be disturbing. The very cordial Elisabetta Bernardini and her friendly staff are happy to make restaurant and itinerary suggestions. Special features are an elevator, central air, and five nice new bedrooms on the top floor with beamed mansard ceilings. A 24-hour snack bar service is available. *Directions*: Rely on a detailed city map to locate the hotel in a residential district, a 15-minute walk from the city center.

HOTEL VILLA DEL PARCO
Hosts: Bernardini family
Via Nomentana 110
Rome 00161, Italy
Tel: (06) 44237773, Fax: (06) 44237572
Email: villaparco@mclink.it
30 rooms with private bathrooms
Lire 290,000 double B&B
Breakfast only
Open all year
Credit cards: all major
Some English spoken
Region: Lazio
www.karenbrown.com/italy/villadelparco.html

With the momentous occasion of the millenium combined with the Holy Year celebration at the Vatican, a myriad of bed and breakfasts popped up in Rome, among them Villa Delros. Offering hospitality to foreigners is nothing new to Swiss-born Rosemarie Diletti, whose daughter, Patrizia, took over the family's Hotel Venezia in Rome (see listing). With the children grown and busy with their own careers, and because she misses the daily contact with international guests, Rosemarie decided to offer accommodation in the family home on the outskirts of the city. The sprawling, very modern home built in the sixties is located on a small road with other large estates and the property extends to the back overlooking lush green countryside. Two spacious air-conditioned guest suites on the upper floor each have a double bedroom, bathroom, corner kitchenette, sitting room, and large terrace. A third suite is located at garden level. With Rosemarie being an antiques collector, the house is filled to the brim with pieces from the baroque period, as seen in the common rooms downstairs as well as in guestrooms. Breakfast is served out on the terrace looking out to the garden and a swimming pool. Transportation to the local train station is provided and the center of Rome is just 15 minutes away from this quiet location. *Directions*: North of Rome 4 km from the GRA ring highway, Via Livigno is just off the Via Flaminia. Call in advance to arrange pickup at a nearby meeting point.

VILLA DELROS
Hostess: Rosemarie Truninger Diletti
Via Livigno 166
Rome 00188, Italy
Tel: (06) 33679837, Fax: (06) 33678402
Email: info@hotelvenezia.com
3 suites
Lire 300,000 double B&B
Breakfast served, dinner upon request
Open March to December
English spoken very well, Region: Lazio
www.karenbrown.com/italy/delros.html

The spectacular 2,500-acre hilltop farm property of Montestigliano, with its splendid full valley and plain views, is a rich combination of woods, cultivated fields, olive groves, and open meadows all surrounding the hamlet dating from 1730. British-born hostess Susan makes sure guests are comfortable in one of the 11 independent apartments within the various houses scattered about the property. All retain their original Tuscan character in furnishings and have a combination of one to three bedrooms, kitchen, living room with fireplace, and essential modern amenities like washing machines. The granary has been restored and converted into a farm shop, recreation room, and dining room where meals are served upon request from Monday to Friday. Groups of up to 12 persons have the opportunity to reside in the main villa, once owned by nobility. Two swimming pools are at guests' disposal, plus many paths and trails for long countryside walks. Montestigliano is a marvelous base for getting to know in depth a part of Tuscany whose traditions and lifestyles have remained intact, while still having Siena, San Gimignano, Pienza, Montalcino, and the Chianti area at one's fingertips. Plenty of shops and places to dine are available in the towns of Rosia and Sovicille. Weekly customized programs such as cooking courses and specialized itineraries are arranged. *Directions*: From Siena (12 km) take route 73 to Rosia, turning left at the sign for Orgia/Torri. The road up left to Montestigliano is immediately after Stigliano.

MONTESTIGLIANO
Hostess: Susan Pennington
Rosia (SI) 53010, Italy
Tel: (0577) 342013, Fax: (0577) 342100
11 apartments, 1 villa
Lire 770,000–4,954,000 villa weekly
* 925,000–2,650,000 weekly per apartment*
Breakfast & dinner served upon request
Open all year
Fluent English spoken
Region: Tuscany

Parma is without doubt the city internationally most known for its Parmesan cheese and prosciutto ham, which you should not fail to sample while you're in the region. Thirty kilometers from Parma are found the curative thermal waters of Salsomaggiore and just beyond town is the Antica Torre, the ancient 13th-century tower that majestically crowns a hilltop overlooking the soft green countryside. The Pavesi family, proprietors of the surrounding farm, offer warm hospitality to its guests within the tower. One bedroom with bath is located on each of the tower's four floors and, in addition, the family has a large two-bedroom apartment available in the main house, ideal for a family. There are four additional apartments recently added within the stone residence. Rooms are simply decorated, and have lovely views over the valley. The barn has been converted into a pleasant dining room where fortunate guests sit down together to a hearty, homemade, Emiliana-style meal, including fresh pastas, vegetables, meat, and poultry direct from the farm (drinks not included in half-board rate). Amenities include a swimming pool, bicycles, and horses. *Directions*: From Salsomaggiore, go through town, following signs for Cangelasio and then Antica Torre, 3.5 km from Salsomaggiore.

ANTICA TORRE
Hosts: Francesco Pavesi family
Localita: Cangelasio-Case Bussandri 197
Salsomaggiore Terme (PR) 43039, Italy
Tel & fax: (0524) 575425
4 rooms with private bathrooms, 5 apartments
Lire 150,000 double B&B
* 100,000 per person half board*
2-night minimum stay, 1 week July & August
All meals served
Open March to November
Very little English spoken
Region: Emilia-Romagna
www.karenbrown.com/italy/anticatorre.html

Though near both Verona and Lake Garda, the busy Ca'Verde farm with its 120 acres feels far away from civilization, immersed in a wooded valley in the Veneto wine country. Nine families got together in the seventies to purchase the unusual stone Provence-style farmhouse, originally a 15th-century convent, and turned it into a busy dairy farm producing goat cheese and yogurt, as well as olive oil, wine and fruit. They adhere to traditional organic production methods without additives or preservatives. Five attic rooms are available for guests in the enormous U-shaped house where three of the families live. Rooms for two to four people are small and utilitarian, with rustic wood beds, beamed ceilings with skylights, and one clean, modern bathroom for every two rooms. Four new, more comfortable rooms with bathrooms have been added (at a slightly higher rate) to another wing. Regional country fare is prepared by a professional chef and is served in three informal dining rooms with red-checked tablecloths and large fireplaces. Guests dine in or out on the patio, and in the summer are treated to outdoor concerts and cinema. *Directions*: From Verona take the A12 autostrada toward Brennero. Exit at Verona Nord, and follow signs for San Ambrogio. Go through town and start up the hill, watching for a small sign for Ca'Verde on the left side of the road. (15 km total.)

CA'VERDE (Co-op 8 Marzo)
Hostess: Antonella Cozza
Azienda Agricola 8 Marzo
San Ambrogio Valpolicella (VR) 37010, Italy
Tel: (045) 6861760, Fax: (045) 6861245
9 rooms, 4 with private bathrooms
Lire 75,000–120,000 double B&B
All meals served
Open May to October
Some English spoken
Region: Veneto

In the southeastern corner of Tuscany is a delightful, yet-undiscovered pocket of absolutely stunning countryside. It was only natural that Andrea, with his expert culinary skills, and his lovely wife, Cristina, a born hostess, should open a bed and breakfast close to their vast 1,000-acre countryside property producing olive oil, wine, cereals and vegetables. La Crocetta sits at the crossroads leading up to the charming town of San Casciano, offering eight guestrooms above the restaurant within the three-story stone house built in the 1930s. You enter the small restaurant by way of a front porch, where meals are also served, into the cozy reception area set around a large sit-in fireplace. Here within the two dining rooms with soft-pink-colored walls Andrea presents his delectable creations featuring homemade pastas with vegetable fillings. Small guestrooms with varying color schemes, each with a new bathroom, are pleasantly appointed with canopy beds and fresh country fabrics used for bedspreads and curtains. Thermal hot springs with spa treatments and horse-riding facilities are located in the vicinity. Orvieto, Perugia, Siena, and the hilltowns of Montepulciano and Montalcino are all at easy touring distance. *Directions*: From the A1 autostrada, exit at Fabro from the south or Chiusi from the north, traveling towards Sarteano-Cetona, then San Casciano.

LA CROCETTA
Hosts: Cristina & Andrea Leotti
Localita: La Crocetta
San Casciano dei Bagni (SI) 53040, Italy
Tel: (0578) 58360, Cellphone: (0330) 549775
Fax: (0578) 58353
8 rooms with private bathrooms
Lire 184,000 double B&B
  138,000 per person half board
2-night minimum stay, All meals served
Open Easter to November
Credit cards: MC, VS
English spoken well, Region: Tuscany

Perched atop a hill and enjoying a 360-degree view of perfectly unspoiled landscape, including a stunning medieval castle, sits the Le Radici farmhouse. Partners and ex-urbanites, Marcello and Alfredo, carefully chose this peaceful spot in order to offer accommodation to those who truly appreciate nature and the sense of well-being it inspires. The two houses have been restored, maintaining most of the original rustic flavor, and divided into four double rooms, three suites, and two apartments. The apartments include one or two bedrooms, living room with fireplace, kitchenette, and bathroom. Wrought-iron beds and antique furnishings adorn rooms, complemented by wood-beam and brick ceilings. Special attention has been given to landscaping around the immediate property, which includes vineyards and olive groves. The real treat is the absolutely gorgeous "borderless" swimming pool with cascading water, which fits harmoniously into its surroundings. An elegant dinner by candlelight is served within the dining room or out on the terrace, using fresh ingredients direct from the property. The hosts suggest many interesting itineraries in this area, which seems remote, yet is only a short distance from the autostrada and bordering Umbria. One can relax in the thermal waters of San Casciano or venture out to the towns of Orvieto, Todi, or Pienza, among others. *Directions*: From the town of San Casciano follow signs for Le Radici (4 km).

LE RADICI
Hosts: Alfredo Ferrari & Marcello Mancini
San Casciano dei Bagni (SI) 53040, Italy
Tel & fax: (0578) 56038 or tel: (0578) 56033
Cellphone: (0338) 5856890, Email: radici@ftbcc.it
4 rooms, 3 suites, 2 apartments
Lire 170,000–240,000 double B&B
  285,000–320,000 suite B&B
  200,000–320,000 daily per apartment (utilities extra)
2-night minimum stay, Breakfast & dinner served
Open all year, Credit cards: MC, VS
English spoken very well, Region: Tuscany
www.karenbrown.com/italy/radici.html

Agritourism and bed-and-breakfast-type accommodations are virtually nonexistent in the northern lake district, so coming across the enchanting Villa Simplicitas was a special treat. The pale-yellow country house of Milanese family Castelli, run by sister-in-law Ulla, sits isolated high up in the hills between Lakes Como and Lugano and is surrounded by thick woods. There is a wonderful old-fashioned charm to the place, enhanced by many heirloom turn-of-the-century antiques scattered about the cozy living and dining rooms. Pretty floral fabrics cover sofas and armchairs, in perfect harmony with the soft-yellow walls bordered with stenciled designs. The same warmth is spread among the ten guest bedrooms with their pinewood floors and *trompe l'oeil* paneled walls, antique beds, and lace doilies adorning dressers. Innovative meals prepared by local chef Maurizio are served either inside or out on the veranda with green-and-white-striped awnings and matching director's chairs. In the evening, impeccably set tables are candlelit for a romantic dinner for two—simply heavenly. *Directions*: From Como head north to Argegno. Turn left, passing through S. Fedele, then just after town at the first bus station, turn left—it is just 2 km up to the house. Alternatively, call from town.

VILLA SIMPLICITAS
Hosts: Curzio Castelli family
Localita: Simplicitas
San Fedele d'Intelvi (CO) 22028, Italy
Tel: (031) 831132 or (02) 460421
Fax: (02) 460407
10 rooms with private bathrooms
Lire 180,000 double B&B
* 115,000 per person half board*
All meals served
Open May to October
English spoken well
Region: Lombardy

San Gemini, in the southwest corner of Umbria, is a jewel of a medieval village, so perfectly preserved that one can easily imagine what life was like in those times. Home also of the famous mineral water, just outside town there are the fascinating Roman ruins of Carsulae (3rd century B.C.). A very special place from which to explore the area is within one of the apartments of the Medici family, who have divided up the 17th-century palazzo where neoclassical sculptor Antonio Canova once lived. The spacious guest apartment accommodating four to eight persons contains two bedrooms, two new bathrooms, kitchen, living room with fireplace, and dining room. Pleasantly decorated with country antiques, rooms are enhanced by the high-beamed ceilings, tiled brick floors, and pastel-colored walls. The bedrooms look out through noble cypress trees towards the main square while the living room opens out to a courtyard where you can have a meal or just relax. A welcome basket of breakfast fixings is offered guests. Congenial hostess and artisan Nelly greets her guests and is on call for any necessary assistance even though she does not live nearby. Another two-bedroom house is available for rental on her small farm property near Lake Bracciano. *Directions*: From the A1 autostrada, exit at Orte and follow signs for Narni, then San Gemini. Palazzo Canova dominates the main square from above.

PALAZZO CANOVA
Hostess: Nelly Medici
Via del Tribunale 69
San Gemini (TR) 05029, Italy
Tel & fax: (06) 9987358
Email: mariqua@tin.it
Mailing address: Via C.G. Sambuco
Bracciano (RM) 00062, Italy
1 apartment, Lire 700,000–900,000 weekly
2-night minimum stay
No meals served, Open all year
English spoken well, Region: Umbria
www.karenbrown.com/italy/canova.html

Il Casale is a highly efficient and very popular bed and breakfast, thanks to warm and dedicated host, Alessandro, who has combined his extensive hospitality experience with a desire to see his great-grandfather's lovely country property restored properly. Six double rooms and two small apartments including bedroom, kitchen/eating area, and bathroom are all housed within the extended stone farmhouse. Another section is reserved for Alessandro and the family who looks after the wine estate. Access to the guest entrance is through a well-kept garden around the back with a small chapel and lovely views over the soft hills. Main areas include a sitting room and beamed breakfast room with fireplace. The spotless home is appointed with scattered antiques, and the very comfortable guestrooms, each with a different color scheme, have new bathrooms and either countryside views or garden or interior patio entrance. Infinite care to details in both the esthetics and service offered is given to guests. The entrepreneurial Alessandro has now restored the stone barn and cantina over in the olive grove, *Rocca degli Olivi*, creating four lovely bedrooms with either mansard or vaulted ceilings, gorgeous views, and a breakfast room. An inviting swimming pool is hidden among the olive trees. Plenty of tourist information is on hand. *Directions*: From San Gimignano follow signs for Certaldo for 3 km. Il Casale is on the left and well marked.

IL CASALE DEL COTONE
Host: Alessandro Martelli
Localita: Cellole 59
San Gimignano (SI) 53037, Italy
Tel & fax: (0577) 943236, Cellphone: (0348) 3029091
Email: info@casaledelcotone.com
10 rooms with private bathrooms, 2 apartments
Lire 180,000 double B&B
* 180,000–250,000 daily per apartment (no breakfast)*
Breakfast served, dinner upon request
Open all year, Credit cards: AX, VS
English spoken very well, Region: Tuscany
www.karenbrown.com/italy/casaledelcotone.html

Due to the ever-increasing popularity of the stunning medieval village of San Gimignano, accommodations in the surrounding countryside have flourished. La Casanova is a typical square stone farmhouse with wood shutters and red-tile roof, which you'll grow accustomed to seeing throughout Tuscany. The bed and breakfast's exceptional feature is that it enjoys a privileged view of the towers of San Gimignano, an ancient town referred to as the "Manhattan" of the year 1000. Roberto and his wife Monica have updated the bed and breakfast, adding amenities in rooms such as air conditioning, satellite TV, and telephone, and have also installed a swimming pool. Their idea is to offer quality accommodation at competitive rates. Breakfast is served on the outside patio where guests are immersed in breathtaking scenery, before heading out to visit intriguing San Gimignano and the many surrounding villages. This is an authentic and simple wine-producing farm with eight double rooms with private baths and one apartment for two persons. Country furniture characteristic of the region decorates the rooms, whose original architectural features have been preserved. *Directions*: From San Gimignano take the road toward Volterra. After 2 km, turn left at the sign for Casanova, **not** Hotel Pescille.

CASANOVA DI PESCILLE
Hosts: Monica & Roberto Fanciullini
Localita: Pescille
San Gimignano (SI) 53037, Italy
Tel & fax: (0577) 941902
Email: pescille@cybermarket.it
8 rooms with private bathrooms, 1 apartment
Lire 150,000 double B&B
  180,000 apartment daily
Breakfast only
Open all year
No English spoken, Region: Tuscany
www.karenbrown.com/italy/casanovadipescille.html

Accidentally coming upon the Casolare, tucked away in the unpopulated hills 8 kilometers past medieval San Gimignano, was a delightful surprise. Just before reaching the bed and breakfast, you'll see a half-abandoned stone convent dating back to 1100 where the hosts reside. The attractive renovated farmhouse, hosted by Andrea, a former art and antiques dealer, and his Spanish wife, Berta, retains all the features characteristic of the original structure. The five double rooms are extremely comfortable and tastefully appointed. Rooms are divided among the two floors of the house, with one being an independent structure poolside. The two suites for two to four persons with terrace and living room have been decorated with refined antiques as well. Original watercolor paintings by a local artist depicting various local sites adorn an entire wall in the inviting double living room. An extra bonus is the breathtaking swimming pool, with sweeping countryside panorama, surrounded by a manicured lawn, fruit trees, and terra-cotta pots overflowing with pink geraniums. It provides refreshment after a hot day of sightseeing, while you anticipate another appetizing candlelit meal at dusk under the pergola. Berta is an excellent cook and prepares very special Tuscan menus accompanied by an impressive wine list. This is a truly tranquil haven. *Directions*: From San Gimignano follow signs for Montaione. Staying left at the fork, turn left for Libbiano and take the dirt road to the end.

CASOLARE DI LIBBIANO
Hosts: Andrea & Berta Bucciarelli
Localita: Libbiano 3
San Gimignano (SI) 53037, Italy
Tel & fax: (0577) 946002
5 rooms & 2 suites with private bathrooms
Lire 148,000–185,000 per person half board
Breakfast & dinner served
Open Easter to November
Credit cards: MC, VS
English spoken well
Region: Tuscany
www.karenbrown.com/italy/casolaredilibbiano.html

The countryside around San Gimignano is becoming like the Alto Adige mountain area where practically every house offers some kind of accommodation, and the competition has created bed and breakfasts with high standards of quality and service. Among these, Il Rosolaccio (the local name for the poppies that cover the hill in springtime) is an 18th-century typical Tuscan farmhouse perched high above the road between Certaldo and San Gimignano. As expected, the view over the vineyards and hillsides is absolutely breathtaking. After a 30-year career running a hotel in Rome, Ingrid Music, with her son Steven and his Russian wife, Natalie, bought and very carefully restored the house which, by tradition, was added on to each time someone in the family got married. All the right ingredients are included for a perfectly delightful stay, with tastefully decorated bedrooms and apartments perfectly in tune with the simple beauty of the preserved farmhouse, warm and discreet hospitality, and marvelous views to be enjoyed either poolside or at sunset with a glass of wine. Common areas include the vaulted dining room and upstairs cozy living room with huge open fireplace and family antiques. *Directions*: From San Gimignano, follow signs for Certaldo and after 7 km at the number 19-XI road marker, turn right at the sign up to Il Rosolaccio.

IL ROSOLACCIO
Hosts: Ingrid, Natalie & Steven Music
San Benedetto 34
Localita: Capezzano Basso
San Gimignano (SI) 53037, Italy
Tel: (0577) 944465, Fax: (0577) 944467
6 rooms with private bathrooms, 5 apartments
Lire 160,000–175,000 double B&B
  1,150,000–1,950,000 weekly per apartment
Breakfast served, dinner upon request (except Mondays)
Open all year
English spoken fluently
Region: Tuscany

After her parents left their native England to settle into life in Tuscany—a dream shared by many—Maria followed suit, leaving behind a career in marketing. Her parents have been offering hospitality for years in four apartments all within one large house next door to their own called *La Fonte*. Maria bought her own property nearby and opened a bed and breakfast two years ago. Turning off the main road, you immediately find a cluster of small houses, one attached to the other, belonging to several different owners. Her own home is next to the guesthouse (originally the priest's quarters, as the name *Vicario* indicates) and chapel with front courtyard. The five bedrooms upstairs off one long hall all have an en-suite bathroom except one, and are decorated with simple country furniture and wooden beds to complement the worn terra-cotta brick floors. A few of the rooms look out to some woods in back and the rest to the front. A Continental breakfast is served either in a little room downstairs off the living room or out on the patio in front of the house. Easy and economical! *Directions*: From San Gimignano, take the first possible right turn north towards Ulignano and after 3 km, instead of turning right for Ulignano, turn left towards San Benedetto and turn at the sign for Il Vicario.

IL VICARIO
Hostess: Maria Bergamasco
Localita: San Andrea 1
San Gimignano (SI) 53037, Italy
Tel: (0577) 941599, Fax: (0577) 945635
5 rooms with private bathrooms
Lire 130,000 double B&B
Breakfast only
Open all year
English spoken fluently
Region: Tuscany

The increasing popularity of this perfectly intact medieval town and the resulting availability of accommodations have made San Gimignano a hub from which tourists fan out to visit nearby, less-well-known treasures such as Volterra, Colle Val d'Elsa, and Monteriggioni. A pleasant, informal stay is very likely at the Podere Villuzza, run by friendly young Sandra and Gianni Dei who opened the doors of their 150-year-old stone farmhouse to guests after extensive modification. Chairs are set up in front where visitors can enjoy the view of vineyard-covered hills leading up to the impressive multi-towered town. Common areas include the rustic living room with ceramic-tiled tables and fireplace where guests convene after a day of touring. While gregarious Sandra pampers guests, Gianni occupies himself with the production of top-quality olive oil. Six double rooms on ground and first floors accessed by several different entrances are furnished in true country style with a mix of wrought-iron beds and antique armoires, complemented by mansard beamed ceilings and stone walls. Rooms have views out over the countryside and town or over back hills. Also available are three small apartments within the house that include a living area and kitchen for weekly stays. A swimming pool just to the left of the farmhouse is a great bonus for guests. *Directions*: Go through town and follow signs for Certaldo. After 2 km turn right and follow signs for Villuzza.

PODERE VILLUZZA
Hosts: Sandra & Gianni Dei
Strada 25
San Gimignano (SI) 53037, Italy
Tel: (0577) 940585, Fax: (0577) 942247
6 rooms with private bathrooms, 3 apartments
Lire 160,000 double B&B
*   200,000 apartment for 2 persons B&B*
Breakfast only
Open March to November
English spoken well
Region: Tuscany

Bagno Vignoni is a charming little village whose unique piazza is actually an ancient stone pool with thermal water. In medieval times the large bath was divided for men and women who came to soak in the rejuvenating waters, hoping to cure such ailments as arthritis and rheumatism. Today, tourists come to view this remarkable place and take advantage of these same curative properties in the nearby falls or modern pool facilities. With the success of their wine bar (*enoteca*) here, it was only natural that the young Marinis should open a bed and breakfast for travelers. The stone building dates to the 1300s and was thoughtfully restored after having been abandoned for more than 30 years. The eight double bedrooms and large living room with loft and grand piano are very cozy and purposely old-fashioned in feeling. The beamed guestrooms and pretty new bathrooms each have their own theme and corresponding soft pastel color schemes and are romantically appointed with lace curtains and pillows, antique beds and armoires, and painted stencil borders. Breakfast is served across the way in the historic *enoteca*, which was once part of the Capuchin friars' monastery. With its informal and warm hospitality, it is no wonder that the bar is a favorite place for artists and writers. *Directions*: Bagno Vignoni is 5 km south of San Quirico. Park in the town lot and walk the short distance to the *locanda*.

LA LOCANDA DEL LOGGIATO   **New**
Hostesses: Sabrina & Barbara Marini
Piazza del Moretto 30 – Bagno Vignoni
San Quirico d'Orcia (SI) 53023, Italy
Tel: (0577) 888925, Fax: none
Cellphone: (0335) 430427
8 rooms with private bathrooms
Lire 250,000 double B&B
Breakfast served, light dinners on weekends
Open all year
Some English, French spoken
Region: Tuscany

During the 18th century under the rule of Leopoldo II, the flat plains to the south of
Cortona were divided into equal farm lots, each having a rectangular-shaped farmhouse
topped with pigeon loft, called *case Leopoliane*. Silvana and Giovanni Bianchi had one
of these homes restored, transforming the former stables on the ground floor into an
elegant restaurant and the first floor into their private quarters along with five guest
apartments. The comfortable apartments for two to six persons are of varying dimensions
and include either one or two bedrooms, bathroom, and living room with kitchenette.
Each is decorated individually with a mix of family antiques and newer reproductions. A
well-known chef from a five-star hotel prepares delicately innovative Tuscan meals for
the dining room with its brick-trim arches and antique rose-colored tablecloths. Meals
are accompanied by an extensive wine list as well as the Bianchis' own production of
wines. Cooking and wine lessons along with organized daily itineraries are arranged for
groups of six or more. A garden lined with overflowing terra-cotta vases of flowers leads
to an enclosed swimming pool. An excellently located base for both Umbria and parts of
Tuscany. *Directions*: Exit from autostrada A1 at Valchiana and head towards Perugia.
Leave this highway at Foiano-Cortona and follow signs to Agrisalotto.

AGRISALOTTO
Hosts: Silvana & Giovanni Bianchi
Localita: Burcinella 88
Santa Caterina di Cortona (AR) 52040, Italy
Tel & fax: (0575) 617417,
Cellphone: (0338) 7378393
Email: agrisalotto@interfree.it
5 apartments
Lire 250,000–450,000 daily per apartment
  1,000,000–1,700,000 weekly July & August
Breakfast & dinner served, Closed November
Some English & French spoken, Region: Tuscany
www.karenbrown.com/italy/agrisalotto.html

Right in the heart of the chic (and expensive) Italian Riviera is a small jewel of a bed and breakfast, hugging the hillside high above the ports of Portofino and Santa Margherita. The young host, Roberto, has restored almost single-handedly the two small stone farmhouses on a piece of his grandfather's property. Nine tastefully decorated double rooms are divided between the two houses, each with private bath, scattered antiques, and lovely panoramic views over the olive trees and fruit orchards and down to the sea. A cozy living room, inviting one to curl up with a book or converse, gives visitors the feeling of being at the home of friends. The ambiance is intimate and welcoming. In the small, beamed dining room or out in the panoramic terraced garden, breakfast and dinner (featuring local specialties such as the famous fresh pesto sauce) are served and prepared by Roberto himself while his darling wife, Simona, serves and attends to guests. From Genoa to the marvels of Cinque Terre, the Ligurian coast holds some very special treasures, and the Gnocchi makes a perfect and very reasonable place from which to discover them. Arrival accepted after 5 pm. *Directions*: From Santa Margherita follow signs to Genova/S. Lorenzo uphill for about 4 km until you see a blue sign indicating an intersection. Just after the sign, about 90 meters before the intersection, take the narrow, winding road on the left with the red-and-white gate down to the end.

VILLA GNOCCHI
Hosts: Simona & Roberto Gnocchi
Via Romana 53
Santa Margherita (GE) 16038, Italy
Tel & fax: (0185) 283431, Cellphone: (0333) 6191898
Email: roberto.gnocchi@tin.it
9 rooms with private bathrooms
Lire 160,000 double B&B
  110,000 per person half board
Breakfast & dinner served
Open Easter to October 17
English spoken well, Region: Liguria
www.karenbrown.com/italy/villagnocchi.html

Bed & Breakfast Descriptions   209

As more travelers realize how close together destinations of interest throughout Italy are, weekly house rentals to use as a home base for excursions have become more popular. One such ideal base is La Sovana, bordering Tuscany and Umbria and equidistant to Siena, Perugia, Assisi, Arezzo, and many other smaller hilltowns such as Montepulciano, Pienza, and Montalcino—the area where Italy's finest wines are produced. Two stone farmhouses were carefully restored to provide comfortable suites for two to six people. Tastefully decorated with local antique beds and armoires, matching floral bedspreads and curtains, each has a fully equipped kitchenette and eating and living area. Guests can dine by candlelight in the dining room in the main house, whose enormous arched window takes in the expansive view of vineyards, wheat fields, and impeccable landscaping. Giovannella and Giuseppe Olivi, dedicated and amiable hosts, and their two children, Riccardo and Francesca, dine with their guests each evening. Potted flowers abound around the farmhouses and pool, where on Saturday nights a sumptuous barbecue is organized to enable guests to meet one another. Two tennis courts, a small fishing lake, and bikes are available. There are additional bi-level suites in a large converted barn in the woods a short walk away from the main farmhouse. *Directions*: Just 2 km from the Chiusi exit of the A1 autostrada. La Sovana is just before Sarteano on the right.

LA SOVANA
Hosts: Giuseppe Olivi family
Localita: Sovana
Sarteano (SI) 53047, Italy
Tel: (0578) 274086, Booking tel & fax: (075) 600197
Email: info@lasovana.com
15 suites
Lire 105,000–155,000 per person B&B
*   150,000–200,000 per person half board*
3-night minimum stay, All meals served
Closed January & November
Some English spoken, Region: Tuscany
www.karenbrown.com/italy/lasovana.html

The stately 16th-century home of Fabio, Italian businessman from Padua, and Yuri, his Japanese wife, painter and musician, is conveniently situated close to many highlights of Tuscany. Their combination of cultures is reflected throughout the decor of the home which they have opened as a very comfortable and refined bed and breakfast. Practically the entire house is open to guests who are made to feel at home in any one of the common areas—living room, terrace, veranda breakfast room overlooking a manicured garden, or swimming pool. The distinguished and impeccable home is appointed with selected antiques, white sofas, Oriental carpets, grand piano, and Yuri's hand-painted porcelain. Four pristine and spacious bedrooms upstairs each have apricot marble bathrooms and elegant touches such as brocaded bedspreads and draperies, wrought-iron fixtures, and gilded mirrors. The suite has a palatial bathroom with Jacuzzi and features a large terrace taking in a sweeping, panoramic view of the unspoiled countryside. From this idyllic location, both highlights of southern Tuscan hilltowns and Umbria are at one's fingertips. *Directions*: From the center of Sarteano follow signs for Chianciano and after 3 km turn right at the sign for Villa Iris. It is the first house on the left.

VILLA IRIS
Hosts: Yuri Hashimoto & Fabio Moretto
Strada Palazzo di Piero 1
Sarteano (SI) 53047, Italy
Tel: (0578) 266111, Fax: (0578) 265993
Email: villairis@ftbcc.it
4 rooms, 1 suite, all with private bathrooms
Lire 250,000–290,000 double B&B
* 350,000 suite*
2-night minimum stay
Breakfast only
Open April to October
Credit cards: all major
English spoken well, Region: Tuscany
www.karenbrown.com/italy/iris.html

Tenuta La Bandita is set amid 150 acres of woods, olive groves, orchards, and meadows within a beautifully undisturbed area south of Livorno near the sea. Dino and Daniela, with their former business and hotel experience, bought the estate not long ago and are in the process of gradually bringing it back to its past splendor. There is certainly plenty to keep them busy since the property includes six additional farmhouses surrounding the 17th-century main villa where most of the guest bedrooms are situated. Their idea was to transform the villa into a bed and breakfast while leaving as much as possible of the original structure and atmosphere of the private residence intact. This was made easier by the fact that the home came with ten furnished bedrooms with bathrooms, situated down one long corridor. The rooms are appointed with original period furniture, chandeliers, and matching drapes and bedspreads. Guests can lounge on the front terrace or in the spacious arched living and dining room downstairs with gray-stone fireplace and framed portraits. Nine additional rooms with private bathrooms are divided within two adjacent houses, between the villa and swimming pool. The formal villa contrasts with the more rugged and natural surrounding landscapes. *Directions*: Exit from S.S.1 at Donoratico and head for Sassetta/Castagneto for 11 km on a winding mountain road. Take the turnoff left for Laderello/Monteverdi (not Sassetta) for 1 km to the La Bandita property. Pass through the gate and go past the first group of houses to the villa.

TENUTA LA BANDITA
Hosts: Daniela & Dino Filippi
Via Campagna Nord 30
Sassetta (LI) 57020, Italy
Tel: (0565) 794224, Fax: (0565) 794350
Email: bandita@tin.it
19 rooms with private bathrooms
Lire 140,000–240,000 double B&B
Breakfast & dinner served
Open April to November, Credit cards: all major
Some English, French, German spoken, Region: Tuscany
www.karenbrown.com/italy/tenutalabandita.html

Saturnia's thermal waters have been gushing from an underground volcano for over 2,000 years, yet only recently have it and the enchanting surrounding Maremma area become internationally famous, leading to new accommodations springing up. One such is the charming Villa Clodia, once home to nobility, now run by former restaurateur Giancarlo Ghezzi. The villa is a curiosity, seemingly built out of the limestone rock, one side overlooking the street and the other an expansive valley of grapevines and olive trees. Because of its unusual proportions, each room is unique in size and decor. A small winding stairway takes guests up or down to rooms, some of which have been literally carved out of the rock. All recently refreshened bedrooms feature scattered antiques, new bathrooms, and valley views, and a fortunate few boast a terrace. Amenities include air conditioning, TVs, and mini bars. Breakfast is offered in a sweet, luminous room next to the sitting room. A lush rose garden and fruit orchard surround the inviting star-shaped pool. Advance reservations are a must and weekly stays preferred. *Directions*: From Rome take the Aurelia highway north, turning off to the right at Vulci following signs for Manciano, Montemerano, and Saturnia. Villa Clodia is in the middle of town.

VILLA CLODIA
Host. Giancarlo Ghezzi
Via Italia 43
Saturnia (GR) 58050, Italy
Tel: (0564) 601212, Fax: (0564) 601305
10 rooms with private bathrooms
Lire 150,000 double B&B
  180,000 suite B&B
3-night minimum stay
Breakfast only
Closed February
Credit cards: VS
English spoken well
Region: Tuscany

North of the beautifully austere ancient city of Bergamo, at the foothills of the Ortighera mountain range right on the River Brembo is the farm property of young local couple, Cinzia and Ferdy Quateroni. They bought the stone farmhouse at the edge of thick woods, which dates to 1850, and completely restored it to include four guestrooms, their private quarters, dining rooms, and small store where they sell their home-produced goat cheeses. The cabin-like bedrooms on the two upper floors are simply decorated in tune with the natural features of the house: stone walls, wood-beamed ceilings, and brick floors. Downstairs in the cozy, arched, stone-walled dining room with large fireplace, gregarious Cinzia serves excellent local fare and an ample breakfast with freshly baked cakes and breads. This is a nature lover's paradise where Ferdy sees to the goats and organizes itineraries by mountain bike, horse, or foot while nearby there are several ski resorts. This is a perfect vacation spot for families. *Directions*: From the A4 autostrada exit at Dalmine (35 km), heading north for Vila d'Alme, San Pellegrino, San Giovanni, and Scalvino. Ten km after San Pellegrino, the source of the famous mineral water, park on the right-hand side of road at the *agriturismo* sign and cross over the footbridge up to the house.

FERDY   **New**
Hosts: Cinzia & Ferdy Quateroni
Localita: Scalvino
Lenna (BG) 24010, Italy
Tel & fax: (0345) 82235
4 rooms with private bathrooms
Lire 120,000 double B&B
  85,000 per person half board
Breakfast & dinner served
Open all year
Some English spoken
Region: Lombardy

Luciana and Luigi from Rome are pioneers in offering accommodation in Sabina, taking advantage of the lovely inherited piece of property, which they have brought back to life in their early retirement. Gregarious Luciana, a former flight attendant, is the hostess *par excellence*. She goes out of her way to see that guests' needs are taken care of and checks their mood and energy level each morning before suggesting one of her many fascinating local itineraries and events—enough to keep one busy touring for a couple of weeks! Accommodation is offered in a variety of apartments divided between the main villa and the well-restored farmhouse down the hill. Each has one or two bedrooms, bathroom, kitchenette, and eating area, while a double living room with enormous stone fireplace is reserved for all guests. The cozy country decor, with its stenciled borders and mix of family antiques, is the result of Luciana's good taste. Apartments on ground and second floors (some with terraces) take in views of the sweeping valley below. Rooms in the villa are more elegant with frescoed ceilings, panoramic terraces, and antique furnishings. In addition to producing wine, olive oil, and fruit, Luigi oversees the business/hobby of raising thoroughbred horses. Luciana also arranges interesting walking tours and courses in Italian and cooking. *Directions*: From Rome, exit from the A1 autostrada at Ponzano Romano/Soratte (new exit and not marked on maps) after the Fiano exit. Drive towards Stimigliano Scalo, turn right in town, and continue until the turnoff left for Forano. After Forano turn left for Selci and before town, turn right on Via Vallerosa.

VILLA VALLEROSA
Hosts: Luciana Pancera & Luigi Giuseppi
Via di Vallerosa 27
Selci Sabino (RI) 02040, Italy
Tel & fax: (0765) 519179
8 apartments
Lire 180,000–350,000 daily per apartment
2-night minimum stay, 1 week high season
No meals served, Open all year
English spoken well, Region: Lazio

Wandering off the main tourist trail in Sicily is recommended for the traveler who truly enjoys contact with local people and their culture (best to have some command of Italian) and is curious and open to new experiences, without being tied to rigid schedules. If you leave yourselves in the hands of the Contes, you will certainly be rewarded with a once-in-a-lifetime stay. Reaching Gangi is an adventure in itself, taking you far away from the main route through the scenic Madonie Mountains cutting across the mid-northern part of Sicily. Villa Raino is just outside Gangi, with its tightly packed houses covering the tip of a mountaintop. Genuine host, Aldo, left the family hotel business in town and restored this 100-year-old brick house once owned by a noble family, offering an excellent countryside restaurant for local families and city people coming from as far away as Palermo. On first and second floors there are ten unique rooms with mansard ceilings, some having a small balcony. A mix of family antiques is scattered about the rooms, which have Tiffany bedside lamps and walls stenciled using an ancient technique giving the effect of floral wallpaper. Bathrooms have brightly colored tiles. All in all Villa Raino provides a delightful opportunity to explore unknown territory. *Directions*: From A19 exit at Tre Monzelli and follow S.S.120 to Gangi for 38 km. A sign before town takes you down a rough, unpaved road to the property.

VILLA RAINO
Hosts: Nina & Aldo Conte
Contrada Raino
Gangi (PA) 90024, Sicily, Italy
Tel: (0921) 644680, Fax: (0921) 644424
Email: villaraino@citiesonline.it
10 rooms with private bathrooms
Lire 130,000 double B&B
All meals served
Open all year, Credit cards: AX
Some English spoken
Region: Sicily
www.karenbrown.com/italy/raino.html

On the southwestern coast between the archaeological ruins of Selinunte and Sciacca with its hot springs, lies the anonymous town of Menfi. Menfi was virtually destroyed in the earthquake of 1968, and consequently is a mix of new construction and devastated areas still awaiting government funds. In the very center of all this sits the splendid 18th-century palazzo of the noble Ravida family, which miraculously survived disaster. One enters the front iron gates from the city street to discover a large stone courtyard with palm trees leading to the U-shaped villa with its solid Doric stone columns. The congenial Baron and his wife, who are in residence seasonally as they live in Rome, offer hospitality in lovely rooms within the villa and garden house wing. The bedrooms are in perfect harmony with the general feeling of the home. There is a perfume of the past as you wander through the frescoed sitting rooms filled with ancestral paintings and period antiques worn by time. Fortunately for guests, the gracious hosts are experts in itineraries throughout Sicily. Their large agricultural property at a short distance from town comprises vineyards, and vast citrus and olive groves. With hundreds of years of tradition in producing oil, it is no wonder that Ravida has received national and international recognition (International Olive Oil Council) as the best producer in Sicily. They also host a week-long cooking course combining daily outings. *Directions*: Follow signs to the center of Menfi and ask for Via Roma or Villa Ravida.

VILLA RAVIDA
Hosts: Nicola & Ninni Ravida
Via Roma 173
Menfi (AG) 92013, Sicily, Italy
Tel: (0925) 71109 or 75836, Fax: (0925) 71180
6 rooms, 4 with private bathrooms
Lire 200,000–240,000 double B&B
Breakfast & occasional dinner served
3-night minimum stay, Closed August 5 to 20
English spoken well
Region: Sicily

The Alcala farm, made up of citrus and olive groves, vineyards, wheat crops, and a wide variety of fruit trees, extends over 75 acres of fertile plain backdropped by the Etna volcano—a picture-perfect setting. Cordial hostess Anna Sapuppo and her young family have taken over the family's agricultural business and have added the hospitality activity as well. The main house is a turn-of-the-century *masseria*, built in several sections, while guests are situated nearby in four different apartment setups (one has handicapped facilities) for two to six persons. Two of them are separate houses and all have terraces of varying dimensions. They include living room areas and kitchenettes and are simply decorated with floral sofas and a mix of modern and old family furniture. Although breakfast is not served, guests can help themselves to plenty of fruits. An occasional typically Sicilian dinner is served in the fascinating rustic wine cantina with its enormous wooden wine barrels or by request in your apartment. Anna, a native Sicilian, gladly assists her guests with touring suggestions, which include Catania city (important where **not** to go), the Taormina coast, Siracusa, Etna National Park, and the temples of Agrigento. *Directions*: Take autostrada A19 from Catania and leave at the first exit for Motta S. Anastasia. Turn left, backtracking towards Catania on route 192, pass the US army base, then turn left again at the Alcala sign (milestone 78)—go to the end of the road.

ALCALA
Hosts: Anna Sappupo family
Casella Postale 100
Misterbianco (CT) 95045, Sicily, Italy
Tel & fax: (095) 7130029, Cellphone: (0368) 3469206
4 apartments
Lire 40,000–60,000 per person daily (depending on apt size)
3-night minimum, 1 week July, August, Easter & Christmas
Dinner served upon request
Open all year, Credit cards: MC, VS
Handicap facilities
English spoken well, Region: Sicily
www.karenbrown.com/italy/alcala.html

The coastal stretch from Messina to Cefalu has special appeal to the off-the-beaten-track traveler who will find the perfect place to stay at Casa Migliaca, a 200-year-old farmhouse nestling in the wooded hills 7 kilometers off the main road. This stone house just outside town, owned by Maria Teresa and Sebastiano, who left the city several years ago in favor of a rural lifestyle, offers a lovely sweeping view over olive and citrus groves down to the sea. The very congenial hosts love to converse with guests around the kitchen table or down in the cool dining room (originally the oil press room) around the press wheel. A special effort was made to keep everything possible intact, giving the house its own very distinct charm, maintaining all original floors, ceilings, beams, kitchen tiles, and furniture, although new bathrooms have been incorporated in most of the rooms. There are even extra showers out in the garden! Guests are offered a choice of three double bedrooms upstairs or five downstairs. For those who desire direct contact with Sicilian culture, Casa Migliaca is a truly memorable experience. *Directions*: From coastal route number 113, just 25 km after Cefalu, turn right at the sign for Pettineo and follow it right past town . Just after a gas station, turn right on a descending gravel road to the house (unmarked) 300 meters from Pettineo.

CASA MIGLIACA
Hostess: Maria Teresa Allegra
Contrada Migliaca
Pettineo (ME) 98070, Sicily, Italy
Tel:(0921) 336722, Fax:(0921)391107
Cellphone: (0335) 8430645
Email: info@casamigliaca.com
8 rooms with private bathrooms
Lire 95,000–105,000 per person half board
Breakfast & dinner served
Open all year, Credit cards: all major
English spoken well
Region: Sicily
www.karenbrown.com/italy/casamigliaca.html

For those who prefer the intimacy of a small pensione, native Salvatore and his amiable Panamanian wife Marisin await you with open arms. The pale-yellow three-story house sits in the quaint town of Scopello with its piazza and three streets. From ancient times this was an important fishing center especially for tuna, and the *Tonnara* stone fishing station down by the sea still stands as proof. The entrance hall is a combination breakfast and dining room with a sitting area in the corner around the fireplace. A central staircase leads up to guestrooms, a few with balconies facing out to the distant sea. The rooms are simply appointed with light-wood armoires, wrought-iron beds, and crocheted white bedspreads. In the evening after a day at the seaside or touring, you come "home" to a delicious three-course home-cooked meal of fresh fish or meat and vegetables from their garden. Enthusiastic Marisin spends time chatting with her guests and advising them what to visit in this culturally rich area. "Must sees" include the ancient town of Erice, the ruins of Segesta, Selinunte, and Agrigento. Well-marked hiking trails cover the spectacularly beautiful Zingaro Nature Reserve along the northern coast (one of its kind in Sicily). *Directions*: From Palermo, exit from autostrada A29 at Castellammare and follow signs for Scopello. The pensione is found just after the bar with outdoor tables.

PENSIONE TRANCHINA
Hosts: Marisin & Salvatore Tranchina
Via A. Diaz 7
Scopello (TP) 91014, Sicily, Italy
Tel & fax: (0924) 541099
10 rooms with private bathrooms
Lire 105,000–140,000 double B&B
  85,000–105,000 per person half board (high season)
Breakfast & dinner served
Open all year
Credit cards: all major
English spoken fluently
Region: Sicily
www.karenbrown.com/italy/pensionetranchina.html

The Limoneto was recommended to us by a reader who raved about the "open arms" hospitality, the excellent meals, comfortable accommodations, and proximity to fascinating Siracusa. We have to agree. At just 10 kilometers from the historical center of Siracusa with its Greek and Roman influences, the orange- and olive-grove farm is a perfectly delightful, safe, and economical base from which to explore Sicily's southeastern corner. Adelina, Alceste, and son, Francesco, make guests part of their family. Guestrooms are split between the refurbished barn and part of the main house, all with individual entrances. Rooms, some for up to four persons, are new with pleasant modern decor and all have spotless bathrooms. Dinner is served either in the spacious dining room where locals come for a Sunday meal, or out in the back garden. You are welcome into Adelina's kitchen to observe and participate in the making of typical regional meals using ingredients fresh from her garden. The warmth exudes and when the evening is just right and the limoncello flowing, she might even read some poetry. Truly unique is the boat tour on the river among the *Papiro* trees of Egyptian origin. *Directions*: From Catania, take the autostrada to Siracusa sud Floridia Solarino exit. Drive towards Floridia on the S124 and turn left at the first intersection for Canicattini B. At the T-junction turn right again for Canicattini: the house is on the left after 4 km.

LIMONETO
Hosts: Alceste & Adelina Norcia
Via del Platano 3, Postal address: Viale Teracati 142
Siracusa (SC) 96100, Sicily, Italy
Tel & fax: (0931) 717352
Email: limoneto@tin.it
8 rooms with private bathrooms
Lire 120,000 double B&B
* 90,000 per person half board*
3-night minimum stay
All meals served, Closed November
Some English spoken, Region: Sicily
www.karenbrown.com/italy/limoneto.html

Taormina is on what could be referred to as the Amalfi coast of Sicily and, although the town is lovely and rich with history, it is very touristy. This of course means that rates are on the high side, but, happily, the Villa Schuler makes it affordable and its location and service are superb. The villa was converted from a private residence to a hotel by the Schuler family at the turn of the century and now grandson Gerardo is the proud owner. The pink façade faces out to the street and has a large raised terrace with potted flowers, palms, and cypresses. A Continental or full breakfast is served either here or in the gazebo where you can enjoy open views encompassing the coastline and the peak of the Etna volcano. To the back is a large and enchanting garden filled with a profusion of jasmine, bougainvillea, and geraniums with several quiet places to sit in the shade. The garden gives directly onto the main street of town and it is just a short walk to the cable car that takes you down to the beach where guests gain free entrance (or you may take the shuttle service). Luminous rooms and five new mansard junior suites have been updated over the past years, all with new bathrooms. Suites have everything, including air conditioning, satellite TVs, safes, and terraces with sea views. For its efficient service, ideal location, and incredibly low rate, the Villa Schuler is a winner. *Directions*: Follow signs through town to the hotel.

VILLA SCHULER
Hosts: Gerardo Schuler family
Via Roma 2
Taormina (ME) 98039, Sicily, Italy
Tel: (0942) 23481, Fax: (0942) 23522
Email: info@villaschuler.com
26 rooms, 5 junior suites with private bathrooms
Lire 180,000 double B&B
  230,000 suite B&B
Breakfast only, Open March to November
English spoken well, Region: Sicily
www.karenbrown.com/italy/villaschuler.html

So very close to Siena, yet having the advantage of countryside tranquillity is the elegant Villa dei Lecci of the Albuzza sisters from Milan. The enterprising and energetic pair left their city careers to resettle in Tuscany, totally renovating an abandoned 17th-century country home to create an upscale bed and breakfast and an intimate and romantic retreat for couples. The yellow bedroom downstairs is a suite with large bathroom adjacent to the frescoed dining room where a generous breakfast is served. A candlelit dinner can also be had upon request here or out in the garden gazebo. Upstairs, where the noble proprietors once lived, the quarters are more elaborate, with painted, wood-paneled ceilings and a large living room and library filled with fine antiques. The Victorian-style Peach Room has floral wallpaper, lace curtains, and silver-framed family photos, while the Alcove Suite is done in golden tones and rich fabrics. Adding to guests' indulgence are a hot tub, exercise room, and sitting area in a frescoed veranda. Altogether a delightful splurge and an excellent base for touring Tuscany. *Directions*: Exit the A1 autostrada at Val di Chiana and take 326 to Siena. Continue straight on to the Siena Est exit, arriving at Due Ponti. Take a sharp right at Bar Due Ponti onto Strada Pieve al Bozone for 2.5 km, turning left at the crucifix onto an unpaved road, Strada di Larniano. Continue 1.8 km to the end of the road and up to the gate of the stone villa.

VILLA DEI LECCI   **New**
Hostesses: Miki & Marika Albuzza
Strada di Larniano 21/1
Siena 53100, Italy
Tel & fax: (0577) 221126
Cellphone: (0339) 1543743
4 rooms with private bathrooms
Lire 400,000 suite B&B
3-night minimum stay
Breakfast & dinner served, Open all year
English spoken well
Region: Tuscany

There is a beautiful stretch of coastline on the Adriatic Sea just south of Ancona, dramatically different from the more flat, uninteresting shoreline to the north and south with its modern hotels and condos. The quaint stone village of Sirolo sits high above the water on a mountainside looking down to the beaches of the Riviera Conero. Delightful seafood restaurants dot the shore, where you might enjoy a plate of pasta with fresh clams while watching the tide come in. Isabella and Giorgio decided several years ago to open a bed and breakfast in 14th-century Sirolo, and offer seven guestrooms above their small, quaint, peach-colored restaurant. The Locanda, dating to 1300, being actually part of the town's walls and arched entryway, is of great architectural and historical importance, so it has taken them many years to acquire permits to restore and renovate rooms. Their patience has paid off and their updated bed and breakfast, respecting the original structure, is a true charmer. Bedrooms, most with sea views, have exposed stone walls and terra-cotta floors showing off wrought-iron beds and antique armoires. Amenities such as air conditioning, telephone, TV, mini bar, and hairdryer were added for guests' comfort. Also available are two apartments nearby overlooking the park and sea for stays of four nights or more. Isabella's highly praised meals feature seafood dishes. *Directions*: The Rocco sits at the edge of the town of Sirolo, after Portonovo.

LOCANDA ROCCO
Hosts: Isabella & Giorgio Tridenti
Via Torrione 1
Sirolo (AN) 60020, Italy
Tel & fax: (071) 9330558
7 rooms with private bathrooms, 2 apartments
Lire 200,000–250,000 double B&B
 160,000–180,000 per person half board
All meals served
Open February to November
Credit cards: MC, VS
Some English spoken, Region: Marches

The real fascination about the gorgeous Val Gardena mountain resort area is that you can actually ski from one connecting valley to the next and end up at the end of the day over near Cortina. Siusi is a convenient place to set up camp in any season. The Aquila Nera with its excellent restaurant and amenities of a hotel is steps up from the very economical bed and breakfast choices of the region. The very cordial Mutschlechner family, with a long tradition in the hospitality business, renovated most of the former private home whose origins date back to 1518. A second building was added on, creating additional rooms (and an elevator), which are freshly new with light-wood furnishings and cheerful fabrics. Downstairs common rooms include a luminous sitting area, a *stube*, breakfast room completely paneled in wood including floor and ceiling, and large contemporary dining room where five-course dinners are served based on a combination of Italian and southern Tyrolean recipes. A small swimming pool at the back, plus sauna, steam bath, and free shuttle to the lifts are added extras. *Directions*: Turn into the main street of town, Via Santner, and take the first right to Via Laurin.

AQUILA NERA
Hosts: Mutschlechner family
Via Laurin 7
Siusi allo Sciliar (BZ) 39040, Italy
Tel: (0471) 706146, Fax: (0471) 706335
20 rooms with private bathrooms
Lire 156,000–274,000 double B&B
* 90,000–150,000 per person half board*
All meals served
Closed April 1 to May 25, Nov 1 to Dec 25
Credit cards: all major
Some English spoken
Region: Trentino-Alto Adige

The Kristiania is a typical bed and breakfast (or *garni* as they are called here) of the Dolomite mountain region west of Cortina where a German dialect is the common language. The area is a favorite among Italians, especially in August when swarms of natives flock here to relax in cooler temperatures, enjoy the scenery, and take advantage of the lower rates. Located in the town of Siusi, near the spectacular Siusi Alps known for its excellent cross-country skiing and hiking trails, the white stucco and wood chalet-style home of the Fill family is surrounded by a garden and looks up to the rocky peaks of the Sciliar. The decor varies minimally from house to house in this area and the Kristiania, as with most of the others, uses wood paneling on walls and ceilings (linoleum floors) as the basic decor. The breakfast room is the common room, with a corner table set around the wood-burning stove heater. All rooms have balconies lined with geranium flowerboxes in the summer and there is also a sauna for guests. The area is truly paradise for nature lovers. *Directions*: Turn into the center of Siusi on Via Santner and turn left at the first street, Via Burgfrieden.

GARNI KRISTIANIA
Host: Josef Fill
Via Burgfrieden 13
Siusi allo Sciliar (BZ) 39040, Italy
Tel: (0471) 706439, Fax: none
10 rooms with private bathrooms
Lire 90,000–104,000 double B&B
Breakfast only
Open all year
No English spoken (German)
Region: Trentino-Alto Adige

To the west of Cortina, the most fashionable ski area in the Dolomites, is Val Gardena, which is almost too storybook-perfect to be true. The valley, once part of Austria, still preserves its Germanic heritage in its language, cuisine, and culture. This very typical bed and breakfast is owned and run by a local couple with four children. The crisp-white house with its old stone-and-wood attached barn has been in the same family for over 400 years and has been renovated gradually over the years. The entrance foyer walls are adorned with antique farm tools, harnesses, and cow bells. On the same floor is a dining room with individual tables where guests enjoy breakfast with a view of the velvet green hillside. The five guestrooms, all but one with snug private shower, are basic and comfortable, furnished with pinewood beds and armoires, bright-orange curtains, and fluffy comforters. Stepping out on the balcony reveals a breathtaking panorama of the pine-covered mountains and dramatic peaks of the Sciliar. The Riers are happy to suggest scenic places to explore by car or on foot (although communication is limited), and know the best places for rock climbing up into one of the most spectacular ranges in Europe. *Directions*: Exit at Bolzano Nord from the Verona-Brennero autostrada and follow signs for Siusi. Beyond town, before Castelrotto, turn right for Alpe de Suisi and San Valentino, and after 1 km make a sharp left turn for Marmsolerhof. Use the back door—grandma lives on the ground floor.

MARMSOLERHOF
Hosts: August Rier family
San Valentino 35
Siusi allo Sciliar (BZ) 39040, Italy
Tel & fax: (0471) 706514
5 rooms, 4 with private bathrooms
Lire 90,000 double B&B
Breakfast only
Open all year
Very little English spoken (German)
Region: Trentino-Alto Adige

In yet another lesser-known pocket of Tuscany halfway between Siena and the sea is the absolutely stunning 1,000-acre property of the Visconti family. Dating back to the 1400s, in its heyday it was a village in itself, complete with the noble family's main villa, farmers' houses, church, nuns' quarters, oil press, and blacksmith and carpenter's shops. These stone buildings are all attached to the villa in a U-shape formation with a beautiful formal garden within. Terra-cotta pots with lemon trees and red geraniums give spots of color among the greenery. Vitaliano and Vittoria, the gracious hosts, whose home has been in the same family since its origins, welcome guests in the restored part of the villa where ten new rooms with private bathrooms have been created including three large triples. All with beamed ceilings and brick floors, they are simply appointed with beds and armoires, looking out either to the garden or woods at the back. Common areas are the living room with enormous fireplace, the dining room where delectable Tuscan country meals are served (35,000 lire), and an upstairs loggia with a panoramic view over the pool and countryside that seems to take in all of Tuscany. Also available on the property are three apartments within two farmhouses for weekly stays. For those who enjoy spectacular scenery in a very special, historical setting, this is the place. *Directions*: From the Florence-Siena highway exit at Colle Val d'Elsa Sud. Follow signs for Grosseto-Radicondoli-Castelnuova Val di Cecina, then Fattoria Solaio.

FATTORIA SOLAIO
Hosts: Vittoria & Vitaliano Visconti
Radicondoli (SI) 53030, Italy
Tel: (0577) 791029, Fax: (0577) 791015
Email: info@fattoriasolaio.it
10 rooms with private bathrooms, 3 apartments
Lire 150,000 double B&B
  1,000,000–1,200,000 weekly per apartment
2-night minimum stay, Breakfast & dinner served
Open all year
English spoken well, Region: Tuscany
www.karenbrown.com/italy/fattoriasolaio.html

The town of Spoleto has gained international fame thanks to the July *Due Mondi* festival, a month-long series of cultural events including ballet, theater, opera, and concerts with renowned artists, which attracts a worldwide audience. Accommodations are reserved from one year to the next. For the rest of the year, however, Spoleto holds its own along with nearby Assisi, Spello, Todi, and Perugia as an enchanting medieval stone town, rich in its historical past. The 14th-century Palazzo Dragoni, situated on a quiet little street in the heart of the town near the famous cathedral, was completely renovated by the Diotallevi family and offers charming accommodation within 15 bedrooms. Son Roberto manages both the bed and breakfast and the main bar in town, while his parents reside in a section of the Palazzo. The spacious bedrooms (larger ones are considered suites) are spread out among the three floors, reached by elevator, and have new bathrooms and many modern amenities including air conditioning. Everything possible has been done to maintain the original architecture and ambiance of a private home, with vaulted and frescoed high ceilings, antique furnishings, Oriental carpets, and Murano chandeliers. The real treat is breakfast served in the glassed in loggia, taking in splendid views of the tiled rooftops and bell tower of the Duomo. *Directions*: Follow signs for the center of Spoleto, by way of Via P. Bonitti, passing the football field (*campo sportivo*). Follow yellow signs for the hotel.

PALAZZO DRAGONI
Hosts: Roberto Diotallevi family
Via del Duomo 13
Spoleto (PG) 06049, Italy
Tel: (0743) 222220, Fax: (0743) 222225
15 rooms with private bathrooms
Lire 230,000–280,000 double B&B
Breakfast only
Open all year, Credit cards: MC, VS
Some English spoken
Region: Umbria

Just north of Spoleto up a winding road is the tiny 14th-century village of Poreta and farther up on the hillside, emerging from lush vegetation, are the remains of the walls of the castle that once dominated the valley. It is here that a group of friends, Luca being the omnipresent, genial host, undertook the task of restoring what was left of the ancient castle and transforming it into a country bed and breakfast. Their idea was to provide not only accommodation but also a special place offering a variety of cultural events such as classical concerts, art shows, poetry reading, and dinners with particular local food themes. The cluster of stone houses where the eight bedrooms are located includes a church restored in the baroque period with original frescoes and faux-marble borders. The small restaurant, which serves seasonal Umbrian fare, is made up of two cozy rooms with beamed ceilings, fireplace, and cheery yellow walls. A clean and pleasant country style pervades the bedrooms with their soothingly soft beige tones and occasional country antiques. They need no elaborate paintings for decoration as the views out the windows suffice. The buildings are united by an expansive brick terrace overlooking olive groves and sweeping views of the valley. Make sure you are back in time from touring for a drink on the terrace to witness the spectacular sunsets. *Directions*: From the N3 Spoleto-Perugia road turn right after 8 km at Poreta and follow signs up to the castle.

IL CASTELLO DI PORETA   New
Host: Luca Saint Amour di Chanaz
Localita: Poreta
Spoleto (PG) 06049, Italy
Tel: (0743) 275810, Fax: (0743) 270175
8 rooms with private bathrooms
Lire 130,000–190,000 double B&B
All meals served
Open all year
Credit cards: all major
English spoken very well
Region: Umbria

On the border of the Liguria and Piedmont regions and conveniently located near the Genoa-Milan autostrada sits the hillside property of friendly hosts, Domenico and Rosanna, president of the regional agritourism association. The house is immersed in woods at the end of a long gravel road and is barely visible through the ivy and rose vines that conceal it—a true spectacle in late May. This gives just a hint of one of Rosanna's two passions: cooking and gardening, both of which guests can participate in by taking lessons. Over 150 rare varieties of roses dot the property as well as 50 varieties of irises. Three bedrooms are situated in the main farmhouse dating to 1714 and in Rosanna's family since that time. The apartments with exposed beams are located next door in the converted barn and are all decorated in pleasant country style with antiques and family memorabilia. Guests sit down together *en famille* at a long table to taste one of Rosanna's delectable meals prepared with their own fresh, organically-grown produce from the garden (Domenico's passion). Guests/friends are made to feel right at home in this informal and tranquil atmosphere, where silence and privacy are highly respected and guests become a natural part of the farm's everyday life. A small pool is hidden among lush vegetation just behind the house. *Directions*: Exit autostrada A7 (Milano-Genova) at Vignole Borbera, following the sign for Stazzano (4 km). Turn right in town at the traffic light and follow the bed and breakfast sign for 2 km on an unpaved road.

LA TRAVERSINA
Hosts: Rosanna & Domenico Varese
Localita: Traversina 109
Stazzano (AL) 15060, Italy
Tel & fax: (0143) 61377, Cellphone: (0335) 494295
3 rooms with private bathrooms, 2 apartments
Lire 130,000 –170,000 double B&B
* 85,000–120,000 per person half board*
* 840,000–1,700,000 weekly per apartment*
Breakfast & dinner served, Open all year
Some English spoken, Region: Piedmont

Now that the owners of agritourism operations are increasingly city people rather than local farmers, Il Tondino, by contrast, goes back to tradition: simple and informal hospitality and board offered on the farmland of a local family. Andrea, his two brothers, and his father divide up the chores on the ranch between them, attending to guests, cooking, caring for the horses, and producing cereal and grains. The property is comprised of three buildings: the family's brick house with attached restaurant in the former barn, stables with living room/game area for guests above, and small guest house where three pleasant air-conditioned bedrooms with quilts, rustic wood furniture, and new bathrooms are located. A low-ceilinged apartment on the lower level of the main house is also available, although very dark. All pasta and breads are homemade and served at long tables in the cheery yellow-sponged-wall dining room with brick-vaulted ceilings. In the area famous for the production and worldwide distribution of Parmesan cheese and Parma prosciutto, eating well has never been a problem. Among the many treasures in the area to explore are the castles of Parma. *Directions*: Exit from autostrada A1 at Fidenza and head towards Salsamaggiore until the sign for Tabiano. After 3 km turn left at the Il Tondino sign and drive for another 4.5 km to the farm.

IL TONDINO
Host: Andrea Bertoletti
Localita: Tabiano 58
Fidenza (PR) 43036, Italy
Tel & fax: (0524) 62106
3 rooms with private bathrooms, 1 apartment
Lire 120,000–130,000 double B&B
* 80,000–90,000 per person half board*
2-night minimum stay
Breakfast & dinner served
Open March to October
Some English spoken
Region: Emilia-Romagna

Halfway between Florence and Siena in the heart of the Chianti region is the Sovigliano farm, restored by a gracious couple from Verona, Claudio Bicego and his wife, Patrizia, and daughter, Claudia, who delight in welcoming international visitors into their warm home. Guests have an independent entrance to the five bedrooms (only two with private bath), each very much in keeping with the pure simplicity of this typical farmhouse. Exposed-beam ceilings and terra-cotta floors nicely worn with time, antique beds and armoires, and bucolic views make time stand still here. Besides three apartments (two with air conditioning) in a separate farmhouse, there is also a spacious two-bedroom apartment within the house, decorated in similar style, with kitchen and dining area and fireplace. The living room, sparsely furnished with the family's antiques, kitchen with country fireplace, TV, and surrounding garden with swimming pool and hydrojet are for everyone's use. Signor Bicego is actively involved in the production of top Tuscan wines in conjunction with several other wine estates, and also coordinates with other area residents to organize lessons in language, history, and culinary arts with local professors. *Directions*: From Siena, exit the superstrada at San Donato; from Florence at Tavarnelle. Follow signs for Certosa-Marcialla and then signs for Sovigliano 2 km from town.

SOVIGLIANO
Hosts: Patrizia & Claudio Bicego
Via Magliano 9
Tavarnelle Val di Pesa (FI) 50028, Italy
Tel: (055) 8076217, Fax: (055) 8050770
Email: sovigliano@ftbcc.it
5 rooms, 2 with private bathrooms
4 apartments (3-night minimum stay)
Lire 170,000–200,000 double B&B
 190,000–390,000 daily per apartment B&B
Breakfast served, dinner upon request
Open all year, Credit cards: AX
English spoken well, Region: Tuscany
www.karenbrown.com/italy/sovigliano.html

With their hearts set on running a bed and breakfast in the Liguria region, young Milanese couple Lucia and Nereo searched hard and long before finding Giandriale. Set high up in the remote mountains above the coast, the 18th-century stone farmhouse is surrounded by a low range of mountains covered with thick woods as far as the eye can see. Utter silence prevails. There are just two guestrooms within their home and four others plus an apartment for four persons in the refurbished stone barn, simply decorated with country-style wood furniture. Guests can relax in one of two comfortable living rooms. Meals are enjoyed in the downstairs dining room with its old-fashioned country stove, which is used occasionally in winter for making polenta. Lucia prepares coffee cakes and jams for breakfast and uses mostly regional recipes in her cooking. Classic sightseeing destinations in the area include the riviera (Portofino, Santa Margherita, Chiaveri), or the Cinque Terre, 45 minutes away. Nereo can also suggest several interesting off-the-beaten-track itineraries beyond Giandriale. Hiking trails and mountain bikes are available. *Directions*: From autostrada A14, exit at Sestri Levante and follow signs for Casarza Ligure, Castiglione, then, after 2 km and many curves, Missano. After a long tunnel turn right for Tavarone and just before town follow B&B signs for 2.5 km.

GIANDRIALE
Hosts: Lucia Marelli & Nereo Giani
Localita: Giandriale
Tavarone di Maissana (SP) 19010, Italy
Tel: (0187) 840279 Fax: (0187) 840156
6 rooms with private bathrooms, 1 apartment
Lire 100,000 double B&B
* 75,000 per person half board*
* 160,000 daily apartment B&B*
All meals served
Open all year, Credit cards: all major
Some English spoken, Region: Liguria

In order to stand out among the crowd of recently opened bed and breakfasts in Italy, many hosts have begun to specialize according to their own personal interests. This is true for enthusiastic and friendly hosts, Alberto and his Brazilian wife Luzia, who opened a gourmet vegetarian bed and breakfast on their isolated 27-acre farm up on a mountain ridge between Perugia and Lake Trasimeno. It is in fact the first of its kind in Umbria and the agritourism law was actually modified thanks to Alberto. An 8-kilometer gravel road ends at the panoramic property with its main house, two stone guesthouses, and cultural center where courses on yoga and meditation, and ethnic music concerts are held. Under the direction of Luzia, an architect, a good part of the construction and restoration was done "in house." An informal ambiance prevails and the total respect for nature and tranquillity is evident among guests who take hikes in the surrounding woods or read poolside, enjoying both sunrise and sunset over the opposite valleys. The ten neat rooms with independent outside entrances are comfortably decorated with rustic wood beds and armoires from Asia and prints brought back from many travels to India. The sun-filled dining room is where guests convene for Luzia's and Alberto's famed fare based on strictly organic produce from the farm. So unique is this bed and breakfast that the BBC did a special documentary on it. *Directions:* From Perugia follow route 220 for approximately 22 km and turn right before Tavernelle at Colle San Paolo.

MONTALI
Hosts: Luzia & Alberto Musacchio
Via Montali 23
Tavernelle di Panicale (PG) 06068, Italy
Tel: (075) 8350680, Fax: (075) 8350144
Email: montali@edisons.it
10 rooms with private bathrooms
Lire 120,000–130,000 per person half board
3-night minimum stay, Breakfast & dinner served
Open March to October
English spoken very well, Region: Umbria
www.karenbrown.com/italy/montali.html

Another one of Italy's best-kept secrets is the Cinque Terre coastline of southern Liguria bordering Tuscany, though this beautiful and quite unique area is now gaining increasing popularity. Its five quaint stone villages hugging the hillside sweeping down to the sea were, until recently, accessible only by boat or by foot and are a delight to explore. Just south of the area right on the Poet's Gulf is the adorable seaside town of Tellaro hugging the rock over the sea, where visitors make a point of stopping to have a memorable meal at the Miranda restaurant. Husband-and-wife team, Giovanna and Angelo, have their own inimitable and ever-varying style of cooking based exclusively on fresh seafood (no meat), which is present in the inexhaustible series of antipasti and pasta plates. Angelo has received plenty of press and praise (Michelin star) for these extraordinary dishes. Meals are served in one of the newly renovated dining rooms, pleasantly appointed with scattered antiques. In the same vein are the bedrooms, most with gulf view, which Aunt Miranda used to rent out and are now in the capable hands of son, Alessandro. A cozy living room with fireplace where guests can convene has just been added. Unique guided excursions of the castles of Lungiana are arranged. Reserve well in advance. *Directions*: Leave the A12 autostrada at Sarzana, following signs for Lerici on route 331. Tellaro is 4.5 km down the coast—the Miranda is on the main road before town.

LOCANDA MIRANDA
Hosts: Angelo & Giovanna Cabani
Via Fiascherino 92
Tellaro (SP) 19030, Italy
Tel: (0187) 968130 or 964012
Fax: (0187) 964032
8 rooms with private bathrooms
Lire 200,000 per person half board
3-night minimum stay, All meals served
Closed February, Credit cards: all major
English spoken well
Region: Liguria

Country tourism has flourished in the last decade, especially in the highly popular region of Tuscany. However, most travelers still flock to the Chianti area, leaving many other parts of Tuscany wide open to discovery. Such is the gorgeous virgin territory of the Valdera Valley between Volterra and Pisa where everything has remained remarkably unspoiled. Affable host Sandro and his family bought the 100-acre farm property 25 years ago and are restoring the ancient farmhouses piece by piece with guests' comfort foremost in mind. So far, six neat apartments with one or two bedrooms and four guest bedrooms have been completed within three adjacent stone houses and are tastefully appointed with local antiques. Within one of the houses is the pleasant dining room with large arched windows where breakfast and dinners upon request are served, all prepared by Sandro's mother, who also conducts cooking lessons. Olive oil, wine, fruits, and vegetables all come directly from the farm. There is a beautiful borderless swimming pool and Sandro supplies guests with mountain bikes and a long list of interesting local itineraries. Easy day trips include Florence, Siena, San Gimignano, Lucca, and Pisa. *Directions*: Il Selvino is conveniently located off the main road 439 from Volterra (20 km) between Terricciola and La Sterza at Pieve a Pitti (marked on most maps).

*IL SELVINO   **New***
Hosts: Alessandro Sgherri family
Localita: La Sterza
Via Pieve a Pitti 1
Terricciola (PI) 56030, Italy
Tel & fax: (0587) 670132
4 rooms with private bathrooms, 6 apartments
Lire 180,000 double B&B
* 100,00–265,000 daily per apartment*
3-night minimum stay
Breakfast & dinner served, Open all year
Some English spoken
Region: Tuscany

Practically 70 percent of the families residing in the Alto Adige mountain region offer bed-and-breakfast accommodations so, unless it's Christmas or August, a bed is not hard to come by. This is a region with a distinct Austrian flavor where more German than Italian is spoken, and where more *wurstel* than pasta is likely to be served at the table. Signora Trompedeller welcomes international travelers to her typical Tyrolean-style home. The six simple guestrooms upstairs each have a private bath and are modestly decorated with basic light-wood furniture and down comforters—a decor common to the bed and breakfasts in this region. The small wood-paneled dining room boasts a splendid panoramic view over the mountain cliffs and green foothills. The house with adjacent barn for the cows is located several kilometers outside the quaint town of Tires on a road that comes to an end at a babbling brook surrounded by hushed woods with hiking trails. Depending on the season, guests can take advantage of the Val Gardena ski slopes or summer mountain climbing. *Directions*: From the Verona-Brennero autostrada, exit at Bolzano Nord and follow signs for Tiers. Go through the town and after 2 km make a hairpin left turn at the chapel and backtrack on a parallel road to the end.

VERALTENHOF
Hosts: Josef Trompedeller family
Oberstrasse 61
Tires (BZ) 39050, Italy
Tel & fax: (0471) 642102
6 rooms with private bathrooms
Lire 72,000–88,000 double B&B
* 55,000–65,000 per person half board*
Breakfast & dinner served
Open all year
No English spoken (German)
Region: Trentino-Alto Adige

Since 1830, the remote 12th-century castle and 4,000-acre farm of Titignano have belonged to the noble Corsini family who in the 1980s decided to offer guests six rooms in the main house, later adding a swimming pool and three new apartments in what was originally the farmer's quarters. They are pleasantly decorated with scattered country antiques. Management is in the hands of Monica and Francesca, delightful hostesses who take care of everything from looking after guests to cooking and serving. Meals are shared at a long table in one of the castle's graciously neglected rooms with an enormous gray-stone fireplace sporting the family coat of arms, and lofty ceilings made of the stamped terra-cotta blocks typical of Umbria. Off the dining hall are the spacious bedrooms, each with modernized pink travertine bathrooms and decorated eclectically with unrefined antiques and wrought-iron beds. They have a worn charm about them. Common areas include a living room with bright floral sofas around a fireplace, a game and TV room for children, and a large terrace with a breathtaking, sweeping view covering three regions. Bikes are available for touring the regional park of the River Tiber (part of the property). *Directions*: Leave the Roma-Firenze A1 autostrada at Orvieto. Follow signs for Arezzo, turning on route 79 for Prodo. Follow the long winding road for 26 km past Prodo to Titignano. (30 km from Orvieto.)

FATTORIA TITIGNANO
Hosts: Monica Gori & Francesca Marchetti
Localita: Titignano
Orvieto (TR) 05010, Italy
Tel: (0763) 308000 or 308022, Fax: (0763) 308002
6 rooms with private bathrooms, 3 apartments
Lire 140,000 double B&B
  100,000 per person half board
2-night minimum stay
Breakfast & dinner served, Open all year
Some English & French spoken
Region: Umbria

The Adriano is a small, family-run hotel with a long-standing tradition in hospitality and exceptionally fine cuisine. The operation has been handed down to the third generation of the Cinelli family—siblings Umberto, Patrizia, and Gabriella. Gabriella works her magic in the kitchen creating innovative dishes using her grandparents' recipes, which won her several European culinary awards. While congenial hosts Umberto and Patrizia deal directly with guests at reception and in the main dining room, Patrizia also finds time for watercolor painting, examples of which are found throughout the inn. Breakfast is served either out in the pretty garden seen from the large windows of the dining room, or in the intimate sitting room just left of reception with large gray-stone fireplace. Upstairs, renovated rooms with all amenities are tastefully coordinated with elegant antiques and rich fabrics. The inn is uniquely situated right next door to the beautiful park and ruins of Emperor Hadrian's villa (circa 120 A.D.), which makes it a quiet spot at night. The park is literally all yours around closing time at sunset. Take a peek at the guest book where such illustrious guests as Queen Elizabeth and John F. Kennedy have signed. Altogether a delightful combination. *Directions*: From either the A24 from Rome, or A1 from Florence or Naples, exit at Tivoli, and follow signs for Villa Adriana, below the actual city of Tivoli.

HOTEL ADRIANO
Hosts: Cinelli family
Via di Villa Adriana 194
Tivoli (RM) 00010, Italy
Tel: (0774) 382235, Fax: (0774) 535122
Email: info@hoteladriano.it
7 rooms with private bathrooms, 3 suites
Lire 220,000–270,000 double B&B
  380,000 suite
All meals served
Open all year, Credit cards: MC, VS
Some English spoken, Region: Lazio
www.karenbrown.com/italy/adriano.html

In the midst of the bucolic countryside surrounding Todi sits the refined bed and breakfast of Poggio d'Asproli. Bruno Pagliari, a sculptor with a long family history in the hotel business, transferred his family from Naples to this 16th-century stone farmhouse and ex-convent several years ago and has succeeded in his aim of creating elegant but comfortable surroundings to make guests feel at home. Each of the romantic guestrooms is unique in style and decor. Rich fabrics draped at bedheads give a canopy effect with matching bedspreads and nice big bathrooms have travertine marble sinks. To the back is a large two-bedroom suite with a separate entrance. The home is filled to the brim with antiques and lovely artwork (some by Bruno's sister, Lilli), which blend in well with the stone walls, worn brick floors, and beamed ceilings. Breakfast and candlelit dinners are served either on the outside terrace or in the elegant dining room. At one end is a cozy sitting area with white sofas around an enormous fireplace. A swimming pool among the trees is a cool spot for relaxing. Daughter, Claudia, is slowly taking over the general management of the bed and breakfast. *Directions*: From Todi, follow signs for Orvieto and take a left at the sign for Izzalini. Before town, take the turning for Asproli and follow signs to the bed and breakfast.

POGGIO D'ASPROLI
Hostess: Claudia Pagliari
Localita: Asproli
Todi (PG) 06059, Italy
Tel & fax: (075) 8853385
8 rooms, 1 suite, all with private bathrooms
Lire 200,000–290,000 double B&B
2-night minimum stay
Breakfast & dinner served
Open all year
Credit cards: MC, VS
English spoken well
Region: Umbria

Fortunate travelers who book a room at the fascinating Tenuta di Canonica will be certain to experience an unforgettable stay. Maria and Daniele, with son Michelangelo, searched far and wide before purchasing the massive stone tower with foundation dating to the ancient Roman period and adjoining turn-of-the-century house. They have transformed it into a bed and breakfast of dreams. Through the arched front doorway to the open ochre-colored entrance, the spacious living room with stone fireplace is reached down a few stairs and looks out over the stunning valley down to Lake Corbara. Outstanding medieval architectural features such as stone walls, brick floors, and high, beamed ceilings have been enhanced by Provence-inspired colors. Stairs lead up to the library and bedrooms are divided between the three-story tower and house, respecting the epoch of each: bathrooms in the medieval quarters have gray stone tiles and travertine, while the others have white tile alternating with terra-cotta pieces. Each tastefully decorated, antique-filled room has some attractive feature, whether it be the more suite-like arrangements with sitting area or the smaller corner rooms with head-spinning views over hills and up to Todi. Common areas include a dining room and large swimming pool with mesmerizing 360-degree views. *Directions*: From Todi take the road for Orvieto, turning right at the sign for Prado/Titignano. After 2 km turn left for Cordigliano and follow the signpost for Tenuta di Canonica to the end of the road (1 km).

TENUTA DI CANONICA
Hosts: Maria & Daniele Fano
Localita: Canonica, Todi (PG) 06059, Italy
Tel: (075) 8947545, Cellphone: (0335) 369492
Fax: (075) 8947581
Email:info@tenutadicanonica.com
11 rooms with private bathrooms, 2 apartments
Lire 200,000 double B&B, 2-night minimum stay
Breakfast served, dinner upon request, Open all year
English & German spoken well, Region: Umbria
www.karenbrown.com/italy/canonica.html

The countryside surrounding Rome has surprisingly few agritourism accommodations, even though attractions of cultural interest are many, so Il Leccio, which offers the peace and quiet of a country home an hour away from the city, is a real find. Cristina and Giuliano, from Rome, carry on their careers as journalist (agriculture and botany) and lawyer besides offering accommodation for guests in one of the two stone houses on their countryside property. The identically sized apartments, one on each floor, include a living room (one with fireplace) with corner kitchen, double bedroom, and bathroom, pleasantly decorated in country style. Both have lovely views over the hilly countryside and although meals are not regularly offered, dinner can be arranged upon request and served under the 300-year-old holm oak, which lends its name to the place. The gracious hosts are happy to suggest local itineraries and also to organize tours of historical private gardens and palazzos (Villa Lante being the highlight) as well as a private French- or English-speaking guide for Rome and the Sabina area (must be booked prior to arrival). This predominantly agricultural area bordering Umbria is dotted with off-the-beaten-track medieval hilltop villages. *Directions*: From Rome, exit from the A1 autostrada at Ponzano Romano/Soratte (new exit and not marked on maps) after the Fiano exit. Drive towards Stimigliano Scalo and turn left in town. Continue past Stimigliano down to the end of the road. Turn right and continue to Torri. Call from town.

IL LECCIO
Hosts: Maria Cristina & Giuliano Fleres
Via Pizzuti 53
Torri in Sabina (RI) 02049, Italy
Tel & fax: (06) 37353076 or (0765) 62412
2 apartments
Lire 180,000 daily per apartment for 2 persons
* 1,000,000 weekly*
3-night minimum stay
Dinner upon request, Open all year
English spoken very well, Region: Lazio

On the northern shores of Lake Bracciano, 45 kilometers from Rome, is the small town of Trevignano where ex-producer and music director Gianni's home is located. A short drive up from town, taking advantage of the high viewpoint over the lake and surrounding countryside, the gate opens to the large four-story house. The *simpatico* hosts' true passion is cooking and entertaining and guests are rewarded each day with a superbly prepared meal based on traditional recipes and accompanied by a wide choice of select wines. Gianni also shares his vast knowledge of Italian cuisine by organizing lessons in his well-equipped kitchen. The five bedrooms on the upper two floors vary in size, from the smaller children's rooms to the master bedroom with Jacuzzi tub, terrace, and stunning lake views. True coziness and comfort is dedicated to the common areas, which include several living rooms with fireplace and grand piano, veranda dining room, manicured garden, and swimming pool. There is also a small apartment for weekly stays with double bedroom, living area with kitchenette, and bathroom. Etruscan history abounds in the area's historical villages, and you can also enjoy Viterbo's thermal spas and a nearby golf course. *Directions*: From Rome's ring highway GRA take exit 5 for S.S.2 Cassia bis to km 35,200. Exit at Settebene Palo and drive 11 km to Trevignano. Via Olivetello begins right in the town. A map is provided with confirmation.

CASA PLAZZI   **New**
Hosts: Gianni Plazzi family
Via Olivetello 19
Trevignano Romano (RM) 00069, Italy
Tel: (06) 9997597, Cellphone: (0335) 6756290
Fax: (06) 99910196
5 rooms with private bathrooms
Lire 150,000–220,000 double B&B
  1,000,000 weekly per apartment
All meals served, Open all year
Some English spoken
Region: Lazio

The Veneto region has so much to offer travelers in art, history, and culture, yet remains terribly weak when it comes to charming bed and breakfasts. This is mainly due to the very strict regulations particular to this region. The Ca'Masieri is a pleasant combination of both hotel and bed-and-breakfast-like accommodation in a country setting. The countryside property has been in the Zarantonello family for three generations and was transformed into a restaurant and inn after Signor Giovanni, a businessman in Milan, made the drastic decision to move here and find a creative way to maintain the farm property. He and his partner, Angelo, opened the restaurant first, creating an intimate ambiance within three stenciled dining rooms in the main villa. The restaurant gained considerable recognition and the next logical step was to offer a place to stay in the stone farmhouse right next door. These two buildings and the attached barn form a quadrangle, with a gated-in terraced swimming pool. The seven bedrooms are very comfortable with many amenities, though their modern decor contrasts with the country setting. The five new suites in the adjoining wing (former stables) are more in keeping with the general ambiance of the place. Signor Giovanni is also on Vicenza's tourism board and can suggest many itineraries in the area (villas of Palladio etc.). *Directions*: Exit from autostrada A4 at Montecchio and go towards Valdagno. After exactly 10 km enter the town of Trissino and follow signs for Masieri up to the Ca'Masieri.

CA'MASIERI
Hosts: Giovanni Zarantonello & Angelo Vassena
Localita: Masieri, Trissino (VI) 36070, Italy
Tel: (0445) 962100 or 490122, Fax: (0445) 490455
7 rooms, 5 suites with private bathrooms
Lire 207,000 double B&B
  282,000 suite B&B
Breakfast & dinner served
Closed Jan 20 to Feb 15, Credit cards: all major
English spoken well
Region: Veneto

When the Marti family from Rome came across the abandoned castle of Montegualandro 17 years ago, it was love at first sight—only pure passion could have driven them to tackle such an overwhelming project as the entire restoration of the property following original plans. A winding dirt road (1.5 kilometers) leads up to the gates of the walled 9th-century castle. As you enter into the open circular courtyard, the main building and family residence lies to the left and immediately to the right is the long stone house, originally farmer's quarters, with small tower, stable, pottery kiln, dove house, and private chapel. Four apartments have been fashioned for guests, cleverly incorporating all original architectural features. All different, each has a living area with fireplace, kitchen, and bathroom and is characteristically furnished with country-style antiques. A walk up in the turreted walls gives a glimpse of the spectacular view out over olive groves (the property produces its own olive oil) to the lake. The Martis' daughter, Cristiana, takes special interest in guests' needs, suggesting easy day trips from the castle and recommending favorite local restaurants. Lovely Cortona is just 10 kilometers away. *Directions*: Montegualandro is marked on most maps. Leave the A1-Perugia highway at Tuoro. Take the road 75 bis towards Cortona and Arezzo. After 3 km, at km sign 44,700, take the road marked Fonte S. Angelo up to the castle or call from town.

CASTELLO DI MONTEGUALANDRO
Hosts: Franca & Claudio Marti
Via di Montegualandro 1
Tuoro Sul Trasimeno (PG) 06069, Italy
Tel & fax: (075) 823026
Email: montegualandro@iol.it
4 apartments
Lire 850,000–1,000,000 weekly
3-night minimum stay, No meals served
Open all year
English spoken very well, Region: Umbria
www.karenbrown.com/italy/castellodimontegualandro.html

La Dogana means customs house in Italian, and the fascinating history of this 16th-century building—which until 1870 served as the Papal customs house for travelers through the Grand Duchy of Tuscany—boasts visits from luminary artists such as Michelangelo, Goethe, Byron, and Stendhal. The 100-acre property belongs to young hosts Emanuele and Paola and, aside from the main villa, includes a stone farmhouse and a building near the stables across the street. In these two "extra" buildings 25 apartment-suites have been created. The guest quarters vary widely in condition, but all feature a living area, kitchen, bathroom, and sleeping accommodations for two to six people. Each apartment is unique in decor, containing mixed antiques, prints, old sofas, and wrought-iron beds. Up on a hillside, guests have a lovely view over Lake Trasimeno whose encircling highway is audible even from here. In the summer months a dining room serving lunch and dinner is open. A small pool for children is on the premises or one can always take a dip in the lake. *Directions*: From Perugia, take N75 toward Firenze, exiting at Tuoro. Turn left at the first intersection, continuing 3 km to La Dogana on the right side of the road.

LA DOGANA
Host: Marchese Emanuele de Ferrari
Via Dogana 4
Tuoro Sul Trasimeno (PG) 06069, Italy
Tel: (075) 8230158 or (0330) 280845
Fax: (075) 8230252
25 apartments
Lire 450,000–1,100,000 weekly per apartment
  (July & August)
Lunch & dinner served in summer
Open all year
English spoken very well
Region: Umbria
www.karenbrown.com/italy/ladogana.html

The area of Lazio north of Rome known as "Tuscia" is rich in Etruscan history, small medieval villages, nature reserves, and three picturesque lakes. It is the homeland of the illustrious and powerful Farnese family whose palazzos and fortresses still stand as monuments of their glorious past. In the heart of this fascinating area not far from the coast is the ancient walled town of Tuscania, completely restored after the dramatic earthquake in 1978. Perla and her Argentine husband José brought back to life one of the buildings right in town and opened its doors as a cozy bed and breakfast and Michelin-star restaurant. A small reception area leads to a lounge and wine bar (over 200 labels) to one side and a courtyard and to the other the cheerful, luminous restaurant with large windows looking out over the tiled rooftops. The *gallo* (rooster) motif is carried out within the three rooms with its checked drapes and tablecloths, antique armoire, and still-life paintings. It is here where José works his magic, serving innovative creations using seasonal local produce. A 10% discount is awarded to our readers for meals. Upstairs each very comfortable and appealing carpeted bedroom has its own color theme in matching floral wallpaper, drapery, and bedspread. They have all amenities including air conditioning and are spacious, with high ceilings and marble bathrooms. Gracious hostess Perla guarantees guests' comfort and assists them in arranging local itineraries. *Directions*: In the center of Tuscania, well marked.

HOTEL AL GALLO
Hosts: Perla Blanzieri & José Pettiti
Via del Gallo 22
Tuscania (VT) 01017, Italy
Tel: (0761) 443388, Fax: (0761) 443628
12 rooms with private bathrooms
Lire 224,000 double B&B
All meals served, Restaurant closed Mondays
Open all year, Credit cards: all major
Handicap facilities
English spoken well, Region: Lazio

Those who have fallen in love with the enchanting countryside of Tuscany, but found its roads too well traveled, should investigate the northern part of the Marches surrounding Urbino. The scenery is magnificent, the ancient towns perfectly preserved, and the ambiance authentic. The Benedetti-Blasi families, hard-working farmers, have dedicated themselves to balancing a productive farm with a bed and breakfast. The brother's side of the family tends to the fields, while Alberto, his wife Maria, and their two sons Andrea and Samuele see to the guests. Three simple terra-cotta-roofed gray houses make up the farm, and horses, cows, sheep, and even peacocks roam the grounds. The guestrooms, each with private bath, are spartan, and the decor uninspired, but the genuine familial warmth of the hospitality, the excellent home cooking, and the value compensate. In the rustic dining room with red-checked tablecloths or out on the porch overlooking the gently rolling, wooded countryside, guests indulge in Maria's spinach ravioli or hand-cut tagliatelle with mushroom sauce, fresh-baked flat bread, and local wine. This no-frills bed and breakfast is an economical choice for those who seek simplicity and authentic farm life. *Directions*: From Urbania head for Acqualagna and turn off right after town to Orsaiola (6 km of country road).

L'ORSAIOLA
Hosts: Benedetti-Blasi families
Localita: Orsaiola
Urbania (PS) 61049, Italy
Tel & fax: (0722) 318988
9 rooms with private bathrooms
2 apartments
Lire 85,000 double B&B
  135,000–180,000 daily per apartment (2 to 4 persons)
All meals served
Open March to Christmas
Very little English spoken
Region: Marches

The Aiola opened its doors to guests four years ago when daughter Federica and her husband Enrico restored the farmers' houses on the wine estate's vast property in Chianti. The family's villa with its ancient origins sits across the street from the guest quarters almost completely hidden by enormous oak and cypress trees. The eight bedrooms, one of which sleeps four persons, are divided between two floors of a stone house, each having a separate outside entrance. Original architectural features have been preserved and rooms are decorated with wrought-iron beds and antique or reproduction armoires. The vineyards come right up to the house and a wide, open view of the hills is offered to the other side. The barn next door includes common areas such as the breakfast room, where Federica's fresh-baked coffee cakes are served, and a living room. With Federica's mother, Signora Malagodi, being the President of the Wine Tourism Association, visits to the cellar and the villa, and wine tasting begin right here at the Aiola. Federica and Enrico's aim to make each guest feel special is evident in the time they dedicate to suggesting itineraries with maps, and making reservations at restaurants, museums, and local concerts. At 12 kilometers from Siena and an easy distance from the highlights of the region, the Aiola serves as an excellent touring base. Total silence reigns here, with only the buzz of cicadas breaking it. *Directions*: From Siena follow route 102 just past Vagliagli—the Aiola property (well marked) is on this same road.

CASALI DELLA AIOLA
Hosts: Federica & Enrico Campelli
Vagliagli (SI) 53010, Italy
Tel: (0577) 322797, Fax: (0577) 322509
8 rooms with private bathrooms
Lire 170,000–260,000 double B&B
Breakfast only
Open March to November
Credit cards: all major
English spoken well
Region: Tuscany

Varenna is a quaint little village sitting halfway up Lake Como's eastern edge. It is situated at the point where the car-ferryboats cross over to the other side of the lake to Menaggio. In the main piazza lakeside is the generations-old family-run Olivedo hotel with its pale-yellow façade where Signora Laura welcomes her guests. Time seems to have stood still within its old-fashioned interior. The reception area and side bar are dressed with faded floral wallpaper, scattered antiques, and a large grandfather clock chiming the hour. Off to the other side of the reception area is a dining room/restaurant with its simple frescoes, serving all meals. A curved stairway takes guests up to the 19 rooms, most with en-suite bathroom and lake views. These are decorated simply with grandmother's furniture and old prints. There is no need to worry about noise except for Saturday nights since traffic is not allowed in the piazza. Bathrooms are being progressively renewed and added. Olivedo serves as a good, economical base from which to explore beautiful Lake Como including its many gardens (Villa Serbelloni, Melzi, and Carlotta). *Directions*: From the Como branch of the lake, head north on either side of lake and take the ferry over from either Bellagio or Menaggio.

OLIVEDO
Hosts: Colombo family
Piazza Martırı 4
Varenna (LC) 23829, Italy
Tel & fax: (0341) 830115
Email: info@olivedo.it
19 rooms, 10 with private bathrooms
Lire 120,000–175,000 double B&B
  100,000–130,000 per person half board
All meals served
Closed November
English spoken well
Region: Lombardy
www.karenbrown.com/italy/olivedo.html

It is a pleasure to be able to include such a perfectly efficient, family-run hotel as the Due Fanali, located in a lovely square next to the 12th-century San Simeon church with its original Tintoretto painting. The hotel is also housed in a 12th-century palazzo, once part of the church complex. The Feron family had the building lovingly restored five years ago to include the sixteen bedrooms (some with smaller "French" double) on the top three floors. A small elevator has been added for the convenience of guests. Extra care has been taken in the selection of appropriate antiques for the guestrooms, reception area, and breakfast room. The soft ambiance is that of an elegant yet warm home, accentuated by lovely Oriental carpets and rich-cream draperies. Breakfast is taken either out in the "garden" in front of the hotel or up in the delightful third-floor veranda, under the open terrace, with its superb view over the square to the Grand Canal. As an alternative to the hotel, there are four independent apartments near San Marco Square, divinely decorated and including bedroom, living room with view, kitchenette, and bathroom with hydromassage tub. Take all these esthetic elements accompanied by the exceptional hospitality offered by Signora Marina and her daughter, Stefania, and you have a true winner of a hotel. *Directions*: The hotel is a five-minute walk from the train station or you can take the No. 1 waterbus to the Riva di Biasio stop.

HOTEL AI DUE FANALI
Hosts: Marina Feron family
Santa Croce 946
Venice 30135, Italy
Tel: (041) 718344, Fax: (041) 718490
Email: request@aiduefanali.com
16 rooms with private bathrooms, 4 apartments
Lire 180,000–360,000 double B&B
  280,000–600,000 daily per apartment
Breakfast only
Closed January, Credit cards: all major
English spoken well, Region: Veneto
www.karenbrown.com/italy/fanali.html

Around the corner from the Santa Maria del Giglio square, sitting on a small private canal's edge is the small and intimate San Moise hotel, named after the nearby church. Hospitality is a tradition in the Donzello family who own three other hotels in Venice, and hostess and owner Signora Irvin obviously takes pride in her work as seen in the attention to detail of her nicely renovated accommodation. Upon entering the pale-yellow 15th-century building, one finds the reception desk and the stairway up to the guestrooms immediately on the right. To the left is the very small but cozy combination lounge and breakfast room decorated with elegant antiques, Murano glass chandeliers, and walls covered with soft-pink flocked fabric. Bedrooms on the second and third floors are in the same vein with variations in the color scheme, some having the advantage of a partial canal view without the usual noise. Rooms are fully equipped with all amenities including air conditioning and satellite TV and you can even leave your gondola at the private dock! *Directions*: Take the No. 1 waterbus to stop 15, San Marco, walk straight up to Calle 22 Marzo and turn left. Pass the church on the left and turn right at the sign for the hotel.

HOTEL SAN MOISE
Hostess: Irvin Donzello
San Marco 2058
Venice 30124, Italy
Tel: (041) 5203755, Fax: (041) 5210670
16 rooms with private bathrooms
Lire 250,000–450,000 double B&B
Breakfast only
Open all year
Credit cards: all major
Handicap facilities
English spoken well
Region: Veneto

With just eleven rooms paired up throughout the six-floor building (luckily with an elevator), the intimate Santo Stefano was actually the watchtower to an ancient convent. The compact hotel, most recently a private home, is right in the middle of one of Venice's largest squares, leading to St. Mark's on one side and to the bridge for the Accademia on the other. Although in close proximity to the busy center, here one can observe the Venetians going about their daily business. The hotel is owned by Roberto and Marcello of the Hotel Celio in Rome (see listing), who have added fresh decorating touches to bedrooms and reception area. Just beyond is a miniature breakfast room, looking out to an ancient well, for days when the weather does not permit having it served out in the front piazza. Touches of elegance in Venetian style follow through in rooms (three of which are slightly larger doubles) appointed with Barovier & Toso chandeliers, coordinated draperies and bedspreads, and painted antiques with floral motif. Many amenities are offered including air conditioning. Roberto and his wife Silvana are experienced and amiable hosts with a definite aim to please their guests. *Directions*: Take waterbus No. 82 to the San Samuele stop or No. 1 to the Accademia stop. Pass over the bridge and go straight into Campo Santo Stefano.

HOTEL SANTO STEFANO
Hosts: Silvana & Roberto Quatrini
San Marco 2957
Venice 30124, Italy
Tel: (041) 5200166, Fax: (041) 5224460
11 rooms with private bathrooms
Lire 270,000–450,000 double B&B
Breakfast only
Open all year
Credit cards: all major
English spoken well
Region: Veneto

With admirable determination and family pride, Alessandro and his darling wife, Debora, took on the task of renovating and running the hotel property, which has been part of the family for three generations. They deserve great credit since they are more concerned with providing warm hospitality and attention to guests' needs than with keeping up with Venice's inflated hotel rates. The spacious and luminous reception area with white travertine floors is a welcome oasis amid the city's more cramped hotels, bustling squares, and crowded narrow streets. Although only a three-minute walk from the Guggenheim collection and Accademia, it has the feeling of being away from the mainstream traffic. The front rooms have water views (higher rate) and all rooms maintain an original flavor with paintings and personal family objects, parquet floors and matching wood furniture, blue-colored armchairs, new bathrooms, and air conditioning. Four bedrooms have private terraces for a higher rate and other guests will enjoy the delightful rooftop terrace. A full buffet breakfast and bar service are offered either in the breakfast room with country accents or out on the large front dock terrace, nicely appointed with large blue umbrellas, plants, and sunchairs, where you can watch the boats going by. Reserve *well* in advance. *Directions*: Take the No. 51 waterbus to Zattere, then follow the quay to the right to the hotel terrace.

PENSIONE LA CALCINA
Hosts: Alessandro & Debora Szemere
Dorsoduro 780, Venice 30123, Italy
Tel: (041) 5206466, Fax: (041) 5227045
Email: la.calcina@libero.it
29 rooms, 26 with private bathrooms
Lire 200,000–300,000 double B&B
Breakfast only
Open all year
Credit cards: all major
English spoken well, Region: Veneto
www.karenbrown.com/italy/pensionelacalcina.html

At first glance the exterior of the Pensione Seguso appears quite bland: a rather boxy affair with few of the elaborate architectural enhancements so frequently evident in Venice. Inside, however, the pensione radiates warmth and charm, with Oriental rugs setting off antique furniture and an heirloom silver service. The hotel is located on the "left bank" of Venice: across the Grand Canal from the heart of the tourist area, about a 15-minute walk to St. Mark's Square (or only a few minutes by ferry from the Accademia boat stop). For several generations the hotel has been in the Seguso family, which provides a homey ambiance for guests who do not demand luxury. In front there is a miniature terrace harboring a few umbrella-shaded tables. Most of the bedrooms have views of the canal (although these are the noisiest due to canal traffic). This being a simple pensione, most of the rooms share a bathroom, so if you are looking for hotel amenities, Seguso may not be your "cup of tea." The pleasant surprise is that the value-conscious tourist can stay here with breakfast and dinner included for the price of a room alone at most Venice hotels. *Directions*: The Seguso is a five-minute walk from the Accademia boat stop. (Vaporetto waterbus Nos. 1 and 82.)

PENSIONE SEGUSO
Hosts: Lorenzo Seguso family
Grand Canal Zattere 779
Venice 30123, Italy
Tel: (041) 5286858, Fax: (041) 5222340
36 rooms, 19 with private bathrooms
Lire 250,000–270,000 double B&B
  180,000–190,000 per person half board
Breakfast & dinner served
Open March to November
Credit cards: all major
English, French, German & Spanish spoken well
Region: Veneto

Just 20 kilometers from the Swiss border, halfway along the shore of Lake Maggiore, at the point where the road curves back down to Verbania, is a farmhouse situated high above the lake (700 meters). It commands a 360-degree view that includes the Alps and Lakes Mergozzo, Monate, Varese, and Maggiore with its miniature Borromeo islands (accessible by ferryboat). A long 5-kilometer road with hairpin turns winds its way up to the turn-of-the-century house with tower. Energetic and friendly hostess Iside Minotti and her family run the inn and rustic restaurant, which is busy spot in the summer when locals come up to dine and take advantage of the cooler air and the spectacular view. Menu ingredients come directly from the vegetable garden and orchards to the kitchen, where sumptuous local specialties are prepared. The 25-acre farm includes riding stables, and the bed and breakfast can also arrange helicopter rides from the property for a breathtakingly scenic tour over the lake, boat excursions, and mountain bike rentals. Nine very basic bedrooms come in various combinations of twins, triples, and quads, each with a snug shower room. *Directions*: On the outskirts of Verbania, at a major road junction with traffic lights (Pallanza), take Via Azari (also signposted Troloss) left for 1 km. Go sharp left at the signpost for Monterosso and up 5 km of winding road (I counted 43 hairpin bends).

IL MONTEROSSO
Hostess: Iside Minotti
Cima Monterosso-C.P. 13
Verbania (NO) 28922, Italy
Tel: (0323) 556510 or 551578, Fax: (0323) 519706
Email: ilmonterosso@iol.it
9 rooms with private bathrooms
Lire 95,000 double B&B
* 80,000 per person half board*
All meals served
Open all year, Credit cards: MC, VS
Some English spoken, Region: Piedmont
www.karenbrown.com/italy/ilmonterosso.html

Bed & Breakfast Descriptions

For years Andrea and Silvia have literally opened their entire home to guests, welcoming and rewelcoming "friends of La Volpaia," their bed and breakfast. International guests gather together in the evenings out on the patio or in the converted barn for one of Silvia's delightful meals based on fresh vegetables and meats enhanced with their own extra virgin olive oil. Conversation is never lacking with meals accompanied by La Volpaia's own Chianti (all beverages are included in the half-board rate). Andrea, a native Roman architect and sculptor, bought the wine estate with its 16th-century farmhouse 17 years ago and his pieces in olive wood are displayed in and about the property. The five cozy rooms are appointed with antiques, as is the large living room with fireplace. Beyond the patio where meals are served is the spectacular swimming pool with its heavenly views of what can only be described as a truly classic Tuscan landscape. Horses, personally trained by the hosts, are available for excursions into the surrounding countryside (experienced riders only). Guests are made to feel immediately right at home in this informal setting and so it is no wonder that many become "regulars" to this idyllic spot so close to the highlights of Tuscany. *Directions*: From the town of Vico d'Elsa follow Via della Villa (on the right) for 2 km, turning left at the wooden signpost for La Volpaia.

LA VOLPAIA
Hosts: Silvia & Andrea Taliaco
Strada di Vico 5–13
Vico d'Elsa (FI) 50050, Italy
Tel: (055) 8073063, Cellphone: (0368) 248287
Fax: (055) 8073170
5 rooms with private bathrooms
Lire 100,000 per person half board
3-night minimum stay
Breakfast & dinner served, Open all year
English spoken well, Region: Tuscany
www.karenbrown.com/italy/lavolpaia.html

In 1999 we came across a recently opened bed and breakfast property that is, to say the least, unique. Situated on Monte Faito between the Amalfi coast and Sorrento, Villa Giusso was a 15th-century monastery for cloistered monks. A long, narrow road takes you up to the isolated, stone-walled property whose entrance is marked by an arched gateway with watchtower leading into a park. From there you take in what is one of the highlights of a stay here— the enthralling view over Sorrento, the gulf, and Naples. The monastery itself is surrounded by a high, crumbling wall within which you find a grass courtyard and ancient well. The Giusso family has owned this beloved property for the past 180 years and now daughter Onorina and mother Giulia have begun the gradual restoration process. Off the one long corridor are two sets of two bedrooms with one bathroom per set, appointed with worn period furniture and huge paintings. Breakfast with fresh ricotta, figs, and cakes is served in the original kitchen completely tiled with Vietri ceramics. Though not for everyone, Villa Giusso is nonetheless fascinating and offers an opportunity to witness the initial stages of the resurrection of this historical place. *Directions*: Exit at Castellammare from the A3 autostrada and follow signs for Sorrento. Drive to Seiano and just after Moon Valley Hotel take a left at the sign for Monte Faito. Drive exactly 4.8 km and turn right on the dirt road with ceramic tile "Passegiate Vicane" to the monastery.

VILLA GIUSSO
Hosts: Giusso Rispoli family
Via Camaldoli 51, Localita: Arola
Vico Equense (NA) 80069, Italy
Tel: (081) 8024392 or 403797
Fax: (081) 403797
4 rooms sharing 2 bathrooms
Lire 140,000–160,000 double B&B
  280,000 suite for 4 persons
3-night minimum stay
Breakfast only, Open April to October
English spoken well, Region: Campania

Villa Verucchio is a small commercial area just inland of the famous beaches of Rimini, the summer playground of young Italians attracted by its nightlife and budget rates. The Tenuta Amalia is a vast property owned by the Savazzi family, divided up into several different businesses each run individually. Case Rosse is the red farmhouse transformed into a pleasant little bed and breakfast and there are also three different restaurants, vineyards, and a 36-hole golf course created around the family's 18th-century villa. Although it is a bit confusing at first, the bed and breakfast is right on the road leading to the golf club entrance. Lucia Gatei welcomes guests to the rustic farmhouse, which offers four double bedrooms upstairs and two on the ground floor. Each is appointed individually with country antiques and yellow bedspreads. Breakfast is served either out on the covered porch or in the beamed breakfast room overlooking a small garden and there is a cozy living room with large stone fireplace. From here you have easy access to the beautiful countryside bordering the Marches with such highlights as the independent state of San Marino, San Leo, Santarcangelo, and Urbino. *Directions*: From Rimini take the S.S. 258 for 12 km to Villa Verucchio and watch for a sign on the right to the Amalia.

TENUTA AMALIA
Hostess: Lucia Gatei
Via Tenuta Amalia 107
Villa Verucchio (RN) 47040, Italy
Tel: (0541) 678123, Fax: (0541) 678876
6 rooms with private bathrooms
Lire 120,000–140,000 double B&B
Breakfast only
Open all year
Credit cards: MC, VS
Very little English spoken
Region: Emilia-Romangna
www.karenbrown.com/italy/amalia.html

On the northern outskirts of the beautiful city of Treviso is a busy farm that was once a convent. The long building has been made into several residences, one belonging to the two Milani brothers, where a restaurant and six bedrooms have been fashioned for guests. All of the bedrooms have private baths, and their decor is very much in keeping with the simple country style of the farm. Typical Venetian antiques enhance the rooms, which also feature homey touches such as white-lace curtains and soft floral armchairs. Guests can observe the wine production taking place on the farm and are also welcome to take horses out on excursions, or take riding lessons if desired. The popular restaurant prides itself on serving local specialties prepared with the farm's fresh produce and game. The restaurant with its large, open central hearth, is a welcoming gathering spot, decorated with lots of pictures, brass pots, pink tablecloths, and fresh flowers. Although the immediate surrounding flat countryside is the not most inspiring, this a great base for visiting Venice, Padova, Vianza, and Verona. *Directions*: From Venice (34 km away), take route N13 through Treviso, and on toward Villorba, turning left at the sign for the Podere. Or exit at Treviso Nord from the A27.

PODERE DEL CONVENTO
Host: Renzo Milani
Via IV Novembre 16
Villorba (TV) 31050, Italy
Tel & fax: (0422) 920044, Fax: (0422) 444783
6 rooms with private bathrooms
Lire 100,000 double B&B
All meals served
Restaurant closed Tuesdays
Closed August
Credit cards: AX, VS
No English spoken
Region: Veneto

Ninni Bacchi has done wonders in transforming her family's 300-acre tobacco and grain farm (just on the outskirts of the city) into a very comfortable bed and breakfast in an area that was once the heart of the Etruscan civilization. The Residence Rinaldone is run more like a hotel—arriving guests are warmly received in the luminous, open living room furnished with antiques surrounding a grand fireplace. On hand for guests at reception is cordial manager, Farid. Downstairs is the large, arcaded restaurant dating back to the 15th century, where guests can enjoy the typical cuisine of the Lazio region or dine outdoors by the pool. The five bedrooms off the courtyard in the main house have the most character with architectural features intact, while the remaining fifteen suites are lined up in two cottage-like wings, and are more spacious and modern in decor. A nice job has been done with the landscaping, pleasingly distracting the eye from the rather bland, flat countryside and encroaching commercial area hereabouts. Tennis, biking, and horse riding, plus the nearby thermal spa are some of the activities available as well as visits to ancient Viterbo and the gardens of Villa Lanti. *Directions*: From Rome (120 km away) follow signs for Viterbo. Take the Cassia road north of Viterbo for 3 km toward Montefiascone, turning right at the Rinaldone sign. 38 km from Orvieto.

RESIDENCE RINALDONE
Hostess: Ninni Bacchi
Strada Rinaldone, 9-S.S. Cassia km 86
Viterbo 01100, Italy
Tel: (0761) 352137, Fax: (0761) 353116
5 rooms, 15 suites with private bathrooms
Lire 160,000 double B&B
2-night minimum stay, All meals served
Open April to December, Credit cards: all major
Some English spoken
Region: Lazio

The northern part of the Lazio region holds many intriguing treasures to explore. Besides being less than an hour from Rome, it is the center of Etruscan history, with lakes, nearby seaside, thermal baths, and lovely gardens. One of the best preserved are the delightful Renaissance gardens of Villa Lante in Bagnaia. Just down the street is the gracious Villa Farinella, a very pleasant bed and breakfast within the 18th-century home of Maurizio and his family. Rita, his mother, lives in a restored farmhouse on the property and has passed her grandfather's ancient home down to her son. In order to revive the home to its original splendor, the bed and breakfast solution was a perfect one. The first floor is entirely dedicated to guests, with four cozy bedrooms entering into one of two spacious living/dining rooms appointed with original antiques and elegant chandeliers. Each quaint bedroom with new bathroom has its own floral theme (wisteria, rose), which is followed through in color scheme, wallpaper, bedspreads, and curtains. One particularly large room has frescoed vaulted ceilings. You will be delighted with the warm hospitality, authentically historic surroundings, and very reasonable rate. *Directions*: From Viterbo drive towards Bagnaia (directly east) on Viale Trieste to the suburb of La Quercia. Just after the Agip station turn left on Via Capodistria past houses to the end of the lane.

VILLA FARINELLA
Hosts: Maurizio Makovec & family
Localita: La Quercia
Via Capodistria 14
Viterbo 01100, Italy
Tel & fax: (0761) 304784 or 344253
Cellphone: (0339) 3655617
4 rooms with private bathrooms
Lire 120,000–150,000 double B&B
Breakfast only, Open all year
English & French spoken well
Region: Lazio

264

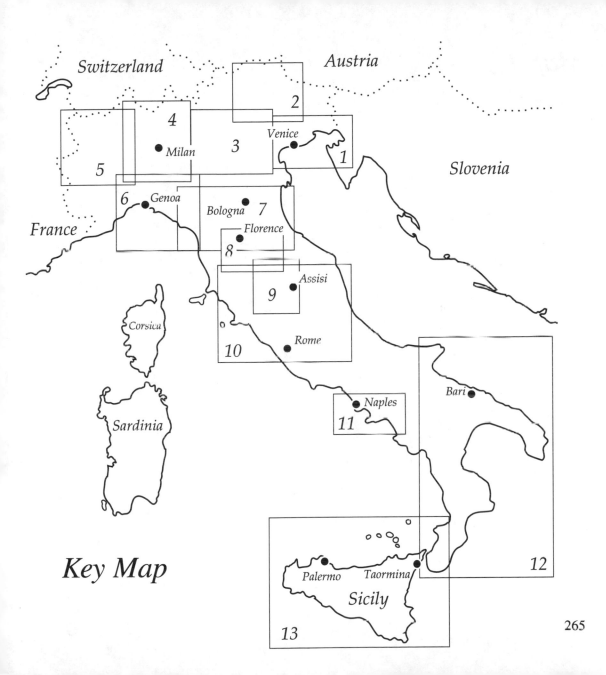

Key Map

Switzerland

Austria

Slovenia

France

2

4

3

Venice

1

Milan

5

6

Genoa

7

Bologna

Florence

8

9

Assisi

10

Rome

Corsica

Naples

11

Bari

Sardinia

12

Palermo

Taormina

Sicily

13

Map 1

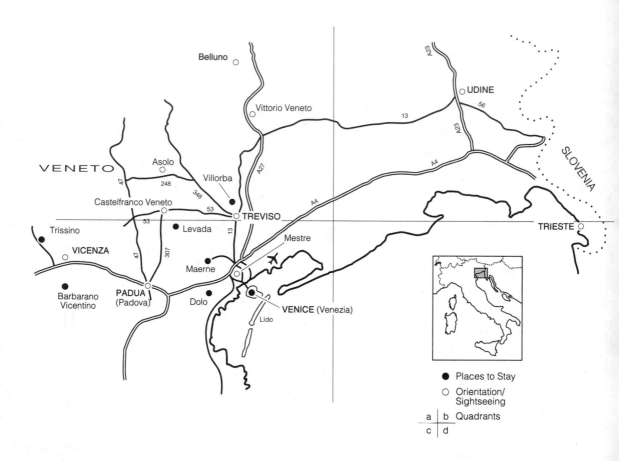

Belluno ○

○ Vittorio Veneto

VENETO

Asolo ○

Villorba

Castelfranco Veneto ○

● Villorba

53

○ TREVISO

● Levada

13

Mestre

● Maerne

● Barbarano
Vicentino

VICENZA ○

Trissino ●

PADUA
(Padova) ○

Dolo ●

VENICE (Venezia)

Lido

A23

● UDINE

56

13

A23

SLOVENIA

A4

A4

TRIESTE ○

● Places to Stay

○ Orientation/
   Sightseeing

a | b   Quadrants
c | d

47

248

348

53

47

307

266

Map 2

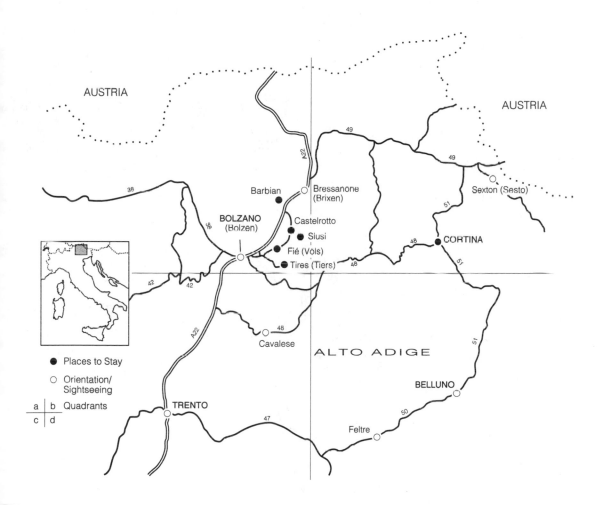

AUSTRIA

AUSTRIA

38

A22

49

49

Barbian

Bressanone
(Brixen)

Sexton (Sesto)

38

BOLZANO
(Bolzen)

Castelrotto

51

Siusi

48

CORTINA

Fié (Vols)

Tires (Tiers)

48

51

42

42

42

48

A22

Cavalese

ALTO ADIGE

51

● Places to Stay

○ Orientation/
  Sightseeing

BELLUNO

a	b
c	d

Quadrants

TRENTO

47

50

Feltre

Map 3

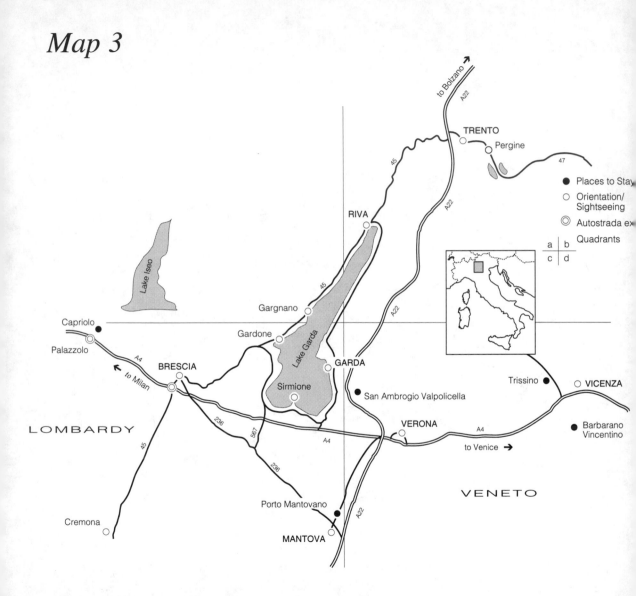

Places to Stay
Orientation/Sightseeing
Autostrada ex
Quadrants

a	b
c	d

to Bolzano
A22

TRENTO
Pergine
47

45

RIVA

45

A22

Lake Iseo

Gargnano

Gardone

Lake Garda

GARDA

Capriolo

Palazzolo

A4

to Milan

BRESCIA

Sirmione

San Ambrogio Valpolicella

Trissino

VICENZA

A22

Barbarano
Vincentino

236

567

A4

VERONA

A4

to Venice →

LOMBARDY

45

236

VENETO

Cremona

Porto Mantovano

A22

MANTOVA

Map 4

SWITZERLAND

LUGANO

Lake Lugano

Menaggio

Lake Como

Varenna

San Fedele d'Intelvi

Verbania

Luino

Argegno

Bellagio

Stresa

Lake Maggiore

Laveno

Varese

LECCO

Scalvino

COMO

Caprino Bergamasco

Alzano Lombardo

Arona

A9

BERGAMO

Malpensa Airport ✈

A8

A26

Dalmine

A4

LOMBARDY

Biella

Candelo

Mottalciata

Novara

MILAN (Milano)

✈ Linate Airport

to TORINO

Vercilli

Morimondo

A7

35

Vigevano

Binasco

A1

Besate

PAVIA

Cremona

ALESSANDRIA

A21

PIACENZA

A21

Tortona

to GENOVA

Borgo Priolo

● Places to Stay
○ Orientation/ Sightseeing
◎ Autostrada exit

a	b
c	d

Quadrants

Map 5

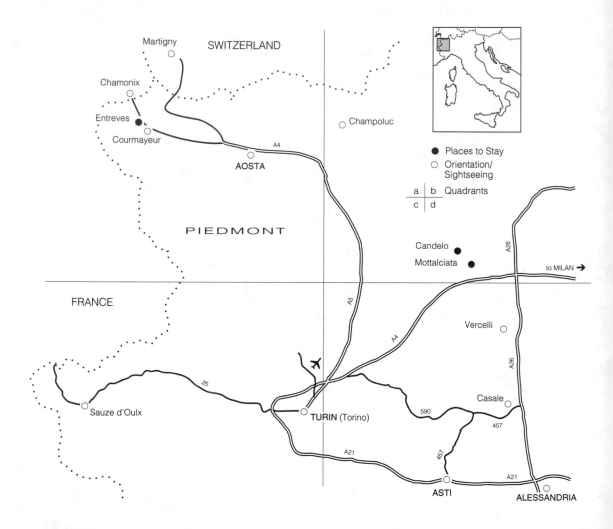

Martigny

SWITZERLAND

Chamonix

Entreves

Courmayeur

Champoluc

A4

AOSTA

PIEDMONT

● Places to Stay

○ Orientation/
   Sightseeing

a	b	Quadrants
c	d	

Candelo

Mottalciata

A26

to MILAN →

FRANCE

A5

A4

Vercelli

A26

25

Casale

✈

TURIN (Torino)

590

457

Sauze d'Oulx

A21

457

A21

ASTI

ALESSANDRIA

Map 6

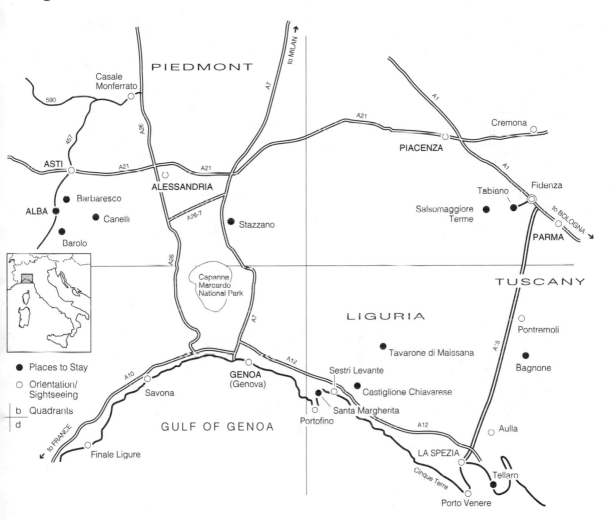

PIEDMONT

Casale
Monferrato

590

457

A26

ASTI

A21   A21

ALESSANDRIA

A26-7

ALBA

Barbaresco

Canelli

Barolo

Stazzano

A26

Capanne
Marcardo
National Park

A7

to MILAN

A7

A21

Cremona

PIACENZA

A1

A1

Tabiano

Salsomaggiore
Terme

Fidenza

to BOLOGNA

PARMA

TUSCANY

LIGURIA

Pontremoli

A15

Tavarone di Maissana

Bagnone

A12

GENOA
(Genova)

Sestri Levante

Castiglione Chiavarese

● Places to Stay

○ Orientation/
   Sightseeing

b
––   Quadrants
d

A10

Savona

Santa Margherita

Portofino

Aulla

GULF OF GENOA

A12

LA SPEZIA

to FRANCE

Finale Ligure

Cinque Terre

Tellaro

Porto Venere

Map 7

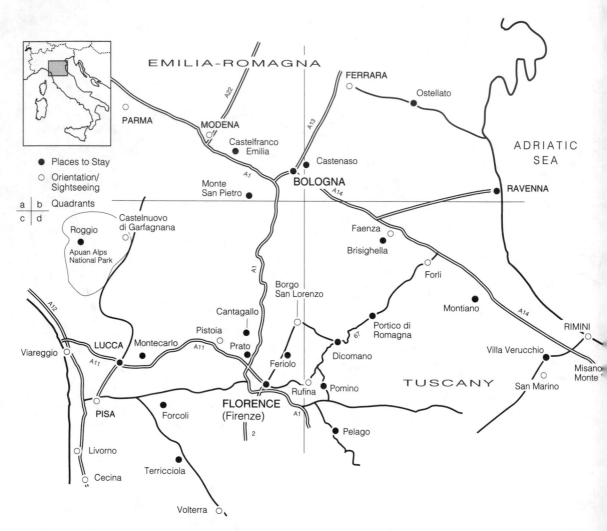

INSET MAP:

EMILIA-ROMAGNA

PARMA ○

A22

MODENA ○

Castelfranco Emilia ●

FERRARA ○

Ostellato ●

ADRIATIC SEA

A13

Castenaso ●

BOLOGNA ●

A1

Monte San Pietro ●

A14

RAVENNA ●

Legend

- ● Places to Stay
- ○ Orientation/ Sightseeing

a	b
c	d

Quadrants

Castelnuovo di Garfagnana ○

Roggio ●

Apuan Alps National Park

Faenza ○

Brisighella ●

Forli ○

Montiano ●

A14

RIMINI ○

A12

Borgo San Lorenzo ○

Cantagallo ●

Pistoia ○

Prato ●

LUCCA ●

Montecarlo ●

A11

Viareggio ○

A11

PISA ○

Forcoli ●

Feriolo ●

Portico di Romagna ●

67

Dicomano ●

Villa Verucchio ●

Misano Monte ○

San Marino ○

TUSCANY

Pomino ●

Rufina ○

FLORENCE (Firenze) ●

A1

Pelago ●

2

Livorno ○

Cecina ○

Terricciola ●

Volterra ○

272

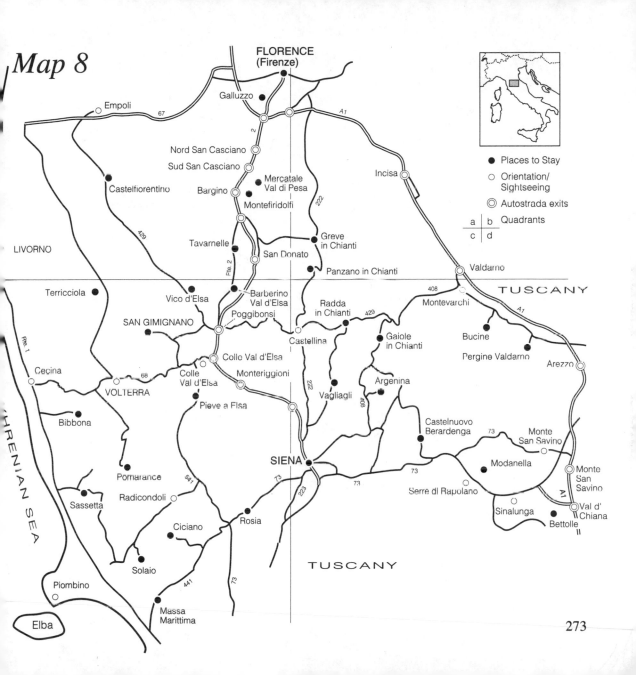

Map 8

FLORENCE (Firenze)

Empoli
67
Galluzzo
A1
2

Nord San Casciano
Sud San Casciano
Incisa

Castelfiorentino
Bargino
Mercatale Val di Pesa
Montefiridolfi

429
222

LIVORNO
Tavarnelle
Greve in Chianti

Rte. 2
San Donato
Panzano in Chianti

Valdarno

Terricciola
Vico d'Elsa
Barberino Val d'Elsa
Radda in Chianti
408
429
Montevarchi
TUSCANY

SAN GIMIGNANO
Poggibonsi
Castellina
Gaiole in Chianti
Bucine
A1

Colle Val d'Elsa
Pergine Valdarno
Arezzo

Rte. 1
Cecina
68
Colle Val d'Elsa
Monteriggioni
Argenina

222

VOLTERRA
Pieve a Elsa
Vagliagli

408

Bibbona
Castelnuovo Berardenga
73
Monte San Savino

541
Modanella

Pomarance
SIENA
Monte San Savino

Radicondoli
73
223
Serre di Rapolano
A1

Sassetta
Rosia
73
73
Sinalunga
Val d' Chiana

Ciciano
Bettolle

Solaio
441
73

Piombino
TUSCANY

Elba

Massa Marittima

273

- ● Places to Stay
- ○ Orientation/ Sightseeing
- ◎ Autostrada exits

a	b
c	d

Quadrants

TYRRHENIAN SEA

Map 9

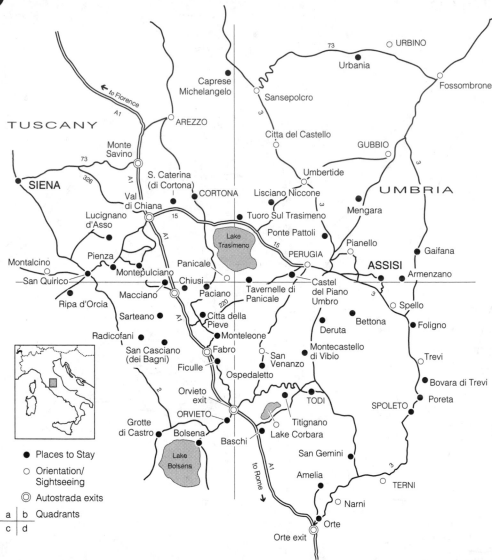

Places to Stay ●

Orientation/ ○
Sightseeing

Autostrada exits ◎

a	b
c	d

Quadrants

274

Map 10

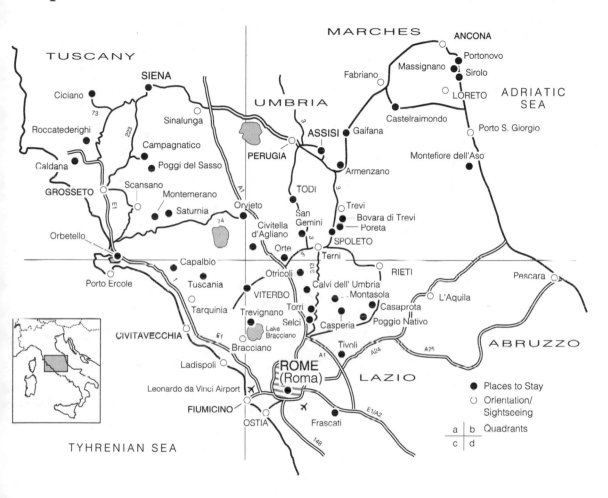

TUSCANY

MARCHES

UMBRIA

ADRIATIC SEA

ANCONA
Portonovo
Massignano
Sirolo
LORETO
Fabriano
Castelraimondo
Porto S. Giorgio
Gaifana
ASSISI
Montefiore dell'Aso
Armenzano

SIENA
Ciciano
Sinalunga
Roccatederighi
Campagnatico
Poggi del Sasso
PERUGIA
Caldana
Scansano
GROSSETO
Montemerano
Saturnia
Orvieto
TODI
Trevi
San Gemini
Bovara di Trevi
Poreta
Civitella d'Agliano
SPOLETO
Orbetello
Orte
Terni
Capalbio
Otricoli
RIETI
Pescara
Porto Ercole
Tuscania
Calvi dell' Umbria
Montasola
L'Aquila
VITERBO
Torri
Casaprota
Tarquinia
Trevignano
Selci
Casperia
Poggio Nativo
CIVITAVECCHIA
Lake Bracciano
Bracciano
Tivoli
ABRUZZO
Ladispoli
ROME (Roma)
LAZIO
Leonardo da Vinci Airport
FIUMICINO
OSTIA
Frascati

TYHRENIAN SEA

● Places to Stay
○ Orientation/ Sightseeing

a	b
c	d

Quadrants

275

Map 11

to Rome

LAZIO

○ Anzio

A2

○ Gaeta

CAMPANIA

● Places to Stay

○ Orientation/
Sightseeing

a	b	Quadrants
c	d	

A30

A16

A16

● Ponza

A30

✈

NAPLES (Napoli) ○

Ventotene

A3

POMPEII
○

Ischia

Castellamare ○

A3

Vico Equense
●

Ravello
●

SALERNO
○

TYHRENIAN SEA

SORRENTO ○

Positano
●

AMALFI
○

CAPRI
●

Paestu

276

Map 12

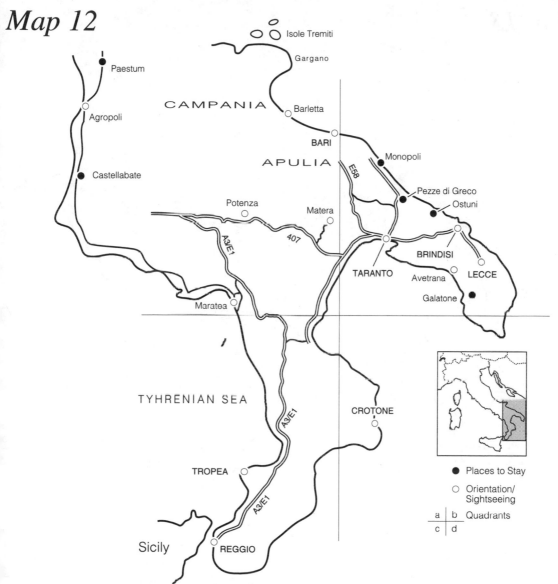

Isole Tremiti

Gargano

CAMPANIA

Paestum

Agropoli

Barletta

BARI

APULIA

Monopoli

Castellabate

Pezze di Greco

Potenza

Matera

Ostuni

E58

A3/E1

407

TARANTO

BRINDISI

Avetrana

LECCE

Maratea

Galatone

TYHRENIAN SEA

A3/E1

CROTONE

TROPEA

A3/E1

Sicily

REGGIO

● Places to Stay

○ Orientation/
  Sightseeing

a	b
c	d

Quadrants

Map 13

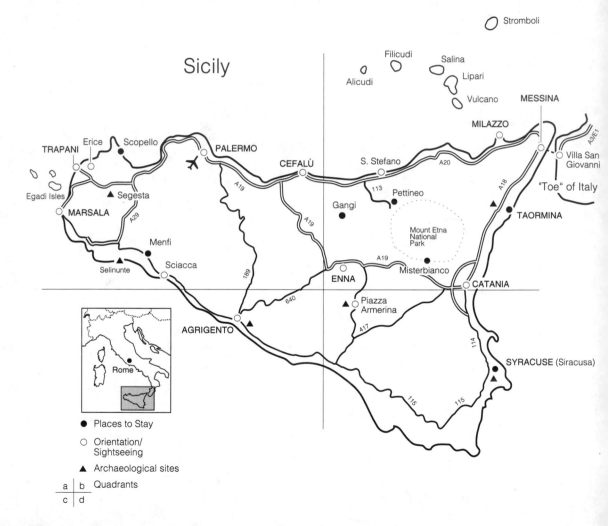

Sicily

Stromboli

Filicudi
Salina
Alicudi
Lipari
Vulcano

MESSINA

MILAZZO

Villa San
Giovanni

TRAPANI
Erice
Scopello
PALERMO
CEFALÙ
S. Stefano
A20
"Toe" of Italy

Egadi Isles

MARSALA
A19
Segesta
A19
113
Pettineo
Gangi
A18
TAORMINA

Mount Etna
National
Park

Menfi
189
Selinunte
Sciacca
A19
Misterbianco
CATANIA

ENNA

640

Piazza
Armerina
417

AGRIGENTO

Rome

114

SYRACUSE (Siracusa)

115
115

● Places to Stay

○ Orientation/
   Sightseeing

▲ Archaeological sites

a	b	Quadrants
c	d	

Valle d'Aosta

Piedmont

Liguria

• Milan

Lombardy

Trentino-
Alto Adige

Veneto

Friuli-
Venezia
Giulia

• Genoa

• Venice

Emila-Romagna

CORSICA
(France)

Sardinia

• Cagliari

• Florence

Tuscany

Marches

Umbria

Abruzzo

• ROME

Lazio

Molise

Campania

• Naples

Basilicata

• Bari

Apulia

Calabria

• Palermo

Sicily

Regions of Italy

Bed & Breakfasts by Region

Apulia

Galatone, Masseria Lo Prieno

Monopoli, Masseria Curatori

Ostuni, Masseria Lo Spagnulo

Pezzi di Greco, Masseria Salamina

Campania

Capri, La Minerva

    Villa Krupp

    Villa Vuotto

Castellabate, La Mola

Paestum, Seliano

Positano, Casa Cosenza

    La Fenice

    Villa Rosa

Ravello, Villa Maria

Vico Equense, Villa Giusso

Emilia-Romagna

Bologna, Hotel Orologio

Brisighella, Il Palazzo

Castelfranco Emilia, Villa Gaidello

Castenaso, Il Loghetto

Misano Monte, I Girasoli

Monte San Pietro, Tenuta Bonzara

Montiano, Le Radici

Ostellato, Belfiore

Portico di Romagna, Albergo al Vecchio Convento

Ravenna, Hotel Diana

Salsomaggiore Terme, Antica Torre

Tabiano, Il Tondino

Villa Verucchio, Tenuta Amalia

Lazio

Bolsena, La Riserva Montebello

Casaprota, Cjase Me

Casperia, La Torretta

Civitella d'Agliano, L'Ombricolo

Frascati, Hotel Flora

Grotte di Castro, Castello di S. Cristina

Montasola, Montepiano

Orte, La Chiocciola

Poggio Nativo, Paese delle Meraviglie

Ponza, Isola di, Gennarino a Mare

Lazio (continued)

Rome, Casa Stefazio

    Fontana Hotel

    Hotel Celio

    Hotel Due Torri

    Hotel Fontanella Borghese

    Hotel Locarno

    Hotel Santa Maria

    Hotel Venezia

    Hotel Villa del Parco

    Villa Delros

Selci Sabino, Villa Vallerosa

Tivoli, Hotel Adriano

Torri in Sabina, Il Leccio

Trevignano, Casa Plazzi

Tuscania, Hotel Al Gallo

Viterbo, Residence Rinaldone

    Villa Farinella

Liguria

Castiglione Chiavarese, Monte Pu

Santa Margherita, Villa Gnocchi

Tavarone di Maissana, Giandriale

Tellaro, Locanda Miranda

Lombardy

Alzano Lombardo, Cascina Grumello

Besate, Cascina Maremma

Borgo Priolo, Castello di Stefanago

Caprino Bergamasco, Ombria

Capriolo, Azienda Agricola Ricci Cubastro

Luino, Camin Hotel Colmegna

Milan, Hotel Regina

Porto Mantovano, Villa Schiarino Lena

San Fedele d'Intelvi, Villa Simplicitas

Scalvino-Lenna, Ferdy

Varenna, Olivedo

Marches

Castelraimondo, Il Giardino degli Ulivi

Massignano, La Biancarda

Montefiore dell'Aso, La Campana

Portonovo, Fortino Napoleonico

    Hotel Emilia

Sirolo, Locanda Rocco

Urbania, L'Orsaiola

Piedmont

Alba, Cascina Reine

Barbaresco, Cascina delle Rose

Barolo, Il Gioco dell'Oca

Candelo, La Mandria

Canelli, La Luna e i Falo

Mottalciata, Il Mompolino

Stazzano, La Traversina

Verbania, Il Monterosso

Sicily

Gangi, Villa Raino

Menfi, Villa Ravida

Misterbianco, Alcala

Pettineo, Casa Migliaca

Scopello, Pensione Tranchina

Siracusa, Limoneto

Taormina, Villa Schuler

Trentino-Alto Adige

Barbian, Bad Dreikirchen

Castelrotto (Osvaldo), Tschotscherhof

Fiè allo Sciliar (Völs), Merlhof

Siusi allo Sciliar, Aquila Nera

Garni Kristiania

Marmsolerhof

Tires (Tiers), Veraltenhof

Tuscany

Argenina, Borgo Argenina

Bagnone, Villa Mimosa

Barberino Val d'Elsa, Fattoria Casa Sola

Il Paretaio

Relais Molino dell'Argenna

La Spinosa

Bettolle, Locanda La Bandita

Bibbona, Podere Le Mezzelune

Bucine, Iesolana

Caldana, Montebelli

Campagnatico, Villa Bellaria

Cantagallo, Ponte Alla Villa

Capalbio, Ghiaccio Bosco

Caprese Michelangelo, Borgo Tozzetto

Castelfiorentino, Le Boscarecce

Castelnuovo Berardenga, Borgo Villa a Sesta

Chiusi, La Querce

Tuscany (continued)

Ciciano, Casa Italia

Cortona, Borgo Elena

    Stoppiacce

Dicomano, Il Cavaliere

Feriolo, Casa Palmira

Florence, Hotel Aprile

    Hotel Ariele

    Hotel Hermitage

    Hotel Silla

    Hotel Splendor

    La Residenza

    La Toricella

    Villa Poggio San Felice

Forcoli, Il Torrino

Gaiole in Chianti, Castello di Tornano

Galluzzo (Florence), La Fattoressa

Greve in Chianti, Casa Mezzuola

Lucca, Alla Corte degli Angeli

Lucignano d'Asso, Lucignanello Bandini

Macciano (Chiusi), Macciangrosso

Massa Marittima, Tenuta Il Cicalino

Mercatale Val di Pesa, Salvadonica

Modanella (Serre di Rapolano), Godiolo

    Castello di Modanella

Montecarlo-Lucca, Antica Casa dei Rassicurati

    Casa Satti

Montefiridolfi, Fattoria La Loggia

    Macinello

Montemerano, Villa Acquaviva

Montemerano (Poderi di), Le Fontanelle

Montepulciano, L'Agnolo

Orbetello Scalo, Il Casalone

    Grazia

Panzano in Chianti, Fagiolari

Pelago, La Doccia

Pergine Valdarno, Fattoria Montelucci

Pienza, Le Traverse

    Santo Pietro

Pieve a Elsa, La Piccola Pieve

Poggi del Sasso, Castello di Vicarello

Pomarance, Casa Zito

Pomino, Fattoria di Petrognano

Prato, Villa Rucellai di Canneto

Radda in Chianti, Azienda Agricola Vergelli

    La Locanda

    Podere Terreno

Tuscany (continued)

Radda in Chianti, Podere Val delle Corti

    Pornanino

    Torre Canvalle

Radicofani, La Palazzina

Ripa d'Orcia, Castello di Ripa d'Orcia

Roccatederighi, Fattoria di Caminino

Roggio, La Fontanella

Rosia, Montestigliano

San Casciano dei Bagni, La Crocetta

    Le Radici

San Gimignano, Il Casale del Cotone

    Casanova di Pescille

    Casolare di Libbiano

    Il Rosolaccio

    Il Vicario

    Podere Villuzza

San Quirico d'Orcia-Bagno Vignoni,
    La Locanda del Loggiato

Santa Caterina (Cortona), Agrisalotto

Sarteano, La Sovana

    Villa Iris

Sassetta, Tenuta La Bandita

Saturnia, Villa Clodia

Siena, Villa dei Lecci

Solaio (Radicondoli), Fattoria Solaio

Tavarnelle Val di Pesa, Sovigliano

Terricciola, Il Selvino

Vagliagli, Casali della Aiola

Vico d'Elsa, La Volpaia

Umbria

Amelia, La Palombara

Armenzano (Assissi), Le Silve di Armenzano

Assisi (Capodacqua), Malvarina

Assisi (Tordibetto di), Podere La Fornace

Baschi, Pomurlo Vecchio

Bettona, Torre Burchio

Bovara di Trevi, Casa Giulia

Calvi dell'Umbria, Casale San Martino

Castel del Piano Umbro, Villa Aureli

Citta della Pieve, Madonna delle Grazie

Deruta, Antica Fattoria del Colle

Ficulle, La Casella

Foligno, Rocca Deli

Gaifana, Villa della Cupa

Lisciano Niccone, Casa San Martino

Mengara-Scritto, Oasi Verde Mengara

Umbria (continued)

Montecastello di Vibio, Fattoria di Vibio

Monteleone d'Orvieto, Poggio Miravalle

Orvieto, Locanda Rosati

    Villa Ciconia

Ospedaletto (San Venanzo), Borgo Spante

Otricoli, Casa Spence

Paciano, Locanda della Rocca

Ponte Pattoli, Il Covone

San Gemini, Palazzo Canova

Spoleto, Palazzo Dragoni

Spoleto (Poreta), Il Castello di Poreta

Tavernelle di Panicale, Montali

Titignano, Fattoria Titignano

Todi, Poggio d'Asproli

    Tenuta di Canonica

Tuoro Sul Trasimeno, Castello di Montegualandro

    La Dogana

Valle d'Aosta

Entreves (Courmayeur), La Grange

Veneto

Barbarano Vicentino, Il Castello

Cortina d'Ampezzo, Baita Fraina

    Meuble Oasi

    Villa Alpina

Dolo, Villa Goetzen

Levada di Piombino Dese, Gargan

Maerne, Ca'delle Rondini

San Ambrogio Valpolicella, Ca'Verde

Trissino, Ca'Masieri

Venice, Hotel Ai Due Fanali

    Hotel San Moise

    Hotel Santo Stefano

    Pensione La Calcina

    Pensione Seguso

Villorba, Podere del Convento

Index

W

Z

CRITIQUE PLACES IN OUR BOOK

We greatly appreciate first-hand evaluations of places in our guides so your critiques are invaluable to us. To stay current on the properties in our guides, we keep a database of readers' comments. To keep our readers up to date, we also sometimes share feedback with them via our website.

Please list your comments on properties that you have visited. We welcome accolades, as well as criticisms.

Name of Hotel or B&B _____

Town _____ Country _____

Comments:

Your name _____ Street _____

Town _____ State _____ Zip _____ Country _____

Tel _____ E-mail _____ Date _____

Do we have your permission to electronically publish your comments on our website? Yes ____ No ____

If yes, would you like to remain anonymous? Yes ___No ___, or may we use your name? Yes___ No___

Please send report to: Karen Brown's Guides, Post Office Box 70, San Mateo, California 94401, USA
tel: (650) 342-9117, fax: (650) 342-9153, e-mail: karen@karenbrown.com, www.karenbrown.com

CRITIQUE PLACES IN OUR BOOK

We greatly appreciate first-hand evaluations of places in our guides so your critiques are invaluable to us. To stay current on the properties in our guides, we keep a database of readers' comments. To keep our readers up to date, we also sometimes share feedback with them via our website.

Please list your comments on properties that you have visited. We welcome accolades, as well as criticisms.

Name of Hotel or B&B _____

Town _____ Country _____

Comments:

Your name _____ Street _____

Town _____ State _____ Zip _____ Country _____

Tel _____ E-mail _____ Date _____

Do we have your permission to electronically publish your comments on our website? Yes _____ No _____

If yes, would you like to remain anonymous? Yes ___ No ___, or may we use your name? Yes___ No___

Please send report to: Karen Brown's Guides, Post Office Box 70, San Mateo, California 94401, USA
tel: (650) 342-9117, fax: (650) 342-9153, e-mail: karen@karenbrown.com, www.karenbrown.com

SHARE YOUR DISCOVERIES WITH US

Outstanding properties often come from readers' discoveries. We would love to hear from you.

Please list below any hotel or bed & breakfast you discover. Tell us what you liked about the property and, if possible, please include a brochure or photographs so we can share your enthusiasm. We keep a permanent database of all of your recommendations for future use. Note: we regret we cannot return photos.

Owner _____   Hotel or B&B _____

Address _____   Town _____   Country _____

Comments:

Your name _____   Street _____

Town _____   State _____   Zip _____   Country _____

Tel _____   E-mail _____   Date _____

Do we have your permission to electronically publish your comments on our website? Yes ____ No ____

If yes, would you like to remain anonymous? Yes ___No ___, or may we use your name? Yes___ No___

Please send report to: Karen Brown's Guides, Post Office Box 70, San Mateo, California 94401, USA
tel: (650) 342-9117, fax: (650) 342-9153, e-mail: karen@karenbrown.com, www.karenbrown.com

SHARE YOUR DISCOVERIES WITH US

Outstanding properties often come from readers' discoveries. We would love to hear from you.

Please list below any hotel or bed & breakfast you discover. Tell us what you liked about the property and, if possible, please include a brochure or photographs so we can share your enthusiasm. We keep a permanent database of all of your recommendations for future use. Note: we regret we cannot return photos.

Owner _____   Hotel or B&B _____

Address _____   Town _____   Country _____

Comments:

Your name _____   Street _____

Town _____   State _____   Zip _____   Country _____

Tel _____   E-mail _____   Date _____

Do we have your permission to electronically publish your comments on our website? Yes ____ No ____

If yes, would you like to remain anonymous? Yes ___No ___, or may we use your name? Yes___ No___

Please send report to: Karen Brown's Guides, Post Office Box 70, San Mateo, California 94401, USA
tel: (650) 342-9117, fax: (650) 342-9153, e-mail: karen@karenbrown.com, www.karenbrown.com

Enhance Your Guides

Online

www.karenbrown.com

- Hotel News
- Color Photos
- New Discoveries
- Currency Converter
- Corrections & Edits
- Property of the Month
- Postcards from the Road
- Links to Hotels & B&Bs

ANY OF THE ACCOMMODATIONS IN THIS GUIDE CAN BE RESERVED THROUGH AUTHOR NICOLE FRANCHINI'S TRAVEL SERVICE, HIDDEN TREASURES OF ITALY.

Reservations provide additional services such as:

- **Personalized itinerary planning**
- **Concert and museum ticket reservation**
- **Private guides, car rental and chauffeured transfers**
- **Special interest itineraries (golf programs, food and wine tours, cooking classes, organized dinners in private historical villas, private garden visits, chartered sailing itineraries to islands).**

Complete wedding/honeymoon planning. Personalized consultation and arrangements for civil or religious wedding ceremonies and reception in the city of your choice. From a private romantic ceremony for two, to a complete wedding in the most enchanting historical places in Italy.

Full pre-payment by check or Mastercard/Visa. Service fees apply.

HIDDEN TREASURES OF ITALY, INC.
55 East Washington Street
Suite 1807
Chicago, IL 60602, USA
U.S. Toll Free Tel: (888) 419-6700

U.S. Tel. (312) 460-8219
Fax: (312) 460-8238
e-mail: info@htitaly.com
www.htitaly.com

HIDDEN TREASURES OF ITALY

ALSO PRESENTS A SPECIAL **"LIMITED COLLECTION"** OF PERSONALLY SELECTED VILLAS AVAILABLE FOR HOLIDAYS, WEDDINGS AND PERSONALIZED PROGRAMS.

THE HIGHEST EXPRESSION OF QUALITY, SERVICE AND HOSPITALITY IN THE MOST CHARMING LOCATIONS.

www.htitaly.com

TRAVELSMITH®

Need a dual voltage hair dryer, a wrinkle-free blazer, quick-dry clothes, a computer adapter plug? TRAVELSMITH has them all, along with an enticing array of everything a Karen Brown traveler needs.

Karen Brown recommends TRAVELSMITH as an excellent source for travel clothing and gear. We were pleased to find quality products needed for our own research travels in their catalog—items not always easy to find. For a free catalog call TRAVELSMITH at 800-950-1600.

When placing your order, be sure to identify yourself as a Karen Brown Traveler with the code TKBX1 and you will receive a 10% discount. * You can link to TRAVELSMITH through our website *www.karenbrown.com.*

*offer valid till December 2001

auto⊗europe.

Karen Brown's

Preferred Car Rental Service Provider

When Traveling to Europe
for

International Car Rental Services
Chauffeur & Transfer Services
Prestige & Sports Cars
Motor Home Rentals

800-223-5555

Be sure to identify yourself as a Karen Brown Traveler.
For special offers and discounts use your
Karen Brown ID number 99006187.

Seal Cove Inn

Located in the San Francisco Bay Area

Karen Brown Herbert (best known as author of the Karen Brown's guides) and her husband, Rick, have put 23 years of experience into reality and opened their own superb hideaway, Seal Cove Inn. Spectacularly set amongst wild flowers and bordered by towering cypress trees, Seal Cove Inn looks out to the distant ocean over acres of county park: an oasis where you can enjoy secluded beaches, explore tidepools, watch frolicking seals, and follow the tree-lined path that traces the windswept ocean bluffs. Country antiques, original watercolors, flower-laden cradles, rich fabrics, and the gentle ticking of grandfather clocks create the perfect ambiance for a foggy day in front of the crackling log fire. Each bedroom is its own haven with a cozy sitting area before a wood-burning fireplace and doors opening onto a private balcony or patio with views to the park and ocean. Moss Beach is a 35-minute drive south of San Francisco, 6 miles north of the picturesque town of Half Moon Bay, and a few minutes from Princeton harbor with its colorful fishing boats and restaurants. Seal Cove Inn makes a perfect base for whale-watching, salmon-fishing excursions, day trips to San Francisco, exploring the coast, or, best of all, just a romantic interlude by the sea, time to relax and be pampered. Karen and Rick look forward to the pleasure of welcoming you to their coastal hideaway.

Seal Cove Inn • 221 Cypress Avenue • Moss Beach • California • 94038 • USA
tel: (650) 728-4114, fax: (650) 728-4116, e-mail: sealcove@coastside.net, website: sealcoveinn.com

NICOLE FRANCHINI, author of *Italy: Charming Bed & Breakfasts,* was born in Chicago and raised in a bilingual family, her father being Italian. She received a B.A. degree in languages from William Smith College and the Sorbonne, Paris, and has been residing in Italy for the past 15 years. Currently living in the countryside of Sabina near Rome with husband, Carlo, and daughters, Livia and Sabina, she runs her own travel consulting business, Hidden Treasures of Italy, which organizes personalized group and individual itineraries.

ELISABETTA FRANCHINI, the talented artist responsible for the illustrations in *Italy: Charming Bed & Breakfasts*, lives in her hometown of Chicago with her husband, Chris, and their two young children, where she paints predominantly European landscapes and architectural scenes. On her annual trip to Italy she enjoys accompanying her sister, Nicole, on her travel research. A Smith College graduate in Art History and French Literature, Elisabetta has exhibited extensively in the Chicago area for the past 17 years, and has had extremely well received shows in Miami, New York, and San Francisco.

JANN POLLARD, the artist responsible for the beautiful painting on the cover of this guide, has studied art since childhood, and is well known for her outstanding impressionistic-style watercolors which she has exhibited in numerous juried shows, winning many awards. Jann travels frequently to Europe (using Karen Brown's guides) where she loves to paint historical buildings. Jann lives in Burlingame, California, with her husband, Gene.

Travel Your Dreams • Order your Karen Brown Guides Today

Please ask in your local bookstore for Karen Brown's Guides. If the books you want are unavailable, you may order directly from the publisher. Books will be shipped immediately.

_____ *Austria: Charming Inns & Itineraries* $19.95

_____ *California: Charming Inns & Itineraries* $19.95

_____ *England: Charming Bed & Breakfasts* $18.95

_____ *England, Wales & Scotland: Charming Hotels & Itineraries* $19.95

_____ *France: Charming Bed & Breakfasts* $18.95

_____ *France: Charming Inns & Itineraries* $19.95

_____ *Germany: Charming Inns & Itineraries* $19.95

_____ *Ireland: Charming Inns & Itineraries* $19.95

_____ *Italy: Charming Bed & Breakfasts* $18.95

_____ *Italy: Charming Inns & Itineraries* $19.95

_____ *New England: Charming Inns & Itineraries* $19.95

_____ *Portugal: Charming Inns & Itineraries* $19.95

_____ *Spain: Charming Inns & Itineraries* $19.95

_____ *Switzerland: Charming Inns & Itineraries* $19.95

Name _____ Street _____

Town _____ State _____ Zip _____ Tel _____

Credit Card (MasterCard or Visa) _____ Expires: _____

For orders in the USA, add $4 for the first book and $1 for each additional book for shipment. California residents add 8.25% sales tax. Overseas orders add $10 per book for airmail shipment. Indicate number of copies of each title; fax or mail form with check or credit card information to:

KAREN BROWN'S GUIDES
Post Office Box 70 • San Mateo • California • 94401 • USA
tel: (650) 342-9117, fax: (650) 342-9153, e-mail: karen@karenbrown.com
You can also order directly from our website at www.karenbrown.com.